FAMILY LETTERS
OF RICHARD WAGNER

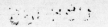

FAMILY LETTERS

OF

RICHARD WAGNER

TRANSLATED, INDEXED, ETC.

BY

WILLIAM ASHTON ELLIS

VIENNA HOUSE
New York

Originally published by Macmillan and Co., Limited
London, 1911

First VIENNA HOUSE edition published 1971

International Standard Book Number:
0-8443-0014-4

Library of Congress Catalogue Card Number: 71-163796

Manufactured in the United States of America

TRANSLATOR'S PREFACE

SOMEWHERE I have recently seen this collection of
" Family Letters" referred to by a well-wishing
journalist in advance of its integral English publication—a few of the letters or portions thereof having
been elsewhere translated by me before—as " a
supplement to Wagner's Autobiography." Upon
the assumption that we yet may be given a reliable
translation of *Mein Leben,* to some extent I can
accept that description, as all the intimate expressions of a great man's personality may be said to
supplement each other in a sense. But the true
counterpart of these letters of Richard Wagner's
to his blood-relatives and connections is to be
found, of course, in those to his first wife "Minna,"
at the end of my preface to which I breathed the
hope, now more than two years since, that they
might "soon be supplemented by an English rendering of the delightful *Familienbriefe* " ; and in fact
it is by the barest chance that the latter rendering did
not then take first place, as was my own desire when
the two collections made almost simultaneous appearance in their original vernacular, winter 1907-8.

For my own part, as between the three works just named, in the matter of self-portraiture I should give decided preference—and should have even before seeing any of them—to the one which displays to us the author in the most levelling of all human relations, that of the member of a large family conclave, and youngest but one of a numerous middle-class brood. Here no possible suspicion of attitudinising can arise in the mind of the most inveterate carper ; if I may be allowed to appeal to personal experience of a similar quiverful, elder brothers and sisters knock all that sort of thing out of their juniors mighty soon. And so we get a picture of the naked human spirit in the driest and most neutral of lights, even the letters addressed to a younger generation, those to two or three adoring nieces, being sobered by the certainty that they will be shewn to the girls' parents. Yet what letters they are, the majority of those to his nieces ! Take No. 65, for instance, with its " I court the affection of nobody, and leave people to think what they like of me ; but . . . if but a finger of true unconditional love is held out to me from anywhere, I snatch at the whole hand as possessed, draw the whole mortal to me by it if I can, and give him, an' it may be, just such a thorough hearty kiss as I should like to give your-self to-day." As pendant to which I may cite that to his brother-in-law Eduard of almost ten years earlier : " I know no first nor last midst those my heart belongs to ; I've only *one* heart, and whoever dwells there is its tenant from bottom to top" (p. 56).

After reading the above pair of extracts, and comparing them with the letters to Uhlig or Liszt, one may be pretty sure that if *this* collection is not ten times its present size, the fault largely lies at the recipients' door ; either in that lack of responsiveness so common among large families, particularly when most of the grown-ups have young progeny of their own to attend to, or in simple neglect to treasure up a store whose future value was not realised (*cf.* p. 278). Yes, and—as my friend Herr Glasenapp informs us in his thumb-nail sketch at this volume's end—it is to the *half-*sister, Cecilie Avenarius, her famous brother's only junior, that we owe the conservation of the main bulk of those family-letters we do possess ; just as it was to her and her husband that by far the chief constituents of its first half were addressed. On the other hand, I cannot quite share the belief my friend expresses, that a want of such care and fore-thought on the part of other members of the family has deprived us of very many fellows to these documents ; themselves they offer too much indication that at various periods in their author's life, e.g. that directly preceding and succeeding his first marriage, all ordinary correspondence with his kinsfolk was suspended for a good long while, as so often is the case with less uncommon individuals in like circumstances.   Nevertheless, it is tolerably certain that letters passed between Richard Wagner and his sister Ottilie Brockhaus or her husband in the summer of 1837 concerning the divorcement of Minna then actively contemplated (*cf.* "*R. to M. Wagner*," p. 502), whilst sister Clara Wolfram's long Zurich visit of the late summer and early autumn 1856 must have entailed at least one letter from her host himself before and after it, to say nothing of his arranging for Minna's visit to her two years previously.   So that there still is faint hope of just a few emerging from some secretive purchaser's portfolio in course of time.

Turning to another aspect of our collection as it stands, one of its distinctive features is that— setting aside a few applications to music-publishers — it presents us with the earliest of Richard Wagner's private missives as yet discoverable ; though in that respect it is run pretty close by the "*Letters to Apel*" quite lately contributed by me to *The English Review*, which in their turn richly supplement our rather scanty record for the 'thirties. The 'forties, on the contrary, here shew a harvest more abundant than in any other volume of the master's letters ; whilst the total time-span bridges nearly all his adult life, little more than its eight last years being unaccounted for besides those earlier gaps.

Regarding the technique of the present edition a very few words will suffice. With the exception of eight letters to Minna included by Herr Glasenapp in the original edition before it was decided to issue the whole of that extensive group apart, nothing whatever has been consciously omitted by me in this Englishing of a correspondence transcribed by my friend and colleague from the autographs themselves; similarly, all the un-signed footnotes are mere reproductions from his. On the other hand, for internal reasons I have transposed the sequence of two or three undated letters, added one of Albert Wagner's narrating the Mother's death (pp. 141-5), and furnished the least possible dressing of what I may term connective tissue,—all such additions of mine being indicated by *square* brackets, as my colleague has restricted himself to curved. Having experimented in the "*Minna*" volumes with "Thy" for the signature where Wagner employs the second person singular throughout a letter, and having found the experiment successful—so far as can be judged from its provoking no adverse comment in any quarter—I have continued it here, as stamping a degree of intimacy for which our own colder nation has no symbol in general use.

In conclusion, I have just one appeal to address

to the reader: an appeal of a practical nature on both sides. Feeling that what has greatly militated against a truer knowledge of R. Wagner's character as man has been a limitation of the sale of kindred volumes by their comparatively high cost, I have persuaded my present publishers to issue this one at a price within the means of all who crowd the cheaper sections of the house at performances of his dramatic works, or take the most modest of parts in their representation. With them and their numberless friends it must rest, alike to justify our present, and to shape our future policy. For at least one more volume of letters is ready for printing in the event of a cordial reception of this.

WM. ASHTON ELLIS.

BRIGHTON, *July* 1911.

TABLE OF CONTENTS

[1] As noted in the body of the volume, Nos. 21 to 23, 36, 37, 39, 43 and 49 of the German edition, having already appeared in the much larger collection of letters translated under the title " *Richard to Minna Wagner,*" are not included by me in the present.—W. A. E.

TABLE OF CONTENTS

TABLE OF CONTENTS

To his Mother on her birthday

MAGDEBURG, *the* 20*th Sept.* [1835].

MY DEAR, DEAR MOTHER—*I am thinking of you to-day
with my whole heart and all the fervour my spirit possesses; and
even though this letter cannot reach you till tomorrow, I find it
sweeter to collect my feelings just* to-day, *when all your children
must be thanking God with such emotion, Who will let you see
this day as oft again, for all our good, as we wish and hope with
all our souls.—*

*Often, right often, my darling, may you witness a happy return
of this day, and be blest with the e'er-renewed feeling how proudly
you can resurvey each year thus added to your life.—O Mother,
do not fret; the Creator meted you a beauteous lot! Is it not
you who, what she gave the world, maintained it also sound and
pure with grandest love and care? On you the glorious gift of
clearest conscience was bestowed in measure as on few besides.
We whom your love and virtue have the most affected, are bound
to plumb them to their depth—eh, rest assured we love and honour
you devoutly—and should every thinkable relation in this life divide
us, our love for you would make us one again. O see, your living
influence will continue thus, and should you e'er be snatched away,
your cherished memory it still will be that binds your offspring fast.*

*It is Sunday, and a fine sunny day; we who form a small
colony here will also keep this day with joy and gladness, and make
of it a feast. Preserve thy constancy and love to us, and we will
thank thee as a Saviour with the offering of our every best wish!
A fond heartfelt Farewell from* Thy

RICHARD.

FAMILY LETTERS
OF RICHARD WAGNER

1. To Sister Ottilie [1]

LEIPZIG, *the 3rd March* (1832).

MY DEAR GOOD OTTILIE—So it is my turn
at last to send a few lines to your far-away
Denmark, after not having seen you for so long
that it has become a positive need to me to have
another talk with you, at least on paper. But
really there's *so much* I should like to tell you
of the year gone by, such a decisive one for me,
that I fear this sheet of paper would never hold it ;
so I must just make shift with what lies nearest to
my heart.

How much it grieved me, that I was unable to
take leave of you when you made your departure
from here ! That is the chief sorrow that has
befallen me in your entire absence, and I felt
quite mopish when I stayed in the same hotel at
Culm where,[2] Mother told me, you bade your last

---

[1] Two years Richard's senior, Ottilie had formed an intimacy with
Charlotte, daughter of the Danish poet, Adam Oehlenschläger, and was now
at the latter's home in Copenhagen on a visit which already had lasted
something like nine months.—TR.

[2] A little place between Dresden and Teplitz where the mother was
wont to take a course of baths each summer ; presumably Ottilie accompanied
her, and started thence for Denmark.—TR.

farewell. However, I suppose it won't be much longer before I see you once more ; for, no matter how you may be enjoying yourself at present, I do hope you will also be longing to get back to us some day, if you sympathise with us else.

And now let me narrate you a little bit about myself; which perhaps will be just what you would like, since you shewed such great concern about me in one of your last letters.

Ah, how it grieves me to have to tell you that I, no doubt, was quite unruly for a while, and had been so turned from my goal through keeping company with students, that it caused dear Mother very much anxiety and pain. But I pulled myself together in the end, and have now been so confirmed in my improvement by my new teacher, that already I stand on a point whence I may view my higher course of life as firmly entered. For you must know that for over the past half-year I have been the pupil of our Cantor Weinlig, whom one may rightly call the *greatest contrapuntist now alive ;* added to which, he's such an excellent man that I'm as fond of him as of a father. He has brought me on with such affection that, to employ his own expression, I may already regard my 'prenticeship as ended, and now he simply stands towards me as advising friend. How fond he is of me himself, you may judge by this: when Mother asked him to name his fee, after half a year's tuition, he said it would be unreasonable of him to accept payment for the delight of having taught me, my industry and his hopes of me were quite enough reward.

Well, you may easily imagine that all this has borne fruit. Last Christmas an overture of mine was performed at the theatre,[1] and actually one at the *Grand concert* last week ;[2] and I would have you know that this latter is no trifle, since before anything is accepted for these concerts from a young composer, his work must be found worthy by all the connoisseurs on the committee ; so my overture's acceptance in itself may prove to you there's something in it. But I now must tell you about the evening of performance, of such moment to me, for sure. Rosalie and Luise [eldest and next eldest sisters] were present. In no case could I expect anything like a rousing success, as in the first place overtures are seldom applauded at these concerts, and in the second, two new overtures by MARSCHNER and LINDPAINTNER had been given a short time previously without setting a single hand in motion ;—nevertheless my suspense was tremendous, and I almost fainted for fright (oh, had you only been there !). So you may guess my joyful surprise when, at my overture's finish, the whole roomful began to applaud just as if they had been hearing the greatest masterpiece ; I hardly knew how to contain myself—I can assure you !— and Luise was so affected by it, that she wept. How I did wish you had been present ; I'm certain it would have given you a little pleasure too ! Enough of that. Now for another piece of

---

[1] This work's identity is a little difficult to establish at present.—TR.

[2] That is to say, one of the regular subscription-concerts at the Gewandhaus. The concert taking place Feb. 23, 1832, this overture was manifestly that in D minor, composed Sept. 26, and revised Nov. 4, 1831.—TR.

news : a pianoforte sonata of mine, dedicated to my Weinlig, has appeared in print this week ; I received a 20 thaler note for it. I would gladly forward you a copy, if I didn't reflect that the carriage would almost exceed the price you can get it for in Copenhagen yourself ; so just go to any music-shop and order it from Leipzig, under the title : "Sonata for the pianoforte by Richard Wagner, op. 1, Breitkopf und Haertel, Leipzig." It isn't very hard, but in case you can't play it yourself straight away, just ask Fräulein Lottchen, in my name, to play it to you ;—I should be so delighted if it pleased you. Quite recently also [Feb. 3] I composed an overture to *König Enzio*, a new tragedy by Raupach, which is performed at the theatre each time the piece is played ; it pleases every one.

And now no more about my products ; as soon as you are back among us, it will give me infinite joy, my dear sister, to shew you everything.

The 21st March.

See what a time I have been without ending my letter ! Meanwhile we have received your last, and as Rosalie herself is answering it, and these lines will be a mere enclosure, it would be needless to present you with our news when Rosalie's letter is sure to tell you quite enough about us all.

How particularly delighted I was to see by your last letter that you are getting a regular longing to be back with us ; it is certain to expedite your journey home. O come right soon, that when Rosalie departs [for Prague] I may not be left with no one who is kin to me through music also ! For which matter, during the break in this letter I've written yet another overture,[1] which I am going to conduct at the Musical Union [Euterpe] myself; perhaps I may manage to promote it to the Grand Concerts as well. Good goodness, there I go starting again about my compositions; to put a stop to that old song, I shall wind up this letter at once. The only thing I'll add to my farewell is : Don't stay away much longer, and God grant that when you do return, you may have kept me thoroughly at heart. Enjoy your final days in Copenhagen as you may, I am sure you will like being here again. Adieu, Adieu. Thy   RICHARD W.

[Between this and the next letter young Richard, still a minor, has made his first launch on the world, starting in January 1833 to join his eldest brother, Albert —singer, actor, and stage-manager—at Wurzburg ; where he soon obtained the post of operatic Chorus-master, and presently commenced his first completed opera, *Die Feen.*—TR.]

2. To SISTER ROSALIE

WURZBURG, the 11*th December* 33.

I must confess to you, my only Rosalie, that your letter made a profound impression on me, coming, as it did, at a time when the sole reason for my silence toward you all had been a certain bashfulness as to how I was to step before you.

---

[1] C major with closing fugue, terminally dated " Leipzig, 17 März 1832 " ; performed also the 30th of the ensuing April at an " extraneous " concert in the Gewandhaus.—TR.

Almost I had to assume that, after the sacrifices
you dear ones had made for me, it would be
extremely disagreeable to you to see their object
unattained, and perhaps you might be angry with
me even for the mode in which I gave you notice
of the failure of that expectation.[1]   Ah, I felt so
strangely depressed when I thought of you all, and
believed I guessed how you must picture to yourselves the reason for my staying on here, as to
whose upshot you could not form the smallest
notion yet.   I cannot possibly describe to you how
much that sort of apprehension tortured me, the
greater its contrast with the feelings woken in me
by my daily occupation with my opera.   God, or
rather yourself, be thanked ! your letter—how shall
I call it ?—your wonder-working letter delivered
me from many discomposures of the kind, although
it caused me fresh disturbance on the other side ;
for, after once reading it, I couldn't work for
two or three days.   I meant to answer you right
away—but—I was still short of my opera's last
finale : the day before yesterday I finished it, and
therewith my whole opera ; it was exactly noon,
and the bells in all the steeples rang 12 as I wrote
Finis beneath it,—how much that pleased me !

So, dearest, the *composition* of my opera is
finished, and I have only its last act left to instrument now !   It is my somewhat pedantic mode of
writing out my score as tidily as possible from the
outset, that has most delayed me in the instrumenting of my work ;—if I am nice and industrious,

---

[1] Evidently regarding that Zurich conductorship which Glasenapp informs
us that Rosalie was so anxious for her brother to accept in the September
just past ; see *Life of R. Wagner*, i, p. 166.—Tr.

however, I expect to have got through even this last stage of work at my opera in something like 3 weeks, and so be able to depart from here in about a month.

But how shall I describe to you the mood I've been working in of late ? How I thought of you all with well-nigh every note—ah, of yourself!—and it was a feeling which often spurred me on indeed, but often also overwhelmed me so, that I had to stop work and seek the open air. That happened to me oft, but ever did I hold it for a glad presentiment ; and how it has delighted me to find your letter bearing witness to an equal sympathy! Oh, God grant I don't deceive your joyful expectations ! But that, that cannot be,—everything has flowed so from my inmost soul,—and they say a thing like that, you know, must likewise pass into the souls of others.

To-morrow there's to be a concert, for which I have been asked to give a couple of numbers from my opera. An amateur with a fine voice will sing Ada's grand aria [act ii.], and then a terzet from it will be rendered by her, Albert, and a young basso. The latter [terzet] joins on to the introduction of the 2nd act, and is the situation where Arindal returns to his kingdom with Morald and is welcomed by his sister Lora. The Chorus greets him as its King with cheers, which he checks, however, with exclamations of sorrow : " O cease these sounds of joy ! They beat on me with fearsome omen ; alas, the mantle of my royal pomp is woven from my father's shroud ! " He has been wafted from the dreams of Fairyland, finds his kingdom laid waste and in havoc, everything recalls his father's death through grieving for him, and added to it all is Ada's warning of the horrors still awaiting him this day,—thus bridging a path for the mood in which he will encounter Ada in the [act's] finale. Lora and Morald, on the contrary, feel uplifted by Arindal's return, and look forward to a happy issue of the battle. This mood is characterised by the new theme of the Allegro [con brio], the exultation of which moved Albert so at the rehearsal, as he assured me, that he let 16 bars pass by before he could go on singing. That miss was more agreeable to me, than if he had come in all right. Yet this is one of my least important numbers, to tell the truth ; for instance, I have a terzet in the 3rd act where Arindal is aroused from his madness and comes to feel that it has vanished through his wife's appeal for help ; where he is emboldened by the two fairies to set Ada free, till at last he picks up arms and rushes off in highest ecstasy to his wife's deliverance ;—from that I count on something more !

But why do I speak of all these things ? 'Tis nothing but the yearning to inform you of just everything. My God, the time is not so distant now,—I shall soon be with you all—with yourself. I mustn't give way to the thought so entirely, though, or I shall be unable to write another word, —and I've such a lot still to tell you, if I could only get it all in trim ! I'm in such an agitated state all day now,—last night again I got no sleep ;— but ah ! what am I saying ? I had to give up

hope of restful nights long since ; I'm thinking of
you all the time—and—immodest fellow !—of my
opera. . .—Of late I've dreamt a deal of all of
you, of my arrival with you, and how I should be
received by you all. Strange ! my dreams of this
sort have resembled one continuous climax :—in
the first my reception among you was no great
shakes—quite coldly casual,—later it already grew
more genial—heartier ;—and now it's fashioned in
my dreams exactly as I'd wish it in reality. I
hope it doesn't mean anything ;—surely you all
will be good to me, even though I have little
deserved it at present.

What you write me about the acceptance and
[proposed] representation of my opera at Leipzig
completely suits me, and I thank you for your
pains and forethought. I really think it will all
work out,—nay, I don't merely think,—I hope it,
and should be greatly frightened at an undeception
of my hopes ! But tell me, among other things
you write me that *Hans Heiling* is taking so well,
and goes on filling the house ;—I must confess, this
news has been extremely disagreeable to me, in a
certain sense. We have given that opera here as
well, and by all means I find the music very pretty
too, especially the single pieces ; but in no other
opera of Marschner's have I met so entire a dearth
of total effect. I can't make it out, but he has
let the best effects pass unexploited : what sort of
things are those for act-ends ;—what unmelodious-
ness in the choruses ! In the 2nd finale he treats
the culminating point of the whole : " He springs
from the realm of gnomes and dwarfs, and is the

mountain-spirits' prince !" so slovenly, and brings off so little climax, that one would imagine something of no sort of consequence was going on. In short, not a single number is arresting,—which, I must admit, might almost betray me into vain hopes for my own opera!

It is distressing that things should be like that with your lady singers,—I much need a reliable voice and emotional acting,—something after the Devrient pattern wouldn't come amiss. From what I know of the Gerhardt as yet, her voice might doubtless prove too weak,—though her having been good as Alice [*Robert*], as you say, has given me hope. Above all, it will be necessary that Eichberger should remain, for the tenor has indisputably the biggest, and certainly also a grateful part ;—if he were to leave, it would be of infinite harm to me! Albert is very fond of this part, and would be bound to excel in it ;—perhaps [that may happen], should he take a starring turn at Leipzig.

Upon the other things you tell me, dearest Rosalie, let me be silent for the present ;—it all affected me too disagreeably, and has wounded me too acutely, for me to be able to discuss much of that sort with you yet ; I shall soon be with you all, and pride myself upon a certain gift now which at least will lighten some of your forebodings, and rob good Mother of many a—crotchet! Yet I thank you for those communications,—the source they flowed from, your loving trust, honours me much! —— ——

How is Mother, and how are you all ? —— —— Ah,

but I shall soon see all of you again! Really, I'm a thorough spoilt child; every instant pains me, when I'm absent from your fold! I hope we two, my Rosalie, may be *a deal* together in this life yet! Do you agree? For the rest, I'm infinitely glad that everything is standing well with all of you,—give the others my best love, and don't let them dread my arrival. It will be about a year, I've been away from you;—God grant it may have borne good interest!

——I perceive I'm winding up my letter most irregularly; ascribe it to the perpetual unrest and agitation which possess me now, particularly when I think of you all and my future! Everything is mixing itself up before my senses, and it's highest time my opera were ended, or my objectivity would have a poor look-out. God willing, however, I shall have finished in 3 to 4 weeks,—then forth to you!

Albert is writing also,—how glad I am that he is relieving me of a duty I can only think of with alarm! I can do no more than beg you all most sincerely for your kindness and indulgence in every way! Good Lord, I'm only 20 years of age as yet!— —

—Remembrances to all once more, and heartiest of all to my good Mother; and tell them a lot about their Richard, who gives them so much care and trouble. But yourself—you remain my good angel, my only Rosalie; remain it aye!—Thy

RICHARD.

[The beginning of 1834 Richard returns to the family fold, where he spends the next few months in vain attempts to get *Die Feen* mounted by the Leipzig manager, one F. S. Ringelhardt. Early in June, however, he sets out on a pleasure-trip, as guest of his well-to-do chum, T. Apel.—Tr.]

3. To the Same

PRAGUE, *the 3rd July* (1834).

MY DEAR ROSALIE—Merely a brief report—what would be the use of a long letter? I shall be back quite soon, you see, and then say more by mouth!

Not until Monday did we leave Teplitz for Prague, after having stayed there a fortnight on account of the baths in particular, which Theodor took seriously, and I rather for amusement. That visit enraptured me, and I shall remember the Milleschauer all the rest of my life. Prague, too, seems quite another city to me now; I can see now what a dull and cheerless oaf I was, when I roamed about it last.[1] We have unimpeachably fine weather, and at the present lovely season of the year that makes everything gay and bright to me. I was delighted with the R's.;[2] they're both quite well. Jenny has a little gone off, Auguste is handsomer than ever; Apel has lost his head. The legatee business has turned out greatly to the girls' advantage; the house belongs to them, and each receives 10,000 fl. Vienna currency from the

[1] With his "juvenile" Symphony in his pocket he had gone there summer 1832, when that work obtained its earliest performance at the hands of old Dionys Weber's pupils in the Conservatorium.—Tr.

[2] The initial given in the German edition; but it plainly should be " P.," as these young ladies, friends of Rosalie's, were the daughters of a Count Pachta, whose guest the budding genius had been two years before. See *Mein Leben* and Letters to Apel.—Tr.

Pravonin estate. Altogether, people set them down at 30,000 fl. ord. curr. apiece. What has much helped them, is the favourable relation with Karl Pachta, who has travelled hither from Milan. He is behaving extremely well to them. I should like to beat that animal, the old woman, whenever I set eyes on her; the girls have a capital chance now,—if they profit by it to get free, they may pull themselves out of the affair quite nicely ;—if not, they can mix with clever people and enjoy themselves : good again!

We have been too short a time here, and I have gone about too little yet, to be able to give you folk much other news. Only to-day am I calling on Gerle, Kinsky, [Dionys] Weber, and above all, Stöger, to whom I've been presented already. He seems to me a splendid chap ; his theatre has a most distinguished footing. The handsomeness of the scenery and costumes transforms the stage here into something so different, that I don't recognise it at all. The Opera is excellent ; among others, the Lutzer has come on, so that she will replace the Devrient for us some day. I'm enraptured with her ;—quite the new young school,—thoroughly dramatic,—a few steps more, and she will be perfect. I shall make up to her,—she'll be a capital Ada. I have copied my text-book out sprucely and neatly, and shall give it to Stöger this very day.

We are having disgracefully good luck ;— yesterday Löwe commenced his starring here, as Garrick : a heavenly treat. But all the rest are good, too,—and they haven't all assembled yet,—

Stöger is still waiting for much, among other
things the filling up of his Ballet.   Prague
must be going to become one of the first - class
theatres !   But the audience is worth it, too.

I'm glad you tell me such grand tales of
Ringelhardt ;—he'll be in fine feather, for sure.[1]
I am writing him to-day, also to the Gerhard ; ah,
and it makes me quite anxious and timid.   Are
the happy days I'm now enjoying about to venge
themselves on me, perhaps ?   That question gives
me a cold shudder from time to time, and then I
often feel what I cannot describe.   I am certain to
be going to face a medley of cross-purposes, for
which I must clothe myself in steel, to conquer
them featly and firmly.   Dear God, pray leave me
my few remaining happy days; for with this
coming winter the chill of life will seize me too,
and my fortune's sun will need to send me of its
warmest rays, if everything's to prosper.   A
torturing unrest on that account now often grips
me, spurring me home with all speed ; I feel as if
something were awaiting me there which I must
confront with all my might.   Your letter, the
very mention of my opera, has made me most
restless, and nothing but the power of the
moment's happiness can stave that feeling off.

Probably nothing will come of Vienna, we've
been too long already ; and that exactly suits me.
We shall travel back by Carlsbad.   So, if you
haven't forwarded the *notes* yet [score of his symphony
or an overture ?], please let that be.— —

1 " Der wird sich gewiss auch tüchtig heben " ; meaning ambiguous in
the absence of data.—Tr.

How are you all? I'm glad Mother has enjoyed herself. How are things standing with Laube? I keep thinking of him, and am much afraid for his sake [political arrest]. You say nothing of Marcus! If he hasn't let himself be heard of any more, he's a miserable poltroon,—and I hope we shall have no difficulty in persuading Caecilie to give him up. My best love to her. Love, too, to Brockhaus [Friedrich] and Luise, — please deliver my message,—I'm taking kindly to him now.

Farewell, my Rosalie, and don't go crying in your bedroom again when you come home at night and undress; I was in your sitting-room, and heard you. Farewell!—Thy RICHARD.

Many greetings from Theodor,—he affords me great hope. Give Mother my sincerest love once more.

How much I wish Julius could make this journey too; he would be bound to return from it *well*. I feel more and more what a glorious blessing Health is; luckily, though, since I am in possession of it, and have no need to long for it,— but I wish it Julius with all my heart!

Please send the [*Feen*] scores to Ringelhardt together with the letter.

[Now just of age, Richard soon became musical conductor at the Magdeburg theatre. At the end of his first season he paid his relations a visit, when he had rather a dismal tale to tell of his manager's impecuniosity; a tale which seems to have met with little sympathy from his brother-in-law, Friedrich Brockhaus, for his mother writes him some months later: "You must not think the family bear a grudge against you. I cannot blame you for avoiding Fritz at present—after what occurred between you and him, it is better that the grass should grow over it and you should have time to give yourself a position in his eyes. He is finding just the same fault with his brother Hermann now, who isn't working hard enough [to please him] and doesn't think enough of money-making ; and the brothers [Fr. and Heinrich B.] have a horror of giving." It would also appear that Richard had been looking out for a fresh berth, though he ended by returning to that at Magdeburg for another season, and letter 4 finds him on a tour of inspection on behalf of his manager, H. Bethmann. It is worthy of note that, albeit the young man had already met and fallen in love with his future wife, Minna, between Nos. 3 and 4—she being engaged as actress at the same theatre—her name is mentioned neither in this No. 4 nor in either of its two successors.—Tr.]

4. To his Mother [1]

Only of yourself, dearest Mother, can I think with the sincerest love and profoundest emotion. Brothers and sisters, I know it, must go their own way,—each has an eye to himself, to his future, and the surroundings connected with both. So it is, and I feel it myself : there comes a time when roads part of themselves, — when our mutual relations are governed solely from the standpoint of external life ; we become mere nodding diplomats to one another, keeping silence where silence seems politic, and speaking where our view

[1] Address : " Ihr Wohlgeb. / Madame / JOHANNA GEYER / pr. Adrss. Fräulein Rosalie Wagner / zu / LEIPZIG — Reichel's Garten, im Hinter-gebäude."

of an affair demands ; and when we're at a distance from each other, we speak the most. But ah, how high a mother's love is poised above all that !

No doubt I, too, belong to those who cannot always speak out at the moment as their heart dictates,—or you might often have come to know me from a much more melting side. But my sentiments remain the same,—and see, Mother— now I have left you, the feeling of thanks for that grand love of yours towards your child, which you displayed to him so warmly and so tenderly again the other day, so overpowers me that I fain would write, nay, tell you of it in accents soft as of a lover to his sweetheart. Yes, and still softer,—for is not a mother's love far more—far more untainted than all other ?

Nay, here I won't philosophise,—I simply want to thank you, and again, to thank you,—and how gladly would I count up all the separate proofs of love for which I thank,—were there not too many of them. O yes, I know full well that no heart yearns after me now with so great an inner sympathy or such solicitude, as yours ; yes, that perhaps it is the only one that watches o'er my every step,—and not, forsooth, coldly to criticise it, —no, to include it in your prayers. Have you not ever been the only one to stay unalterably true to me when others, judging by mere outward results, turned philosophically away? It would indeed be exacting beyond measure, were I to ask a like affection from them all ; I even know it is not possible,—I know it from myself : but with *you* all issues from the heart, that dear good

c

heart I pray God e'er to keep inclined to me,—for
I know that, should all else forsake me, 'twould
still remain my last, my fondest refuge. O
Mother, what if you should prematurely die, ere I
had fully proved to you that it was to a worthy
son, of boundless gratitude, you shewed so great a
love! But no, that cannot be; you still must
taste abundant fruits. Ah, the remembrance of
that latest week with you; it is a perfect feast to
me, a cordial, to call before my soul each several
token of your loving care! My dear, dear
Mother,—what a wretch were I, if I could ever
cool towards thee!

For the future I shall tell the family but little
of my doings,—they judge by the outward results,
and will learn those without my assistance. In
whatever fashion it has come about, I'm independent now, and mean to stay so. O that
humbling before Brockhaus is graven deep into
my heart, and the bitterest self-reproaches torture
me, that I should have given into his hands a right
to humble me. I shall get even with him in time,
but never, never at one with him; and should
that be wrong of me, I prefer to bear that wrong
into the grave with me: I withdraw from them
entirely. Each side cannot be right, and I was
wrong;—yet I will never admit it—*to them*, but
place myself in such a situation that I've nothing
to admit to them,—whereas my recent great fault
was having played into their hands, given them
the very smallest right against me. For that
matter, we stand so far from one another, that it
would be absurd of me to want to be at one with

him. Yet, how I do rejoice at this catastrophe,
which has brought me full recognition that I have
nothing to expect from anybody in this world, but
must stand on my own pair of feet ! I feel independent at last. It was this feeling I lacked, and
that lack which made me negligent and easy-going ;
—I had a certain vague reliance on some backer,
which foolishly did not restrict itself to Apel, but
also took other fantastic directions that almost
make me laugh at my stupidity. Now I'm
undeceived about all that, and very glad to be.
My softness needed these experiences,—which will
profit me in every way. Only, I straightway beg
them to deny me any sympathy,—'twould irk
me ;—yourself, your heart, your love shall be my
only stand-by, my refuge and hope in every trouble
of my coming life. Maternal love requires no
reasons,—all other seeks to fathom why it loves,
and therefore turns to nothing but regard.

I have been to Teplitz and Prague, and found
nothing there beyond the confirmation of my plan
not to go to Vienna, and advice to pursue the
direction I already have struck.[1] Moritz was in
Prague, and gave me many a hint in this respect.
From Prague I wrote to all the individuals I have
my eye on, so as to know beforehand where I
stand with them, and take no road in vain. I am
expecting their answers at Nuremberg, whither I
go to-morrow or the next day, as I'm only waiting
for a letter from Magdeburg to conclude my

---

[1] Namely, to look in minor cities for the singers his manager needed.
The actor Moritz of the next sentence had once played Romeo at the
Prague theatre to Rosalie's Juliet.—TR.

business here.   I shall make a halt at Nuremberg ; when a company is being disbanded, one easily picks something up ;—moreover, the Wolframs can give me a deal of information, so that their opinion, perhaps, will save me a journey or two.

My dear, dear Mother,—my good angel,—fare heartily well, and don't fret ;—you have a grateful son who never, never will forget what you are to him.—With the tenderest remembrances,   Thy

RICHARD.

[On his way back to duties at Magdeburg he paid a flying visit to Leipzig again, temporarily exchanging his trunk there for Rosalie's hand-bag, as may be judged from the end of No. 5.   Now in the possession of Wagner's nephew, F. Avenarius, this No. 5—so Glasenapp informs us —is in a most dilapidated condition, much blotted with a corrosive ink which has made the paper so brittle that some of the ends of the lines have dropped away.—TR.]

5. To Sister Rosalie

MAGDEBURG, *the 3rd September* : 35.

MY DEAR ROSALIE—I will just give you in brief the needful news you wish for.   In any event Wolframs are firmly engaged here,[1] and urgently expected ; but their travelling money— 50 thaler, not 100—unfortunately went off to them from here only the day before yesterday. So, if they had started already, they won't have received it ; if they have managed to pull through as far as here, though, they'll receive it *here*, since

---

[1] Sister Clara (his senior by 5½ years) and her husband Heinrich, both of them stage artists at this epoch.   They do not appear to have retained their Magdeburg engagement very long, as they soon discovered how the managerial land lay.—TR.

it will be returned here if it didn't catch them at Nuremberg. It therefore is merely a question whether *both* the Wolframs have left Nuremberg together. Cläre wrote you, you know, that she would be starting this week in any case ;—consequently it might be that *Cläre* has arrived alone, and Wolfram stayed behind ;—if so, please tell her that, in receipt of the travelling money, Wolfram would follow her now. In any event don't let her waste a single minute,—they're counting on her here already as on their daily bread. So, if they both left Nuremberg together, and have pulled through so far, they'll receive the money here. Cläre mustn't think of accepting any other offer,— but both must come here very, *very* quick.

Please go this instant and enquire at both the Letter and the Parcel Post whether a poste-restante letter with 5 Friedrichs d'or for me is lying there. Bethmann has shewn me the certificate; it was despatched to Frankfort, and, according to orders I left there, will either have been forwarded to Leipzig—or if not, it will return here to-day or to-morrow. I will write you to-morrow if Freimüller [tenor] turns up,—no doubt . . . [dropped away]. For that matter, things are quite passable here . . . [ditto] our people are getting their pay. I saw the . . . [ditto] *of Women* yesterday, which was really quite charmingly played, at the least just as well as with you. I believe we shall have a great success with the Opera here ; every one is [looking forward to] Wolframs ;—mind they come.

You'll get your travelling-bag back by the same [messenger] who is to fetch away my trunk.

Love to all—most hearty love, and excuse this hurried scrawl.—Thy   RICHARD W.

[Owing to Bethmann's insolvency, this Magdeburg operatic season came to a premature end with a disastrously scrambled production of Wagner's only just completed *Liebesverbot*, March 29, 1836. After hanging on there another few weeks, meantime opening vain negotiations with Leipzig Ringelhardt for acceptance of that second opera in default of his shelved first, the already-affianced proceeds to try his luck with it about the middle of May in big Berlin itself.—TR.]

6. TO HIS MOTHER [1]

BERLIN, *the* 31*st May.* 36.

DEAREST MOTHER—You must have been expecting a letter from me for some time, especially after your being here and our not meeting. Not until the evening after your departure, did I learn from Eichberger that you had been here. I had heard from the Gerhardt before, that you were here with Mad. Berthold ;—but I didn't quite believe it, and thought that if you really were here, you would surely have informed Laube of it, as you couldn't well know where I was lodging. I went to Laube,—but he knew nothing about it, and doubted it as much as I,—and—so I was quite thunderstruck when I learnt it at last, but too late, from Eichberger. So far as I made out from him, moreover, my letter from Magdeburg

---

[1] Address : " Ihr. Wohlgeb. / Madame / JOHANNA GEYER. / LEIPZIG. Reichels Garten, Hintergebäude, rechts."

didn't catch you at Leipzig ; and that was doubly
disagreeable to me, since you didn't even know
that I intended going to Berlin. Ill-luck and
misfortune, however, has been my constant lot
of late; my flesh creeps still when I think of
it all.

My Berlin expedition has turned my evil star
at last a little. I and Cerf[1] are the most intimate
friends in the world, embracing as often as ever
we meet. I pleased the fellow, and he promptly
regretted having signed a contract with his
musikdir. Kugler for another year. For the
present, only thus much :—Kapellmeister Gläser
has a long leave this summer, and during his
absence I'm temporarily to step into his shoes
and pay. While I thus have the reins in my
hand for a time, I shall get up my opera here, and
produce it; and when Gläser returns, I shall
descend from my perch again. To be sure, I
shall have to accept a fresh engagement for a
while then, but hope to have my next year's
contract with Cerf in hand by then as alternating
Capellmeister ; and in the worst event I shall be
winning myself renommée here, when I can retire
with a better face. Laube and his literary retainers,
such as Glasbrenner, are making a terrible fuss of
me as the foremost genius in the world ;—but you'll
be equally able to read in the *Konversationsblatt*
the printed announcement of all that I've told
you above. There's nothing else for it, I'm

---

[1] Lessee and manager of the Königstädter theatre in Berlin. From this
point onward it is scarcely necessary to warn the reader against taking too
greatly in earnest a harmless mystification of the anxious mother.—TR.

bound to make my fortune here, and that's just what I lacked ;—I couldn't have come to Leipzig, the air is not good for me there [Mendelssohn ?]. I hope this will ease your mind a little, should it require it.

So Cläre is staying with you,—the dear good creature ! But how are things going with her husband ? In my direst want and desperation I wrote him once from Magdeburg,—but got no answer. Wohlbrück from Riga is here ;—a new theatre is being built there, and will be opened this autumn. Perhaps I may go there ; but I want to make my name here first.

Excuse me, I must be off to my good friend Spontini, or the man will be dropping in here ; he is beside himself that *he* can't give my opera ;— but why did he apply so late ? I cannot oblige him ! My good friend the *King* has offered me Spontini's post ; but what good would that be to me ? At this moment six writers are craving an audience of me ;—there's a regular rush for me,— I can't stand it much longer,—particularly as *I haven't a farthing* in my pocket. My good friend— Theodor Apel—also sent me a very pretty *unfranked* letter to Magdeburg, in which he told me they were rebuilding at Ermlitz, and so there'd be no room for me ;—I maintain that's another new joke from his latest comedy. Quite frankly, dear Mother, I have even a mite of suspicion that it was you who set this gentleman a little on to me as well ; I have my grounds.[1]

[1] " Recht offen, liebe Mutter, ich habe selbst Dich ein wenig im Verdacht, dass Du mir auch diesen Mann etwas auf den Hals gehetzt hast, ich habe

There you see how splendidly your son is faring. Cerf, among other things, can't control his affection for me ; he's sure to strike his children from his will and put me there instead,—often he quietly beweeps upon my breast the woes of his directorate. He's just as much a blackguard, as of use to anybody who can manage him. My whole policy, just now, is to pack Gläser off to the baths as quickly as possible ;—he must catch a thorough chill there,—for I don't believe he is intemperate. God grant me His assistance ! Till then fare right heartily well. Love to Cläre and the whole family a thousand times from Thy

RICHARD W.

[After kicking his heels for two months in Berlin to no purpose, Wagner followed Minna Planer to Königsberg, on the chance of an appointment there, which he did not actually obtain until the theatre was on the eve of bankruptcy. Meanwhile he married her, November 24, 1836 ; but his wife ran away from him just half a year later, and did not rejoin him till some few weeks after his installation as Kapellmeister at Riga, September 1837, where he began the composition of *Rienzi*. Ousted from his post through the intrigues of a false friend, Heinrich Dorn, he leaves Russia the end of June 1839, and, after a perilous sea-voyage of over three weeks, reaches London with his wife and dog the beginning of August, *en route* for that imagined El Dorado, Paris.—TR.]

---

dazu meine Gründe." The meaning here is somewhat obscure, though possibly connected with Frau Geyer's objection to her son's proposed marriage.—TR.

7. To Eduard Avenarius [1]

BOULOGNE, *the 23rd August* 1839.

MOST ESTEEMED SIR AND FRIEND—Please let me call you by that intimate name at once, since for my own part I already feel so prepossessed by all that I have heard about the amiability and uprightness of your character, that I shall do everything I can to earn the corresponding rights and title of a friend.   Forestalling that, I have repeatedly troubled you before through my good sister Cäcilie ; and the readiness with which you undertook a fairly difficult transaction for me is warrant that I shall not completely put my foot in it with the request that forms this letter's chief occasion.   No doubt you have already been made acquainted by Cäcilie that my present somewhat daring, nay, haply adventurous object is Paris ; how far I am prepared to face that mass of obstacles undaunted, you will judge for yourself when you have had the obligingness to lend ear in Paris to what I think of and propose ; a matter in which I also reckon mainly on your good advice, for whose bestowal I beg you in advance most keenly.

After a ghastly and very perilous voyage of nearly 4 weeks, I arrived in London on a sailing ship about 12 days ago, and was forced to spend a week of gold-fraught days on its expensive pavement through the muddling of my captain,

---

[1] Avenarius was then betrothed to Wagner's half-sister Cecilie, whom he married March 5 of the ensuing year.   Address of this letter : " à/Monsieur/ Monsieur AVÉNARIUS/pr. addresse :/la LIBRAIRIE DE BROCKHAUS/ET AVÉ-NARIUS/à/Paris./Franco." Pcstmark : " Boulogne-sur-mer, 24 Août 1839."

who had played silly tricks with my luggage. On the 20th I came by steamer to Boulogne, where I made haste to take as cheap a lodging as I could get for a few weeks in the country, that is to say a little under half an hour's walk from the town. I chose this halt for several reasons : 1°, I believe I am unlikely to find sundry persons of weight for my project in Paris just yet ; 2°, I have still a few weeks' work ahead of me on what I should like to bring to Paris *finished*, in order to begin my machinations there immediately after arrival ; 3°, I really wished to be able to rest off some of the jolting I have gone through, before plunging afresh into such a hurly-burly as the Parisian is certain to be.

Might I therefore beg you in the meantime to find me a lodging in Paris, kindly observing the following :—An ordinary room with an alcove is fully sufficient, of course, for myself and my wife ; a larger room *without one* would also do at a pinch. It will have to be furnished in fact, though we possess our own bedding and linen, table-gear, candlesticks, utensils, as we have brought almost our whole small outfit with us, and merely sold the most untransportable in Russia. My wife will do the housekeeping herself, *i.e.*, buy our victuals, cook, and so on ; therefore needs no other service than of a charwoman to assist her in the roughest work. Naturally, I can only hire the lodging by the month, and as I don't quite know the price one has to pay for such a thing in Paris, I won't name any fixed one, but leave it to necessity and your own obliging nous. I hardly need assure you that in every respect I should prefer not to live too far away from you. So, would you have the kindness to look around you in a leisure hour for what I ask, and report to me hither thereon, Boulogne poste restante ? In that case I would write you again before my departure from here, telling you the exact day of my arrival in Paris, so that you might be so good as to engage the apartment from that day, and spare us having to alight at an inn.

I know I am begging no trifling favour of you, but nevertheless nurse the perhaps impudent trust that, of all people, you are in a position to make me the sacrifice. At the same time I also beseech you to write me how your and Cäcilie's affairs are standing now. It would very much rejoice me to hear something joyful in that regard, more especially as I unfortunately have been unable to get any tidings from home for ever so long. If I might hope to see good Cäcilie in Paris soon, all my hopes of a favourable issue to my future endeavours would really become the fonder and more precious in no small degree. God give his blessing, and let all honest folk prosper !

Looking joyfully forward to a letter from you, I commend myself to your regard with all the cordiality of which my heart is capable.—Yours most sincerely,

RICHARD WAGNER.[1]

---

[1] Note by recipient : " Answered 27, viii. fr. poste rest."

8. To the Same[1]

BOULOGNE, 13th Sept : 39.

MY MOST VALUED SIR—If I am so late in answering your very kind and attentive letter, it is because *this* letter of mine was at the same time to inform you definitely of the day of my arrival in Paris; which on various grounds, in turn, has only become possible to-day. For the self-same reason I am also writing but a few lines now, as I hope to be very soon able to greet you in person and discuss everything by word of mouth ; for I leave here by diligence Monday, the 16th of this month, and shall therefore reach Paris quite early on Tuesday. So, to come to one of the main points straight off, I will avail myself of your not sufficiently to be acknowledged kindness, and beg you to hire a room big enough for myself and my wife in a hôtel garni to begin with, according to your own suggestion, and for the present *by the week*. What you say about my plan of a lodging to manage oneself is perfectly right, and that is a point you will permit me to discuss by mouth with you and quite clear up. You write me, one can get a very decent chamber in a hôtel garni for as little as 30 francs a month, and I must confess that I hadn't supposed one could do it so cheap ; consequently, if you will engage that sort of thing for me, I beg you not to be afraid even if the rent should amount to 40 or 50 francs ; I had set

---

[1] Address : " Monsieur / AVÉNARIUS / libraire / à / PARIS / No : 60, rue Richelieu." Postmark : " Boulogne-sur-mer, 15 Sept. 1839." Paris postmark : " 16 Sept. 39."

down that much for this purpose in advance. Naturally, however—the cheaper the better. But as I shall in any case be arriving in Paris *very early Tuesday*, and should really not care to alight at an inn, you would infinitely oblige me if you would give yourself the great trouble to write a couple of lines with the address of the hôtel garni in which you had engaged my room, and leave them at the Barrière St. Denis, which we shall pass on our way from Boulogne, so that I may find them on my arrival, and be able accordingly to drive to my refuge at once.

That is the chief thing I wanted to ask you beforehand. Only don't let it alarm you ; I mean to moderate my future claims as much as possible.

Once again I reserve for oral conversation whatever else may be worth the telling now. Only thus much about my affairs : in no case should I have remained at Boulogne so long, with these English prices to pay, if a lucky chance had not ordained that I was to meet Meierbeer here ; who may be of incalculable weight for my project, and with whom I already have struck up as much friendship as possible. But upon that too—by mouth, as also concerning all your news about my family.

That I really am *sincerely* looking forward to making your personal acquaintance, I scarcely need assure you. With that presumption I most heartily commend myself and wife to your friendship and favour.—Yours very sincerely,

RICHARD WAGNER.

9. To the Same [1]

4.30. [*Autumn* 1839.]

Most estimable Friend—Tired and done up
as hardly ever before, I have this instant come
home after knocking around at the Garcia's, Joly's,
Dumersan's, Meyerbeer's, etc., since 10 o'clock;
so I must heartily thank you for your offer to
take me to the Italian Opera to-night, but hoard
it for another time. For which matter, in the
Garcia I have made the acquaintance to-day of a
most amiable and obliging creature, who has
volunteered to assist me in everything I ask of
her,—consequently I am hoping she'll also be able
to procure me tickets for the Opera, etc., from
time to time.

I'm as tired as a dog! Heartily wishing you
much enjoyment—though without me,
Yours sincerely,   Richard Wagner.

In great haste, and knocked to pieces.

10. To the Same [same address.]

[*End of* 1839 ?]

Most valued Friend—My wife very, very
warmly entreats you to be so kind as to send her
10,000 francs per bearer;—should that be impossible in such a jiffy, at least she implores 12
hours of your excellent coffee-mill, which you shall
receive back to-morrow morning.

I am invited to dinner at Dumersan's to-day.
—Till death Your   Richard Wagner.

[1] Address: "à Monsieur/Monsieur/Avénarius/rue Richelieu, No. 60."

11. To the Same [same address.]

[PARIS, 4th Jan. 1840.]

MY VALUED FRIEND AND BENEFACTOR—Please answer me quite simply, Yes or No, whether it stands in your power—(would to God it were only your will!)—to increase the sum of my indebtedness to you by another fifty francs; which would make that sum exactly round, or rather, square. No doubt, with the present complexion of the debt itself, I feel that this request of mine almost borders on effrontery;—nevertheless Want not only teaches importunity, but also a certain grade of impudence, which *you*, however, will perhaps excuse more readily than any other man. To pay my rent, etc., I visited the pawnshop yesterday with the last things we could spare, yet without being able to raise sufficient; so, as it is a matter of no more than exactly fifty francs cash, I am having recourse to yourself again (and for the *last* time). If you are able to round off an affirmative answer with the actual nervus rerum, you may easily imagine how welcome it will be to me.—Your   RICHARD W.

I found it impossible to bring this query past my lips yesterday.[1]

---

[1] Draft answer, on the reverse side : " 4th Jan. 1840. I forward you, dear Friend, the 50 fr. you wish for—making 400 fr. in all—and will see what I find your Frau sister [Luise ?] disposed to. With the *best* will, however, I *cannot* go beyond ; as, to obviate any possible misunderstandings, I ought not to conceal from you.—Ever yours,   E. A."

12. To the Same [same address.]

Dear valued Friend—You will have been unable to explain to yourself why you didn't receive that letter of my wife's for kind despatch to Cäcilie long ago. She begs you herewith to excuse this delay, since I *myself*, or rather, my illness has been cause of the lengthy postponement. You will remember that a sudden toothache seized me, the last evening we spent together. That was the beginning of it : a couple of days later I nearly went mad with neuralgia ; after which I got fever, and had to keep my bed ; now I'm merely suffering from a stiff neck, but daren't go out yet. My wife accordingly has not felt fit to write a fluent letter till to-day, as you may well conceive. Voilà tout ! Heartiest thanks once more. Regards from both of us. Your

Richard Wagner.

13. To the Same[1]

PARIS, 29 *April* 1840.

My most honoured Friend and Brother-in-law—I enclose a letter for Fr[au] Dr. Laube, whom I am asking to combine with my sister Luise and send you as quickly as possible the needful authority, or whatever else is required, to advance me 200 francs. I beg you, in the first place, to be so kind as to forward this letter with your [Leipzig] budget of to-day.

[1] Address : "Monsieur / Monsieur E. Avénarius / librairie Allemande / 60, rue Richelieu."

To be sure, my dearest Avenarius, it would be a shorter and far less circuitous method of arriving at the same result, if you could make it possible to advance me this *extra* 200 fr. for a month yourself, and recoup yourself out of the money I have to receive on the 1st of June. For I hereby declare that it's only a question of another 200 fr. which I must have at once to cover my requisite outgoings ; since, fully recognising that I should be unable to sustain my life much longer this way, I have already taken steps of such a kind that, beyond these instantly lacking 200 frs, I shall need to make no more appeals on that side. I beg you not to treat this as bombast, but rest assured that if I don't at once *inform* you whence this extra assistance is coming to me [1]—I feel pledged to that course. Merely I repeat that you now may set your mind entirely at ease about my future, and I shall be provided with everything needful till the time I begin getting returns.

To confirm you in that belief, I cannot tell you how much I should have wished not even to need to beg of you these 200 frs themselves. Rest assured that I am only turning to you now because I've tried *all* other ways of obtaining what I need for the moment *in vain*. I therefore confess that I feel greatly humbled at being compelled to turn to you once more, after I already had promised to leave you henceforth at peace with that sort of thing.—But—the time was *too* short, and my instant

---

[1] Perhaps referring to hack-work such as the "arranging of airs for all the instruments under heaven" to be undertaken for publisher Schlesinger (cf. *Prose Works*, i. p. 18).—Tr.

demands are too pressing, for me not to enquire once again in the likeliest quarter, namely of you who have done me the service of intervening to procure me a stipend, and charged yourself with its disbursement to me.—

This, dearest Avenarius, was all I meant, too, when I remarked to you the other day that " You were my nearest resource." Your answer shewed me that you somewhat misunderstood me, and I therefore repeat that I merely viewed you as the " nearest " for *so* long as you still should have donations to disburse for my support.

For the very reason which engendered that misunderstanding the other day,—or rather, to avoid it,—I prefer writing, to speaking to you about this last money-matter between us ; more especially as it is difficult to get a word with you alone, and I don't care to discuss that kind of subject with you before Cäcilie.

Once more, then, the last plea of its sort :—If it is *possible* to you, would you have the kindness to advance me 200 frs, in return for which I hereby formally make over to you what you would be paying me the 1st of June on behalf of Fr. Dr. Laube and Luise. In that case I would beg you not to forward the enclosed letter to Frau Laube, but to keep it back, as it would only give rise to a needless confusion.—If you don't care to, or cannot do this, please have the kindness to send that letter off to-day. But as an answer can't arrive so quickly as I need the money for my maintenance, I would beg you, in perfect confidence that the authorisation to take this step will reach you ere long, to try and procure me the 200 frs in advance. Should none of this come off, it would really be the first time that anybody who had something falling due to him—and moreover, who in a few weeks will be placed in the position of seeing his future ensured him—should have to go hungry for those same few weeks !

How much and sincerely I deplore, dear Avenarius, your having reaped nothing but disturbances of this kind from your acquaintance with me so far,—please be convinced ; for I know they form the very greatest upset to the regulated life of a business man ; moreover, I already have seen how estranging has been their effect on two couples who otherwise, perhaps, would be standing in the frankest and most sociable intercourse. But as no one feels this more than I, whilst no one more heartily wishes that intercourse to become what it unfortunately is *not* at present,—so I hereby beg you once again to be fully assured that it isn't empty boasting when I tell you that this shall have been my last relation with you in the pecuniary line—at least of an unpleasant nature—and with the ceasing of those relations I cordially look forward to entering a closer and more intimate communion with you both, which at least shall be interrupted no more by invasions of this sort : a thing, I'm aware, that will only be possible when those questions shall never re-arise between us which really have hitherto troubled our intercourse more than is fit. Adieu, dearest Avenarius ! Your faithful brother-in-law

RICHARD WAGNER.

14. To the Same

DEAREST AVENARIUS—Do you know, you could do me a very great favour : to wit, if the state of your affairs permitted you to advance me five-hundred francs till Easter. Schlesinger, for whom I've undertaken work to the tune of three-thousand fr.— namely, complete arrangements of two operas, the Favorite and Guitarrero—has already paid me the half, fifteen-hundred fr. cash ; but, as I'm only just about to commence the second opera, I fear, and with very good reason, I shall be unable to obtain another lump payment quite so soon ; whilst I have various personal grounds for much preferring to have no need to dun him for money again till I've completed everything and can demand the whole. The beginning of April I shall have finished Guitarrero also, and thus be able to dispose of such a tidy sum in the course of that month that I can firmly promise repayment of what I ask to-day by Easter ; in fact, despite my recently-acquired distaste for notes of hand, I even might offer to draw you one up with good conscience.

To repeat : if it could be done without a certain sacrifice on your part, you would render me a very great service by granting my request, a service I should be only too eager to return you

---

[1] By a palpable slip of the pen, Wagner has written " 1840," the post-mark being " 23 Février 1841 " ; which latter year-date agrees with the draft reply of Avenarius,—who in his turn, as will presently appear, must have made a similar error in the day of the month. The address is : " Monsieur / Avenarius / librairie de Brockhaus et Avenarius / 60 rue Richelieu / Paris."

some day ;—for, however far I may have pulled myself out of my horrible fix already, there's enough of it left still to shew me a threatening look. Let me remove that instanter, and if possible without having to sound Schlesinger for another advance,—to avoid which I've a thousand present reasons,—among them I will merely mention this : only to-day have I learnt that Schlesinger is accustomed to pay nearly half as much again for some arrangements I shall also have to make ; —I should like to make use of this knowledge to speak seriously to him about raising my fee, and that will be impossible if I go and ask him for a big advance.

So, if it is possible, please try and render me this friendly service, whereby you may gain me a profit of 300 to 400 fr. in the happy event of my drumming my representations into Schlesinger's head.

Well, you will see what you can manage, and be sure of my thanks in advance. Begging for a couple of lines in reply, Your faithful brother-in-law
RICHARD WAGNER.
25, RUE DU HELDER.[1]

---

[1] Draft of Avenarius' reply, on an accompanying loose sheet : "P. 22 Febr. 1841.—Believe me, dear Wagner, perhaps none of your connections would be readier than myself to assist you with a loan, if I could do it. But I have no money to dispose of,—I require my earnings from the business for my really very modest house-keeping, and draw them at stated intervals ; whilst the capital of the bus. does not stand at my private command.—I may direct your notice to a combination which perhaps can be carried out. Get a payment on account of Guitarrero made you by Schlesinger in the form of a bill dated 6th May, or still better, June. That way you would spare him a payment of cash for the nonce, which he always likes avoiding, and I will try and get the bill discounted for you at no great loss. Yours . . ." Beneath which these words are struck through : " If you can come to me Friday. . . ."

15. To his Mother [1]

MEUDON, 12th Sept: 1841.

MY BEST LITTLE MOTHER—It is *my* turn at
length to be able to offer you an equally joyful
and hearty congratulation on your birthday!
Please do not think I have ever forgotten you,
even when I was silent and let nothing be heard of
me. Ah, I believe I've told you once before,
there have been times when I really avoided
arousing your interest anew in my fortunes.
Then I prayed God in silence to preserve your
life and health, since I hoped in time to reap a
reward from even my endeavour that should make
it more gratifying to me to shew you my face
again. Let those who don't know me say : " He
should have acted so—he ought to have done this
or that," as much as they like,—they all are
wrong ! So long as it comports with one's inner
sense of right and wrong, every man who would
attain to true inner and outer independence ought
decidedly to strike the path his own more serious
inclination and a certain irresistible inner impulse
bid. Without needing to be particularly magnani-
mous, the world may very well forgive him the
sufferings he thus draws down upon himself ;
only who would fain relieve those sufferings, has
the right to tender him advice,—but whoever is
unable to relieve them notwithstanding, must eke
put up with seeing his advice not followed after
all. I'm sure I am none of your headstrong,

---

[1] Address : " To Mother " ; an enclosure to another letter.

unbendable characters : on the contrary, I am
rightly accused of too feminine an inner mobility ;
but I have quite enough staying power to keep
me from abandoning a road once struck, before I
have convinced myself of all its bearings.   And
that's what has happened to me with Paris :—

I have won the firm conviction that for at
least as long as I can only wage the contest with
my personal powers, it is absolutely impossible for
me to prevail here.   To those who predicted me
pretty much the same, I reply that their mere
forecast on hearsay could have carried no weight
with me.   When such a man as Meyerbeer, on
the contrary, emboldened me to rush into the
fray, hardly any one will be surprised that a young
man like myself preferred trying—to turning tail
without a stroke.   And Meyerbeer was right ;
the qualifications I lacked—renown and money—
might be very well made good to me by others,
and he offered to lend a helping hand himself
through his considerable influence.   Meyerbeer's
having been obliged to keep away precisely all
this time from Paris, *that* was the misfortune in store
for me ;   for operations at a distance count for
nothing in Paris,—the personage is everything.

Consequently I had soon to see myself con-
strained to prosecute with my own powers a battle
I had undertaken in reliance on the aid of others.
And *that* attempt I had to venture also.   Had I
been one of those frivolous creatures of the present
mode, had I any sort of flashy talent for the salon,
it would doubtless have been possible to push my
way into this or that coterie which perhaps would

have given me a lift at length, even without
intrinsic merit.—Well may I say : Thank God
I'm *not* cut out for that ! I have been bound to
despise whomever I have seen succeed in that way ;
such an indomitable disgust has seized me at these
good-for-nothings, that I really account myself
lucky not to have taken their taste at all.—So,
what is left me with Paris, is to devote to my
frugal subsistence the resources of an arduous
métier I have opened for myself here with a
music-publisher, and calmly thus abide the time
when luck and chance shall help me whither I
would go. Moreover, that is what I shall be
compelled to fall back upon, provided the good-
fortune now presenting itself to me from another
quarter should not attain complete fulfilment.—

That good-fortune is the definitive acceptance
of my opera for Dresden. In my last letter I
made you all acquainted with the position of my
Dresden affairs, at the same time informing you
of the steps I had taken toward the success of my
enterprise. Those steps, my dear Mother, it
heartily rejoices me to be able to tell you,—have
completely succeeded. As early as the beginning
of July I received LÜTTICHAU's letter, announcing
to me in the most flattering terms that, after
mature examination of its text and score, my
opera " Rienzi " had been accepted for representation in Dresden, and would be produced the
beginning of next year at latest.—

Even in this announcement, best Mother, I
have to recognise an extraordinary piece of great

good luck. If one reflects that I still am without any name as composer, and considers of what a genre my opera is, one will understand what I mean : a point I've already dwelt on in my last letter. Winkler has assured me they would do everything with my opera to shew off the new theatre in all its glory ; so, if they meet my requirements, they'll have enormous expenses ; since the *first* production of an opera like this, which I strictly had reckoned for Paris, must be attended with all possible luxury. But nowhere—not even at Berlin or Vienna—could I find a more excellent cast, than in Dresden, for the leading rôles of my Rienzi :—the DEVRIENT and TICHATSCHEK—I surely need say no more.—In short, if God disposes all things happily, this may prove the lucky turning in my life.—

I have made up my mind to start for Dresden about a fortnight before the performance ; so I shall see you again, my good motherkin, at last—at last !—You may imagine the delight this thought, this certainty affords me !—Heaven will grant me to find you quite safe and sound ; and if a down-right fine success is reserved for me at Dresden in addition,—I fancy such wishes may form my best congratulation to you even to-day.—How many, many years have I waited, fought and struggled, to be able to rejoice you with a piece of news like this. It gives me a positive shudder, to think that, at my next glimpse of you, almost *six* years will have flown since I parted from you last : great God, who would ever have thought it ! I shall find you all again—except dear Rosalie ! ! Ah, it had always been so fond a thought to me to make precisely *her*, who had watched the throes of my development at such close quarters and often with such painful feelings, a witness also of the happier issues of my frantic efforts,— —and now I must approach her grave !— —God, God but keep my darling Mother in good health, and grant her still the strength to revel in her children's prospering !

We shall not come to harm ! Even Albert won't, shan't, and cannot ! Let Fortune only smile on one of us,—the good luck of one is the other's also. Perhaps Heaven may even make myself the channel, and prepare me an engagement in which I can push Albert's best wishes !—I don't want to look ridiculous through speaking out what I am thinking, what I hope,—for what are thoughts and hopes ?—but things *must* mend, and he is worthiest to taste good luck, who comes home from out the storm with all the teachings of misfortune !— —

Best love to each and all ! We soon shall meet again, and let things around us figure as they may, —our hearts will have remained the old ones, and — —everything's *bound* to come right ! Preserve thee, dear Motherkin, for Thy faithful son

RICHARD.

16. To EDUARD AVENARIUS [1]

MOST VALUED FRIEND AND BROTHER-IN-LAW —A couple of words in confirmation and reinforce-

[1] Address : " Monsieur/Monsieur E. Avenarius/Librairie Allemande de Brockhaus et Avenarius/60, rue Richelieu/à/Paris."

ment of faith! The overtures you made to me yesterday re your possible intervention in the matter of my furniture-selling are of the greatest moment to me. As I build on them the solitary valid hope of a prosperous answer to the question discussed, please do not take it ill of me if I'm writing you thereon again to-day,—since time pressed for my departure yesterday, and I should like to leave Paris untrod for the nonce both to-day and to-morrow; whilst on the other hand, this business weighs too much upon me. So listen, dearest friend :—If, as Hr : Vieweg gave me to understand, Hr : v. Rochow wants to buy furniture from me to the tune of 300 fr. net,—further, if you would have the kindness to undertake disbursement of that sum yourself directly the bargain is struck ; and lastly, if it suits Hr : v. Rochow for you to advance him this money on his receipts,—*I shall be completely helped over the stile.* For, with these 300 frs I can pay what I owe at my flat,—therefore can insist on immediate release,—which—as the concierge assures me—can't be refused me in case I'm placed in that position before the 15th inst. Purchasers have also been proposed to me for other single articles ; so that I may even hope to be able to stop my cabinetmaker's mouth with something, —when I shall move the remnant of my furniture to a small apartment, and transfer it to the cabinet-maker in part payment when I leave for good,— and everything would be fairly quits.

This would be the best and most desirable expedient in all respects ; for, if I can only get rid of that fatal flat at once, I'm *certain* of a great economy.—Yourself alone could make this possible through intervention,— wherefore, if your good will succeeds in it, you'll pledge me to the greatest thanks.—Best love to Cäcilie and Max from me and Minna, Yours RICHARD WAGNER.

MEUDON, 2 *Octobre* 1841.

17. TO THE SAME[1]

O MY CHERISHED BROTHER-IN-LAW—Couldn't you carry out the proposal once made me, and forward this letter for Meyerbeer to Berlin, accompanied by a few lines to your correspondent there? —In that case you would have to beg the gentleman to take the note to Meyerbeer himself and wait for an answer.—I have cut my lines very short, and told him that, to make his answer easier for him, I have asked a friend of my brother-in-law's to receive it from him orally and report to me hither. I merely want him to declare in brief whether he has received my "fl. Holländer," and whether he has anything in mind with it?—Please do so this very day!—In spite of her inward repugnance, my wife is commissioned to hand you the postage. God bless yourself and wife and child!—Thine ever, RICHARD.

2 *March* [1842].[2]

---

[1] Address (in German this time, the letter being evidently conveyed by Minna): "Sr. Wohlgeboren/the/distinguished Bookseller/and excellent/Brother-in-law/in/Paris."

[2] Draft on the back, in Avenarius' hand: "3 März 1842/Hrn. Asher & Co. in Berlin/Permit me to claim your obligingness in a small private matter to-day. I beg you, to wit, to send one of your assistants to Herr Meyerbeer with the enclosed letter and ask him for an answer, which you

[The 7th of April Wagner leaves Paris for good, with his wife, to push forward the lagging Dresden preparations for *Rienzi*; very soon also taking a flying trip to Berlin to try to float that stranded *Holländer*.—TR.]

18. To EDUARD AND CÄCILIE AVENARIUS [1]

BERLIN, 21 *April* [1842].

DEAREST EDUARD, DEAREST CÄCILIE !— —So it really is a whole fortnight since I went away from you—and I'm writing you only to-day ! Vivid as few events in all my life, the hour and moment of our parting stands before my soul ; never shall I forget it, for 'twas it that first brought fully home to me how very precious you two had become to my heart. When I left you, I certainly didn't think I should be able to hold out so long without sending you tidings : at each station I wanted to write to you ; at Chalons, in fact, the paper lay spread for it. The farther we travelled, however, the more our journey engrossed us ; it was fatiguing, especially for poor Minna, as we preferred not to halt even at Frankfort, for reasons

will doubtless have the kindness to convey to me in your next.—The enclosure is from Hr. Richard Wagner, who is acquainted and in connection with Hr. Meyerbeer, and sent him the full score of an opera The flying Dutchman some time ago, without, however, getting news about it from Herr Meyerbeer as yet, who appears to be no very punctual correspondent.

"Herr Wagner would therefore like to know whether he [M.] received the opera, and what he thinks of doing with it ; and I trespass on your kindness to procure my friend and relative this information—at the least to leave him in no doubt as to the score's safe receipt.

"You would much oblige me, if in your next business letter you would include a word how the matter stands, *in any event*. Kindly forgive the trouble caused you, etc., etc."

1 Address : "Monsieur/Monsieur/E. Avenarius/60, rue Richelieu/à/ Paris " ; postmark : "Berlin, 21.4.5-6."

easy to be understood, and so were a little over 5 days and nights en route. At Dresden we therefore took a good day's rest without compunction ; then a day got lost on errands and apartment-hunting ; and then I went to Leipzig. There Mother, whom I found in capital condition—thank God!—Luise, Hermann and Ottilie, yes, even Julius and Fritz, took such entire possession of me from hour to hour of my three days' stay there, that at length I postponed writing you till my first quiet morning at the Berlin inn. I arrived here the night before last, and squandered a whole day yesterday in quest of Meyerbeer, with whom I only got a hurried conversation in the evening. He has given me a rendezvous for 2 to-day ; so half a day is left me at last to turn back to both of you in peace.

That is the history of my past fortnight's experiences, by way of brief preamble : now for an intimate word !—Never has a parting come harder to us than that of Paris ; Lord ! what are all the sorrows we endured there, against the sense of so sincere a friendship which we have borne away ?— What witchcraft have you played with Minna ?— Decidedly *you've* turned her heart about, so that Paris now seems nothing to her but a paradise. The whole journey she never ceased weeping ; hardly had she grown a little calmer, than the only answer she could make to all the comforting I felt obliged to give her, was " Mayn't I cry again ? "— Her relations—everything was quite indifferent to her,—and when I took farewell of her to go to Dresden [meaning Leipzig] she very naively admitted that she by no means wept since I was leaving her, but because she didn't know how to get back to Paris.—Oh, my dear children, just believe me, I also share her feeling : I'm still quite lukewarm in pursuit of my affairs, for my mind's too full of Paris and the dear good hearts I also know are beating for me there. I'm living little in the present yet, and it almost strikes me as no great misfortune should it turn out bad ; for a good-fortune to be tasted by me *without you two* I don't reckon of much account. Howbeit, Heaven will soon take care that things shan't go too gilded with me.—Minna *wants* them to turn out amiss, that I may make a contract with Schlesinger and return to Paris :—the poor woman has no thought for anything save Paris.

For my own part, this fortnight is a dream to me already ; my waking senses are with you. In that dream did Mother and the rest of us recur to me : the streets and houses where they live have altered much, themselves but little ; the young brood that has shot up in their midst forms the single change. Horror takes me at the thought that perhaps I'm also not to see your Maxel any more till he has shot up too ! If Minna sobbed out Maxel's name betwixt her tears, she was sure to set myself in tears at once. In the memory of that dear babe concentres all our sadness. Maxel ! Maxel !—

Ottilie's children pleased me ; the eldest is somewhat spoilt, the younger a droll little rogue. How envious they all were, when I told them tales of Maxel !

On every side, though, you were asked about
with great affection ; I went up in Mother's estimate when I assured her you were fond of me.
The portraits of both of you hang in her room :
your picture, dear Cäcilie, pleased me best, though
it is outré in various features ; yours, good Eduard,
has a certain resemblance, but is rather ordinarily
conceived and executed : but both drawings took
me thoroughly back to you, ay, I even had a little
chat with you. When Maxel's picture comes, the
Devil's certain to break loose again ; I shall be
unable to look at it without poignant emotion.
For which matter, they are *all* looking eagerly
forward to it. Will it come soon ?—

I know that Minna bitterly regrets being unable
to write to you this time with me. As soon as
I've returned to Dresden, we will both sit down
and execute a writing duet ; and that's why I
have had to promise Minna to get back sharp.
I hope it will soon come off too, as I can't do
much here for the moment ; since the new
Intendant, Küstner, has not arrived yet, and
Redern, so Meyerbeer assured me, neither can nor
may fix anything regarding the date of my opera's
production. It's almost immaterial to me, though
—I would I were with you.

What I'm going to live on, this summer, I do
not yet know. Luise, who is occupying herself
much with my immediate requirements unasked,
sees insuperable difficulties in the way of collecting
the means ; she wants to leave Schletter [a rich
Leipzig business acquaintance], whom Mother keeps
most casually suggesting, altogether out of count ;

E

and Luise is right,—there are many objections.—
So : I'm still the same old Out-at-elbows—with
splendid prospects and an empty pouch.—

I was very sorry not to find Clärchen as we
expected ; she had returned to Chemnitz : should
it prove impossible for me to visit her just yet, the
dress shall be sent on to her. Albert's on tour,
and doing well,—as Mother assures me. For the
present it will be difficult for me to see him either ;
such joys need money—confounded money.

Most ingenuously I informed Heinrich Brockhaus that you, dear Cäcilie, implored him *not* to
come to Paris, as that would be your only chance
of carrying out your pet idea of coming with
Eduard to Germany. Of course he had to laugh,
for he could see well enough by my face that it
really was *my own* wish.—

Yes, dear children, if you could make that
feasible,—if you both could come to us, to say
nothing of Cäcilie and Maxel staying with us at our
ideal Töplitz,—*that* would be something to fling
up one's cap over. Oh, do try and manage it :
you, Cäcilie, travel in front, and let Eduard fetch
you in the autumn ; you'll do that, won't you ?—
If Rienzi has come out by then, I'll defray your
return journey. Ah, what would I not do !

Only rejoice us with a couple of lines, and that
full soon ! But *both of you*, mind ; and reflect
that, if Minna isn't writing with me this time, it's
simply due to circumstances. Tell us all about
yourselves and dear, dear Maxel. Tell us also of
Herr and Mad. Kühne, to whom I only don't
write this time because I'm saving it up till I can

do it with Minna; assure them of the greatest affection and gratitude we haven't ceased remembering their excellent selves with every day. So let me bid you all the heartiest and most fervent farewell; may you prosper and remember us! For, however long we do not see you, our eyes will grow moist as often as we think of you. A thousand thousand greetings from Your

RICHARD.

P.S.—I am seated in a dubious Berlin inn, and the remnant of my Paris cash is pulling still more dubious faces at me ; so pardon if my letter reaches you unfranked this time : it shan't occur again. But I didn't want to forward through the firm, for once, so that at least you might receive these lines quick in the end.—

Our Dresden lodging is *Töpfergasse No.* 7.

19. TO THE SAME [1]

DRESDEN, 3 *May* 1842.

BEST EDUARD! DEAREST CÄCILIE!—I sent you from Berlin my first dazed lament for our parting, and so it's nothing but devoir and duty that I should inform you briefly of the facts of our position in a clearer mood. The first truly crushing impression, which my separation from you both was bound to leave upon me for a goodish while, has at length been effaced, in a measure, by too material contact with the present;

---

[1] No address ; written on very thin note-paper, the letter is an enclosure per the firm of Brockhaus.

and I can only congratulate myself thereon, for I couldn't possibly have continued in that torpid reverie, into which I was plunged at the first, without serious harm to my nature and purpose.

My first shaking-up came in Berlin. True, it wasn't possible to do anything decisive towards settling the date when my opera is to be produced there, as Küstner was still on his travels ; yet I made the acquaintance of Hr v. Redern, who received me with great distinction, and indulged my wish so far as to promise to arrange the present repertory so that my opera should be the next to be got up after the production of the Huguenots (which is to take place the end of May). So Küstner would require to set himself in flagrant opposition to arrangements made already, if he meant to put my Holländer upon the shelf. Of course he won't do that, though, as in the first place Mendelssohn (with whom I have struck up quite friendly relations) has assured me he's convinced that Redern will in any case exert supremacy for the first half-year, and in the second, every measure has been taken to win over Küstner to my interest ; [1] but that means my having to go to Berlin and Leipzig a second time, the middle of this month, which is pretty hard on me.

My pecuniary affairs have taken a turn I really much prefer. The best of it is that it didn't cost myself a word : Luise, Ottilie and Hermann had put their heads together and arrived at the conclusion (as they told me) that it was their personal

---

[1] In his capacity of Munich Intendant, he had recently rejected this same *Flying Dutchman* as " not at all suited for Germany.'"—Tr.

duty, without dragging in any stranger, to offer me as much as I considered needful to maintain me during the next half-year, in which I could count on no takings. On my return from Berlin, accordingly, they asked me what sum I required ; when I put it at 200 thaler [£30] for the half-year, they appeared to think that less than they expected, and offered to let me have it in monthly instalments from their own monthly moneys, so that the thing might be kept entirely to ourselves ; which naturally was very welcome to me.

In general, best children, I must confess it strikes me as if all our folk had greatly changed to their advantage : that odious hot temper seems to have somewhat died out from our family ; and in this respect I was particularly pleased with Julius, whom I found better in every way than I anticipated.—The Mama is living quite in clover now, and really has a pleasant time of it : at any instant she can either be alone or in society ; she has a marvellous flat, big and comfy, for which you'd envy her with your entire household. All the same, she intends going to Töplitz this year as well, and wants to chum with Minna there : how would it be, good Cäcilie, if you really came too? Just listen ! We would engage a lodging for you, in fact in the same house with ourselves. In *August*, as irrevocably fixed now, my Rienzi is to be brought out here : good Eduard shall run over for that ; I'll pay off my debt to him out of my fee, which will be something toward the journey back. Couldn't all that be arranged ? Your Eduard need give you little money,—we'd club our housekeeping together. Natalie[1] could be disposed of somewhere by then,—perhaps through the good Kühnes.[2]—Ah, that would be fine! You'd be giving everybody great delight. Maxel's portrait, which really has arrived at last, has made a prodigious sensation (as was to be expected); Mother described to me the impression it produced on her most touchingly: when the chick's here in natura, he'll play the devil with them all. True, our sisters are a wee bit envious,—never mind; better be envied, than have to envy. But you all are coming, aren't you?

There's very little for me to tell you of Dresden, after all. These people look upon me as a golden calf, and will certainly do everything I wish. They're to begin studying my opera the commencement of *July*; from most sides I'm congratulated on being able to be present, as it will have the best of influences. Reissiger is continually falling on my neck, and smothers me with kisses whenever he gets the chance; moreover, every one assures me he really means square by me and feels the best will: but the man has turned into such a lazy philistine, alas, that I should be terribly off if I left the artistic execution of my opera to his tender care alone.

I had just got thus far, and Minna had just finished her letter to Cäcilie (—she began hers first—)—when your joint letter arrives!—That releases the Devil—I weep—and Minna howls! A

---

[1] Formerly regarded as Minna's youngest sister, but openly avowed in the master's *Mein Leben* to have been her love-child from several years before he made his first spouse's acquaintance.—TR.

[2] Who kept a private school in Paris; see *Mein Leben*.—TR.

nice to-do ! The most sensible thing for me to do would be to leave again straight off ; since nothing can come of my opera now, I've such a fearful opponent to conquer—an intriguer beyond match, —my own wife ! Amid a flood of tears, she has just informed me she would put forth all her might to make my opera fail, as there'd be nothing else for me to do then but return to Paris !—Great God ! neither have I any zest remaining for the thing myself, or at least I should lose it if I often received letters like to-day's, which make my heart so heavy. Believe me, dear best children,—it's the same with us as with yourselves : only, as to *one* point I'm more cheerful :—*I believe in a quicker reunion than you do.* God in Heaven—after all, one's only slave for just so long as one *can't help it ;* but whoever can help it first, there really can be nothing better for him to do, Heaven knows, than institute a Wiedersehen between us ! In this sense it has a double value to me when I look towards the smile of Fortune : with *gainings* in my purse, I'm *free* and can do what I will ; and my *will* is, to *see you both again straight off :* whether in Paris or at Töplitz, is immaterial. We shall *meet again* soon ; that's my belief and Minna's consolation !— The good soul looked over the first page of your letter with me,—after that she could see nothing more, her tears rolled down thick and prevented it ; and yet it was a proper joy, for there's no true joy without them ! Precisely in that style will we all of us weep and rejoice, when we do meet again.—

Nothing beyond a general outburst of feeling,

dear Cäcilie, can be my answer just yet to your dear, darling letter. It is impossible for Minna to add even a line, since she's *dissolved*. Eduard's lines have touched me to the quick ; if only that fatal " dernier des derniers " hadn't figured among them ! Lucky it's French, and so I see you merely meant it as a joke, dear Eduard, else I should have felt mortally offended. I know no first nor last midst those my heart belongs to : I've only *one* heart, and whoever dwells there is its tenant from bottom to top ; how you get on together in it, is no affair of mine.— —Children, children, buck up ; good times are close ahead ! Away with tears ; save them all well up for *Wiedersehen!*— —Maxel ! Maxel ! ! !—Ah, that's another story,—it bubbles from one's heart into one's eyes : the babe, that babe !—There goes Minna giving way again !—I must shut up ; not another sober word will come !

I intended writing also to the cherished *trefoil* [Lehrs, Anders, and Kietz],—but this letter burns beneath my fingers, I must get it out of the house at once. I will write to the others to-morrow.— Everything goes through the firm [of Brockhaus], so you'll shortly get another letter telling you whatever I've omitted in my turmoil of to-day.—

God bless you ! God preserve you ! We'll have another talk soon. A thousand salutes and kisses ! Tears, laughter and sobs ! Ever both of Yours, RICHARD.

20. To Sister Cäcilie Avenarius

TÖPLITZ, 13 *June* 1842.

DEAREST AND BEST—Here we are at Töplitz, the Schlossberg in front of our noses, a cowshed beneath us,—and here we sit and think of you— of both of you! Your excellent letter, good *Cäcilie*, we laid in the family-archives ; its words stand graven on our hearts. You faithful creature with your staunch attachment, how dear and ever near you are to us ! We shall never forget either of you, not for so much as a day ; and there are many hours in our days we fill with memories of both of you in all we speak or think of. Your being robbed us for this summer, is a woful grief that ne'er forsakes us, and dims our mirth. Only stay near to us in spirit through your kindness and fidelity, the least trace of which attends our steps with blessing, when courage and endurance must e'en conquer separation! How do things look ; have you no prospect ?—Is nobody coming from Leipzig to Paris,—or can Eduard contrive no business pretext for paying the Leipziger Quer-Gasse a visit ? It isn't far from there to Dresden.—Ah God, that these should be mere empty phrases, at which you'll only twitch your lips, dear Eduard, if your confounded business leaves you even time for that. What is one to do, so long as one's a slave ? Enjoy what presents itself at no expense, hope in the future, and—hold each other dear, be it from afar or near !—

Yes, *we* are at long-promised Töplitz ! How

we all raved about it when we were together! Then let this year but be the opener of a happy turning in my fortunes, the next is bound to make my luck complete,—and with us you must be!

Ah, this Töplitz with its remotest precincts is perhaps the loveliest spot I know! Our coming here had been delayed by the uncertainty I was hovering in at the end of last, and beginning of this month, whether I should have to run over to Berlin a second time or no. I had already got as far as Leipzig again the 2nd of June, to go on from there to Berlin, when I received a letter there from Küstner telling me pretty well all I could anyhow have learnt by mouth. Since he is only just entering the Intendancy amid a thousand cross-currents and chicanes, Küstner could say nothing more definite at present *re* the date of my opera's first performance, than that it should take place as soon as ever circumstances allowed. Accordingly I abandoned pro tem a useless and expensive personal visit, and, with a man who is shewing himself so punctilious as Küstner in epistolary dealings, in any case I hope to arrive at the best possible results on this road also. So I went straight back to Dresden and arranged our departure for Töplitz with Minna, who has brought with us her excellent sister [Jette] (a good housekeeper). No doubt Minna, who has just taken up her pen, will give you fuller details of our journey, as also of our installation on the spot ; so I will only say that we're lodging " *zur Eiche*," the last house on the Turnaer Wiese, a mere matter of some 50 paces from the Turna

Park. We are living at a farm, entirely by our-selves,—but, as said, you'll hear all that from Minna. At the first start on our lodging-hunt we came across the Rosenlaube, your quondam home, dear Cäcilie, but every room there was already taken.

We had meant climbing the Schlossberg this morning itself, to be able to report if we found your and Eduard's names there still; but Minna had cramp in the calf, and begged me to postpone that expedition for the nonce.—The Mama, who wrote to you a week ago, is also here; she travelled from Dresden *the same* day as ourselves, but in another carriage: her eternal indecision, as to whether and when she would come, hadn't permitted her to give me definite orders for booking a seat. So Mother and Minna met here for the first time, naturally in the attitude of two people who want to make one another's acquaint-ance at last. Mother seems very glad of our society; despite her stiff knee, she came hobbling up the Schlackenburg after us the day before yesterday, as I had told her we intended going there. She asked Minna to provide her with baked meat from time to time,—yesterday we sent her roast veal; whereupon she paid us a call, and got treated to cream. She is quite chirpy, and prattles to herself by the hour; really she's looking remarkably well, and in spite of her lean-ness I have firm hope that God will preserve her to us for a long time to come.[1] For that matter,

[1] Her age was then just three months short of 68; she died over five years after, see p. 141.—Tr.

she is living in deuced fine style here, in a brand-
new house (" the Blue Angel ") on the main
thoroughfare, close to the baths, first étage, and
pays 10 thaler a month without including linen :
I wish her joy of it with all my heart ! She's very
fond of you, dear Cäcilie, and upon the Schlackenburg the other day it was amid brimming tears
she recalled her last visit to Töplitz with yourself ;
you may guess if we chimed in ! Ah, would you
were here, with that Devil's-imp, that Max !— —

Ottilie very much wants to run over to Töplitz
for a week, with her children ; but Mother thinks
nothing will come of it. Shall see ! I should like
it, for I've grown quite fond of her afresh.—Luise
will also arrive at Carlsbad in the next few days ;
I am heartily attached to her.

Holla ! Rienzi is to cross the boards the end
of August in full harness ! You'll be there, of
course ? I will see to your lodgings.—All's well
with it in Dresden ; nowhere have I met any
hostility yet.—Apropos, I have been to see Albert
at Halle ; I found him better than I expected ;
moreover, he had been a little maligned as to his
"comedian ways" at Leipzig.—I slept 2 nights
in his diggings, and had long and hearty talks
with him. A better engagement must be obtained
him in time, that's certain,—nevertheless there was
a crumb of comfort :—*he gets his salary punctually !*
One knows what that is saying. His wife's as
beautiful as ever ; Johanna can play-act quite well,
and—has a voice that justifies *great* hopes, under
Albert's tuition.—I was unable to visit Cläre, but
then *she* had spent *two* days at Dresden with her

husband, and—never looked me up!—True, Mother hadn't written her my address, but she might have guessed I was in Dresden, and Wolfram only needed to enquire at the theatre and he'd have learnt it. A thing like that's incomprehensible !— However, probably there was nothing sinister behind it !— — —

Before winding up, I have something else to request you, good Cäcilie : to tell Kietz that I should have liked to write him too to-day, but have refrained from doing so because I can learn nothing definitive re his money affairs for *another few days*; I have done what there was to do, and have good hope that my steps will have the best results. I am expecting a letter from Leipzig about it, on receipt of which I will write him instanter and post him the letter direct ; in this way he perhaps may get his letter even earlier than the present one, which I'm sending through the firm, will reach yourselves. Heine [F.] will write him in two or three days also, with lots of fine things about our drawings [for *Rienzi* ?] and the caricature, which he greeted with a regular guffaw. I had a singular feeling myself, when I set eyes again in Dresden on the long-awaited drawings : O Paris ! O sorrows and joys ! O you friends ! O remembrances !!—

Children, fare heartily well ! I don't want to break down again, for if my tears were to fall on this infernally thin paper into the bargain, my letter no doubt would present an emotional, but by no means a legible look. Farewell all of you, farewell ! Eduard, eyes right ! Muster yourself

also, next time, for a couple of lines to your
Paris ex-pest!—Write us, both of you, soon ; let
the huge delight you'll give ourselves be your
reward !—

God keep you! Onward, Max! Remember
your glorious uncle, but on no account follow his
footsteps!—Onward, Natalie! Grow tall and
slim !—To me, to us, you dear ones never to be
forgotten! Dearest Sister, best Brother-in-law!
Ever all of yours,   Richard W.

[Nos. 21 to 23 of the German edition constitute letters
1 to 3 of the " Minna " volumes.—Tr.]

24. To Eduard Avenarius [1]

24 *August* (1842).
Dresden.

Best Eduard—I can't and won't reply to your
and Cecilie's letter with these scanty lines, which I
only address you because of an instant occasion.
That shall be done in a fortnight at latest, however,
not before when shall I be able to write to you
clearly and fully about a weighty question [*re* Natalie ?]
raised in Cecilie's letter. So, everything suspended
until then! I should like these lines to reach you
very quickly ; hence I'm writing on the moment's
spur and in all brevity.

Hr Ferd. Heine, my and Kietz's friend, has
called on me, an instant back, and begged me to
address you an enquiry and prayer on his behalf.
He is a thorough French scholar, to wit, and

---

[1] Address : "Herr/Eduard Avenarius/in/Paris./Urgently recommended
by Richard Wagner for kind enclosure in the next [business] letter going
off."

from time to time translates French books, novels etc., as only the other day a novel for Collmann of Leipz.; for his salary is small, and he finds himself obliged to earn a little extra off and on. Well, an obscure Leipzig bookseller, named Zirges, has just offered him the job of translating two books whose appearance the Parisians are keenly looking forward to : namely, an Histoire militaire de l'exped. de la *porte de fer*, p. F. duc d'Orléans, and secondly, Memoires du Maréchal Soult, duc de Dalmatie. Heine, however, who has no particular belief in the said Zirges, thinks that *you* would be getting these books translated in Paris at once in any event, since they're very interesting; and so, in case you feel disposed to, he begs you to commission *him* with that translation, which would be highly desirable to him *for the simple reason* that he would be entering relations with a solid firm. If his guess is correct, and if it's all the same to yourself *who* supplies the translation, you would be doing me a very great favour if you would think of Hr F. Heine for it;—he's an excellent fellow, and vowed heart and soul to my interest, to which he already, in fact, has rendered substantial services.—Please do what you can !—

Two words more.—My opera, which we have been getting up since August 1, isn't to come out till the beginning of October, to open the subscription series.— —I can't write to Kietz, either, for a fortnight : the experiences I am reaping with his affairs are most *instructive* to me ; nevertheless I hope to be able to send him money—how and in what fashion, he shall hear in a fortnight. A

thousand greetings to all from Minna and me.—
Detailed letters soon from Thy

RICHARD W.

25. TO EDUARD AND CÄCILIE AVENARIUS [1]

BEST BROTHER AND SISTER—You have sent us
such plenteous and beautiful gifts once again, that
we remain re-engaged to fresh thanks. The
colder and more indifferent to us our present
surroundings, the greater the warmth with which
we look into the distance and the past! So our
wish to meet again this summer didn't come to
fulfilment; will it next year?

To let you both quite realise how much your
letters have delighted us—especially that great
surprise, the dear birthday-letter [for Minna's Sept. 5]
—and what friendly sunbeams they appeared to
us, I merely need give you a faint sketch of our
life here; a colourless, cold tedium, only relieved
from time to time by money bothers. Splendid
relief! The 18th July I left Teplitz for good, to
flick up my Dresden drones a little; Minna and
mother stayed behind till August 1. To tell the
truth, we can't say we much enjoyed Teplitz: we
didn't make a single expedition,—Minna went up
the Schlossberg, to the Schlackenburg, and the
Obere Bergschenke, in fine, just wherever one
decently can go on foot; beyond which, as she
wasn't allowed to take long or tiring walks, she
knows little, or as good as nothing, of the Teplitz

[1] Address : " Monsieur / EDOUARD AVENARIUS / Rue Richelieu, No. 60 / à /
Paris."

environs. I won't grumble at that, however, for
Teplitz did us both a lot of good, and particularly
to Minna ; she began a regular thorough cure at
last, to which it was granted me to devote all
possible care. We were recommended to the
bath-house doctor, Ulrich, who diagnosed Minna's
complaint most correctly ; at any rate, he told her
it was highest time to pay exclusive heed to her
recovery, and in particular he put her on a very
strict diet. She took comparatively few baths, and
those of sulphur, but had to drink the more of
Eger-Franzen water. Her malady is naturally of
a kind in whose regard there can be no talk of a
rapid recovery ; nevertheless, Minna already feels
better in sundry respects. Her presentation to
our mother formed a red-letter day for her. As I
wrote you before, Mother lodged some distance
off from us at first ; in the end she moved into
our house, for several weeks. When I departed
from Teplitz she was a trifle ill, and I left her in
bed ; Minna nursed her most devotedly. For all
that, her state of health is very reassuring,—the
baths did her a heap of good ;—during the short
time she stayed with us in Dresden she sprang
about the promenades like a young roe.—

So we've both been back in Dresden since the
1st of August. I couldn't avoid taking a somewhat
respectable lodging here, nor hiring a grand piano :
the two together ran away with over the half of
our monthly money ; so, with the present dearness,
we have a terrible pinch to keep up appearances,
which I am bound to maintain much more in my
position here than was needed in Paris. Often I

F

could positively bellow for the time when we shall cease being beggars in decent clothing ; lucky those who needn't fear to sport their rags upon their limbs !

As to the state of my opera I wrote fairly [minutely] to Kietz, who will have passed it on to you and so spared me the trouble of relating it over again ; in any event, the production of Rienzi will take place in about a month. Your good wishes, dear children, are all the more welcome to me, as they are cordially meant :—I rather think they'll be fulfilled. Only let me make one thorough hit —and within a year there shall be high jinks !— —

It quite alarmed us, dear Cecilie, what you told Mother and us about the danger, now happily surmounted, that threatened your health. Ah, how much I wish you, too, the chance of soon being able to exclusively attend to a cure ! In fact, Eduard gives us quite serious hope that both of you will come to Germany next year ; and as *he* expresses it, I also firmly trust to see it realised. —Should all go according to my wish, we shall visit you in Paris winter come a year ; oh, my plans are all laid ! What you write me of your trip to Bellevue touched me much. Ah, believe me, there comes a soft spot in our heart whenever we think of you : *this* 5th of September, and that of last year ! ! ! O Heavens, what a contrast ! ! ! I hardly congratulated Minna at all, my dumps were so deep :—then came the letter from you two, and made us fully feel again what a godlike power resides in friendship ! You sat at table with us, and we kissed each other and rejoiced as if we had you tête à tête ! Never, never, good Cecilie and best Eduard, shall we forget your loyalty and love, and our full thanks shall reach you yet. Three cheers for the sorrows of Paris, they have borne us glorious fruit!

Dear good children, keep us in friendly remembrance—as indeed you are certain to—and rest assured that none save a good fortune *in common* can ever come our way. So pray for *Rienzi*, you also; you soon shall know the lot appointed it. Farewell! Ever and eternally both of Yours with heart and soul,

RICHARD W.

WAISENHAUS-STRASSE, No. 5,
  DRESDEN, 11. *September* 1842.

(*P.S.*)—Best thanks, dear Eduard, for the kind answer to my enquiry about translations for Hr Heine; if you really can give him employment in time, you'll please me greatly, for he has deserved it of me through unfeigned and self-forgetting sympathy.—

There's *no* foundation for Cecilie's chaff about *children* as yet: as we still have no prospect of *human* young whatever, we have to continue making up with dogs. We've another now, only 6 weeks old, a funny little chap; his name is *Peps*, or *Striezel* (because he looks exactly as if he had come from the gingerbread market). He is better than our late Robber [stolen in Paris]; still, it's hard on us to have to go on eking out with such unthinking creatures. I'd much rather have a Maxel—but there can only be *one of that* in the world at a time.

Children, a letter takes really too long through the firm; I'm sending this by post, and that *unfranked*—for mere safety's sake;—true, I also have no money,—but that would be the smallest reason : I'm too fearful of losing the porterage, especially when I can't pay it!

26. To EDUARD AVENARIUS [1]

DRESDEN, 8. *October* 1842.

BEST EDUARD—It's true I wrote you both last time that I shouldn't be sending you news of myself again until after the production of my opera; however, it strikes me as getting too long to leave you on the qui vive as to the date of that production, just when you are certain to be thinking of me with additional interest. Really I intended writing yourself in particular as early as the 5th; but I was so extraordinarily busy that day, that I had only time to remember you duly and with fitting emotion, good Brother-in-law, at my and Minna's very frugal dinner. We had no wine, to toast you properly upon your birthday,—so we did it with a hearty hand-shake : he's a rogue, who does more than he's able. We'll retrieve the toast with wine, though, next time we're all together—let's hope, next summer. To resume, that day it still stood settled that my opera should be given on the 12th inst.; so I put off writing you till the 13th : but, for very good reasons and with my full consent, after allowing for every

---

[1] Address : " Monsieur / Monsieur / Edouard AVENARIUS / Libraire / Rue Richelieu No. 69 / à / Paris."

unforeseen occurrence, the first performance now
is definitely and most positively fixed for Wednesday the 19th ; and that's how I have time to write
you both again so early.

√ Yes, dearest Eduard, on the 19th the Devil
breaks loose with lightning and thunder ; I can
tell you, I'm looking forward to this production
with high glee, for it will be *excellent!* Singers
and band are rehearsing with well-nigh more than
affection ; from all sides I receive the most
encouraging wishes, and every one anticipates an
extraordinary success. Certainly it's rare that
any one can say upon such an occasion : I've
nowhere come across a malcontent as yet. First
singers, who only have insignificant parts in my
opera, and therefore began with some grudging,
were soon drawn into the general glow, and now
co-operate as zealously as if they had the most
grateful rôles. The band exclaims : " For once
we really have a job it's worth while taking pains
with." In spite of a sore throat and not feeling
well, the Devrient hasn't missed a single rehearsal ;
and through her enthusiastic remarks wherever
she goes (so I'm told) she has contributed no
little to gaining my opera such credit with the
public, in advance, that everybody is looking
towards the production with all the intentness due
to something quite out of the way. Tichatschek
declares Rienzi will be his most brilliant part,
since there's no other in which he finds so many
opportunities.—The only one who might have
been set against me by jealousy, Reissiger—seems
to forget all egoistic regards in personal affection

for me : at least, he consistently behaves in such a fashion, especially behind my back too, that it is impossible for me to harbour any mistrust of him. You see, best friend, that's how things stand ; so let the Capitol crash in on Wednesday the 19th, if my evil star pales out to boot ! God place within my hands the means to shew you both my gratitude as I could wish, and you shall be pleased with me, I promise you. Devil take it, how's Max ? — — —

Really I oughtn't to have plagued you with such silly chatter ; your domestic affairs will be giving you worry enough, and we unfortunates have increased it for you to a certain extent. Only suffer it for my sake a little longer,—something is certain to happen to me soon, to cut the knot whose tightening still forces me to send you this letter unfranked to-day, and made me propose your health on the 5th without wine.—Ah, how I long for a glass of good wine—you know the sort ; often I'm so washed out by these terribly exhausting rehearsals, that a frivolous craving for a drop of fire-water perhaps is excusable in me. Never mind, do you my drinking for me ! Things soon shall turn better ; cheer up, my darlings ! Peace and blessing to you also, Mr. Loizeaux [his tailor], Draese,—Schuster [cobbler ?], and whatever you're called ! But a curse on that atrocious *Kietz*, who, in return for my last letter, for my most sacred entreaties to keep faith in times of pinch with *sterling art* and console himself with that—as I did,—could find no other answer to all this I wrote him, than his chicken-hearted

letter to Laforgue, with the declaration that he should now hang art upon the peg and turn his hand to pot-boilers! Fine fellow that, who can help none but others o'er a stile, and not himself! He shan't have another line from me till I can send him *money* with it. *Money! Money!*— — Bah!—
Now greet and kiss Cile most fervidly for me, and Maxel most tenderly.—I embrace all my friends, and declare to them : " The knot's bound to be cut! "—God protect you, dear good Eduard ! Stay true to Thy   RICHARD W.

But doesn't my wife greet and kiss you all, too?.! Do I need to assure you it ? Of course not.

27. TO EDUARD AND CÄCILIE AVENARIUS [addressed as last]

Na, dearest Children ! Played out as I am, at least I must send you a hasty line to-day to tell you what happened yesterday. I would rather you heard it from others, though, for—I'm bound to say it—*never* before, as *every one* assures me, has an opera been received on its first appearance in Dresden with such enthusiasm as my *Rienzi*. It was a commotion, a *revolution* throughout the city ;—*four* times over was I tumultuously called. People assure me that Meyerbeer's success with his production of the Huguenots here wasn't to be compared with that of my *Rienzi*. The second representation is the day after to-morrow :—every seat is taken for even the third. I am fearfully tired and run down ; after the second representation

I'll write you *in detail*. The performance was *transportingly* fine—Tichatschek—the Devrient—everybody—everything in a perfection such as had never been witnessed here. Triumph, triumph, you dear good, faithful souls! The day has broken ; it shall shine *upon you all!* Your

　　　　　　　　　　　　　RICHARD.

　　DRESDEN, *the 21st October* 1842.

The opera will be given at raised prices for several performances more.

I got Cecilie's letter this morning—with what feelings we read its good wishes ! ! !

(In Minna's hand, on the margin): Children, I am too happy, my utmost wishes are attained !—MINNA.

28. TO THE SAME

TO MY DEAR ONES IN PARIS—To which of you shall I write in particular? Shall I give each single one of you a separate piece of news ? Or am I to believe I have a secret to impart to one of you which the rest are not to know? Assemble the Holy Synod of Five, grant *Cecilie* the honour of the chair—you owe it her, were it only as the sole lady among you—and hear how things go with your brother !

I ought to have written you all again long ago ; but I was partly withheld by exhaustion, pressure of business, visits from members of my family, partly also by the circumstance that I wanted to wait for a few more settlements in my affairs before writing you at length. Added to which, *Heine* told me he had sent Kietz a circumstantial account of the production of Rienzi—which, to be candid, just suited my book, as I gladly left somebody else to report details it would have been hard for myself to collect. So you had all been primed with my success—I hope—through Heine, and I might confine myself to giving you a mere outline of facts ; with which I intend at least commencing.

Children, it's quite true,—my opera has had an unexampled success here ; and the greater's the marvel, as it was the *Dresden* public that pronounced this success. Bear in mind : a public which had never before been placed in the position of having to pass a *first* verdict on any considerable dramatic product. Was it not to be supposed that, with an entirely unknown author's name in front of it, these people would be shy and diffident about delivering judgment, were it only through sheer philistricity [*sic*] ?—So my foremost thanks are due to the whole personnel of our Opera ; for, as the practising progressed, alike singers and musicians waxed more and more enthusiastic for my work, and spread such an opinion of it through every circle in the town, that every one at last agreed there had never reigned so promising a curiosity among the public here about any coming opera—as in anticipation of something quite out of the common. This lucky circumstance entirely redeemed the disadvantage of my unknown name : the public was expecting something quite out of the common,—a representation ensued such as had never before been given with like enthusiasm on every hand ; and the one that didn't lag behind in its enthusiasm was the audience.

But you've been informed of the success of the first representation—so not another word about it ; it made an epoch in the annals of German operatic performances. Since then the opera has been given for a fourth time, and—unheard-of case— invariably at raised prices and to an overflowing house ; nor do I believe those prices will be lowered in a hurry, as the rush is still the same : tickets are never to be had from one performance to the next. At the second representation again I was called, with the company, after the second and last acts. For the third representation I arranged with the regisseur that—in case there were any more calls—I should no longer appear on the stage, so that the singers should have the whole honour in future. At that performance, accordingly, there were calls after the 2nd, 3rd and 4th acts, with my name above all again ; but the singers had to come forth alone, and immediately the rumour got about that I had left for Paris already. At the fourth representation the singers were vociferously called again twice. In short, the thing's assured, and there's no telling *when* the success will diminish. What's most remarkable to myself is the audience's *endurance :* I've cut as much as possible, but the opera still goes on till half past 10, and yet we haven't seen a seat vacated during a single performance ; everybody sits it out with the very keenest attention till the last fall of the curtain : which, for Dresden, is something to say. When I began the shortening, I had strange experiences to make : the singers said, " To be sure, it's fearfully taxing," yet none wanted anything struck from his part.   I regularly went down on my knees before Tichatschek, to let something be dropped from his appallingly fatiguing part : no possibility !   His constant answer was : " No, for it's too heavenly ; it's too heavenly ! "—

After all this, I really had some curiosity about my fee.   The most unheard-of fables went the round : some said the first 3 takings would belong to me,—some that I should get 2000 thaler, etc. Instead of which, after the third representation I received a letter at last from his Excellency, telling me, with the most flattering expressions, that he was assigning me a fee of 300 thaler [£45] for my " so capital and beautiful work, albeit the customary honorarium for an opera only amounted to 20 louis d'or ; but he could not resist making an exception in my favour, to testify his thanks to me."   Thus you see how one fares here, so long as one's obliged to leave this sort of thing to an Intendant's generosity ; my only comfort is the knowledge that the page will soon turn over for me, and upon similar occasions in the future *I* shall be able to *demand*.   So, dear children, I cannot help any one much with this first receipt of mine : for, in the first place I have to pay debts to the Brockhaus's out of it ; secondly, my old Magdeburg creditors are threatening me with pro-secution—and I shall have to appease them so far as possible ; then our bodily outfit—shirts, linen etc.—is in a condition at present that's indescribable, and cries aloud for restoration ; and so on.   *But,* after such a fabulous *success* it's really inconceivable that things should remain for long at this *one* receipt; it is to be hoped I shall soon sell the score to a few other places, at least; moreover, a good publisher—one who'll pay me decently—cannot be very far off. With this forecast, which is surely not flippant, I will console you and my Paris creditors for a wee time yet, and promise—to set apart my very next taking exclusively for them. It isn't to be imagined that that should be long deferred; *so comfort with a good conscience whomsoe'er you see pining for me ! ! !*—

And speedy takings on another path, too, will not be lacking. Only fancy!—KÜSTNER, the present Berlin Intendant, wrote me that he couldn't give my "fl. Holländer" before next February, as he means to and must bring out the Lachner opera first [*Catarina Cornaro*]; whereon comes Lüttichau and begs me let him have that opera of mine as well, that he may produce it on the heels of my Rienzi. So I had to write Küstner to send me back the score of the Holländer posthaste, since, as he cannot give the work till February, he would have the score quite time enough if I returned it to him the end of December. Then Küstner answers me evasively, not trusting himself, on account of Redern and Meyerbeer, to leave hold of the score of a composer who now has been crowned with such fame. But I have replied to him at once most determinedly : either he lays everything else on one side and gives the "Holländer" straight off, or he must remit me the score ; otherwise I shall hold him responsible for any damage that may accrue to me from the delay : for, why doesn't he keep his former promise ?—So in any case a thing unparalleled will happen : at one and the same theatre two [new] operas by *one* composer will have been given in immediate succession. The scenery is already ordered here, and, fortune favouring, the first performance of my " Holländer " will take place a month from to-day here in Dresden. See, children, the commencement is made ! !—

But I must still entertain you with something most comic, namely the rumours current here about me.—Naturally, every one has been asking : " What does it all mean? Who *is* the man ? One had never heard tell of him, and of a sudden he pops up with a work putting Meyerbeer, Auber, in short, all our recent notabilities to flight ! Is it a beginner's effort, this Rienzi ? That isn't possible ! Under what name can he have been writing operas before? " etc. But then they see I'm still a youngish man, and their per-plexity goes on increasing.—At last it transpires that I'm a Leipziger, and was lately in Paris : of course—I'm a pupil of Meyerbeer's. The happy family B. skims the fat off it, though : B. sent me to Paris for three years, people say, to " study " there and write Rienzi ; I drew 100 thaler a month from him, and he has contrived to get this opera produced in Dresden.—Children, this gossip will drive me to the grave with vexation ! Really, it's abominable that the stupid world should be used to ascribing triumphs to such people as these . . . ! !

For the first representation came Ottilie and Hermann, in the first place, then Luise with Bochmann ; Fritz [Brockhaus] hasn't been at all yet, as the editing of his journal [*Deutsche Allg. Ztg*] detains him. The one I still like best is Hermann. Luise, who is so fond of ecstatics, and jumps out of her skin at whatever's the mode, expressed her satisfaction with my opera, etc. Mother came for the second performance ; she lodged with us, and was thoroughly amiable, as she still knows how to be. Julius came to the third performance : a good fellow with whom things are now going heartily ill.—It was good Clärchen, however, who gave me and Minna the greatest delight : she stayed twelve days with us, and felt and made us very happy ; an excellent dear creature, full of feeling and without a grain of affectation. She is certain to have written you by now, dear Cecilie : Minna has quite become her sister, as already yours ; what a deal we three did talk about you ! And the two of us, I and Minna, who are alone again now, how often and with what feelings do we think of all of you ; upon my word, intoxicated with all the elating things that have come my way here, I was about to call the time just past the happiest in my life, when bitter tears gave me the lie, and recalled to me the incompleteness of my luck since *you*, all *you* still failed me. Jesus Christus, what wouldn't I have given to have had you here ! For listen : we're quite forlorn still ; of an evening we sit all alone, all *alone*, and no one drops in as of yore : ah, what sweet remembrances the sorriest plights in life may leave behind them !—Heine's are the only ones with whom we can seek compensation ; they belong to our bond out and out, have cares and troubles and are akin to me. After the dress-rehearsal of my opera Heine became my brother : he's a splendid fellow !—Children, we *must* come together again ; only let my opera bear interest, and when the creditors (*Gläubiger*) are polished off, the believers (*Gläubigen*) shall have their turn. It must be ! Who knows what news I shall be giving you next ? " Have trust in me, the tribune ! " God will vouchsafe me not merely to remain the same, but to go on increasing.—

Now give my heartiest regards to all acquaintances and sympathisers. Tell Kühne and wife the minutest item, and assure them that I and Minna are always thinking of them with the warmest thanks. God keep you all, my precious dear ones ; I bring you my whole heart as greeting ! All of Yours, RICHARD W.

DRESDEN, 6. *November* 1842.

To-morrow I shall send off a parcel through the firm with playbills and text-books of Rienzi.

29. TO EDUARD AVENARIUS [1]

MY GOOD EDUARD—Not to mix up what's of common interest to you all with trivial specialities, I am writing you a couple of lines in particular, to beg you to oblige me by undertaking a small commission for Hofr. Winkler. For all his

---

[1] Undated enclosure in No. 28, with special address " To Eduard."

selfishness, the man has really been of use to me, and played no insignificant part in the happy march of my affairs. He is now on the track of another new piece of Scribe's, which is to come out at the Théâtre français in a week or two. This child of man besought me fully 10 days back to execute the job I'm only seeing to to-day ; but God knows I couldn't get to writing, and therefore I'm afraid it has already grown too late through my fault. What he wants, is to buy this latest play of Scribe's, in its first proof-pulls, on the same terms as the " Chaîne "—namely for a payment of 200 fr. So please address yourself this instant to the publisher, Mr. Beck, and offer him the 200 fr. if he will forward Herr Hofrath Winkler the proofs of this new piece as quickly as in the case of the " Chaîne." Should it already be too late through my fault for such a bargain, then write me—I entreat you, for the love of God !—a letter informing me that you duly received mine of the 26th October (—do you twig ?—), but unfortun- ately the commission was no longer executable because, etc. . . . In an adverse event, this is the only way for me to pull myself out of the hole as regards Winkler.

Don't be cross with me—there's a good chap ! There was really nothing else for it.—

So you're coming to us soon ? ? ?
Hurrah ! Hurrah ! Hurrah !

Private letters, especially to good Cecilie, will follow shortly.

30. To Albert Wagner [1]

BEST BROTHER—The less I'm to be excused for
my long silence, the more I must beg you to shew
me indulgence, as otherwise we shan't ever get
straight. That charge of haughtiness, if you
meant it seriously, could only hit me had I suddenly
gone mad : had I any tendency to haughtiness,
I might have been equally haughty *before* my
Dresden success as *after* it, since I imagine myself
to have been entirely the same person before as
after ; what lies between is *luck*,—and on a piece of
luck I can't well plume myself.—Stuff and nonsense ! If you could cast a glance into my present
and lately-past life, you'd quickly comprehend how
it could occur that for so long a time I couldn't
get to writing you a copious letter—the only kind
you ought to have from me. You've no idea of
the distraction in which I am plunged through
continual excitements from every side ! Naturally, my whole life has altered at a blow ; though
I remain the same myself, everything around me
has become different. It will therefore serve me
as my best apology, if I relate to you in brief
what has happened to me since I received your
letter before last—on the day of my opera's first
performance.

You know pretty well what the success of that
first performance was ; literally, it made a furore.
I owe all my luck to our singers, and after them,
to the musicians of our capelle. Picture to your-

---

[1] Address : " Sr. Wohlgeboren / Herrn / Albert Wagner / Sänger und
Schauspieler / in Ballenstädt / frei."

G

self a place, or rather, a public like the Dresden, which has not been wont for untold ages to pass a *first*, decisive verdict, but had always been able to wait and hear what sort of verdict was expressed elsewhere,—this public, tepid in and for itself, for the first time finds itself faced with such a pretentious work, whose author bears the least-known name in all the world! This highly critical position, for me, by no means escaped either myself or my friends from the first, as a single shoulder-shrug by one of the gentry of the Opera here would have sufficed to undermine my work in advance ; but Heaven so ordained it that with each rehearsal the singers evinced more attention,— then interest, affection, and finally enthusiasm for my work ; and bit by bit that feeling got imparted by them to the public to such a degree, that it at last was looking forward to my opera's appearance as intently as to something quite unheard of. Thus it came about that the success of the very first representation was so complete that nobody here can recall anything equal to, or even resembling it. *And this despite the fact of the first performance having lasted till ¼ past 11 !!! [1]* They tell me, every one sat out that first performance with the greatest attention till the very last note,— which, for *Dresden*, was my crowning triumph.

That first representation was given at raised prices, and all were of opinion that from the second performance onward the opera would be put on at ordinary ones ; however, the rush has continued so great, that it was given a week ago

---

[1] Commencing at 6 P.M.—-TR.

for the *sixth* time at raised prices, and to a house as packed as ever. So Lüttichau has determined to make a break in the performances of my opera till the New Year, and then resume giving it at raised prices. I will spare you an enumeration of the special honours done me by the audience at those performances, merely telling you that the sixth representation, which I conducted myself, was if anything more enthusiastically received than the first.——What affected me most, however, was my experience with the whole company, but with Tichatschek and the Devrient in particular, when I began shortening the opera : none of them wanted anything cut ; so that I had a regular tussle, and only brought it off by so manœuvring my cuts that as little as possible was taken from the principal singers. The opera only lasts till half past 10 now ; but many voices have been raised among the public in protest against my dropping this or that passage.—— ——

Well, after the second performance, Lüttichau proposed to me to have my second opera, " der fliegende Holländer," also given in Dresden at once,—as it couldn't be brought out in Berlin, you see, till February or March. You will easily comprehend what an exceptional flattery there lay in that offer for me, and I gladly accepted it. So towards Christmas my second opera will be produced here too ; the Devrient has begged for the chief feminine part in it—which I naturally have had to alter a bit for her. You may well imagine that this concurrence usurps my whole mental activity : I'm superintending the copying of scores,

alterations, cuts, arrangements, etc. I have been
to Leipzig a couple of times, too, and the last time,
in fact, took part in a concert of the Devrient's
there. Every day I receive letters concerning my
affairs, many of which still lie unanswered. But
most disturbing of all are the *invitations :* time was
when never a cock crowed after me, and now I can't
get away from it, especially as my friends all declare
I must go everywhere : in brief, I'm the fashion
here.[1]

But what also has set and still keeps me in great
commotion, is the situation into which the so
surprisingly sudden death of poor Rastrelli has
brought me. At once all eyes were turned on me
as his successor in office ; it was mooted at Court,
and Lüttichau had me sounded. I am still battling
hard with myself. Naturally, I should wish to
stay free for the coming few years : I'm at my
best time of life now, when productive powers are
at their freshest ; I have already sketched two
subjects for new operas,[2] and might have composed
them in course of two years if I remained free. I
confess I would gladly have bought that freedom
for a few anxieties in the pecuniary regard ; and,
after all, I surely may count on some handsome
returns yet with my two completed operas. Per
contra, all proceeds slowly and deliberately in our
Germany ; I'm too unexpected an arrival for the
generality of theatres, and before they find time to

---

[1] In confirmation of which, in his latest edition of vol. i of *Das Leben
R. W.'s* (1905) Herr Glasenapp quotes Minna's own complaint, from a billet
to Cecilie dated Jan. 5, 43, that " in many a week we scarcely dine at home
twice."—TR.

[2] *Tannhäuser*—of course—and *Sarazenin*, or *Bergwerk von Falun ?*—TR.

shovel me into their repertory no doubt I may have to suck my thumb awhile. To be sure, I've a provisional order for the score from Brunswick through Schmetzer already ; yesterday I also had a letter from the Aachen Director, in which he begged me for the score : nevertheless, even should I begin picking up a trifle here and there, my old debts lie heavy on my neck still, in particular the Magdeburg ones, and I am a long way off seeing the time when I'd be rid of money worries. Therefore, and especially as I had been upbraided for not speaking up, I made a clean breast of it to Lüttichau a few days back, and told him that, although I strictly should have liked remaining free, yet the prospect of having at my disposal such an extraordinary ensemble as the Dresden Opera now offers for the highest art-efforts was something so seductive to me that I might easily renounce my earlier design ; but, as a subordinate position such as Rastrelli had occupied did not present to me that prospect, I could not contemplate the vacant place. Thereupon Lüttichau explained to me that it wasn't his intention to fill up the berth *precisely* as Rastrelli occupied it, but since he could repose the needful confidence in Reissiger no longer, owing to his too great indolence and shiftlessness, he proposed setting another *Kapellmeister* by side of him, who at the least should share completely equal rights.—So I am standing like Hercules at the parting of the ways : —whoever has none save my material interest in eye, will naturally admonish me " Lay hold ! "— but is that really everything?— —

So you see how it fares with me : my head's continually chock-full—now with art, now with— mart.—I should much have liked to see you here ; are you really so frightfully busy ? If I haven't written you before, for a long time the circumstance was partly to blame, that I didn't know *where* to write to. But you're all back at Ballenstädt now, and things are going as well with you as could be hoped, are they not ?

I rather think we'll wait a while *re* my Rienzi. Don't you consider it as well, yourself, if it were first given at some second leading spot ? I don't depreciate—Lord knows—the flattery implied in your enquiry, and if you have better grounds for giving the opera so soon at your theatre, why, tell me them and teach me. In any case it shews great trust on your director's part, and I thank him for it heartily. The fee will be no great obstacle between us ; and moreover, I'm so rearranging the score that a performance won't put minor stages in too great a fix. At all events it will be interesting to me, to see and hear you as Rienzi ;[1] so write me soon, please, what you have to reply to my demur.

And now—how goes your family ? How's the wife ? What progress are the children making ? I often speak of yourself and Johanna here. Please write me out the latter's repertory ; all sorts of idiots get débuts or trials here, so why shouldn't one give a beginner a chance who promises so well

---

[1] Needless to say, Albert never sang in any of his brother's operas ; excepting such a rôle as Eric, the tenor parts must have been quite beyond his powers.—Tr.

under your instruction? Where there's a will, there's a way.—

My wife sends cordial thanks for your greeting, and reciprocates it. Contrive for us to see each other soon ; perhaps the opportunity may present itself, if you're going to shift your tent to Bernburg? You can put up in my rooms yourself. Fare perfectly well, and don't be cross with me any longer. Best love to all your family from myself and wife. Ever and always Thy faithful brother   RICHARD WAGNER.

DRESDEN, 3. *December* 1842,
MARIENSTRASSE No. 9.

31. To Cäcilie Avenarius

DRESDEN, 5. *January* 1843.

MY BEST CECILIE—It's a long, long time since I wrote to you, as I know you cannot regard even my last letter as any special intercourse between us two ; for, lengthy though it was, that letter contained nothing but a detailed report on the success of my Rienzi, a report addressed to *all* my Paris friends, not to yourself in particular. You were to have had a private letter besides, discussing everything that concerns our own affairs,—so I intended when despatching that report ; and it is my not having been able to bring myself to write that letter yet that places me under a very unmerited cloud on the one side, but on the other, has worried me for months. To make it comprehensible to you how I came to be so behindhand with

fulfilment of a duty as important as agreeable, I
absolutely must give you first a survey of my
recent life.

Down to this moment I have never come to a
rest, and if at last I set apart this forenoon for a
letter to yourself, you may be sure I'm leaving
jobs undone which to other folk would seem too
urgent not to be discharged before all else. With
the success of my Rienzi I have made a giant's
stride into publicity, and therewith fallen prisoner
to the thousand and one considerations of a public
name. The trouble of maintaining one's repute,
and spreading it, is now in full swing ; within the
last 2 months I've received more letters than
during the whole of my stay in Paris. Notwithstanding my resolve to take no steps myself to
offer other theatres my opera, I very soon had to
answer direct and indirect enquiries after it. Then,
scarcely had I got out of the commotions caused
me by the performances of Rienzi, than the fresh
labour with my "Flying Dutchman" raised its head.
I had undertaken to rehearse and conduct this
opera myself ; before which I had a fine ado to
recover my score from Berlin. Twice over I had
occasion to journey to Leipzig. On the top of
all which came the death of Rastrelli, which has
thrown me into a quite unexpected situation as
regards the post so suddenly left empty at the
theatre here. I couldn't but look for a speedy
conclusion of everything involved in this development : will you make it a serious reproach to me,
that I wanted to be relieved of many a doubt
before I could feel composed enough to write

you ? Moreover—I cannot write to yourself without remembering your good husband, whom I knew to be burdened through me with so much that positively cried for removal before I could face you both again with tranquil heart. Enough if I inform you that, while writing you to-day, I've a letter received from Vienna a month ago, about my Rienzi, still lying unanswered in front of me ; that I have left an order to adapt the book of Rienzi for the Prague censorship un-executed for a fortnight ;—let this suffice to prove to you that lukewarmness at least is not my reason, if I haven't written you before.

Only to-day do I arrive at telling you how in-finitely you delighted us by your so surprising news that you'll visit us with Eduard in the dear father-land next spring. Can you really believe we could accept news like that without recognising in it the promise of fulfilment of our fondest wishes ? In that case you'd be taking all we wrote to you before as flagrant lies. On the contrary, that piece of news quite lulled us, in a sense : we saw fulfilment of our wish attained, and had no further cause to pester you to make your journey possible ; the thing seemed to us settled, leaving us nothing but to look with longing toward your actual arrival. But your easily accountable, however unjust pique against me seems to have infected all my Paris friends : not one of them gives even a sign of life, and I'm getting quite afraid lest the whole lot should be dead. Has no one any mercy for my situation, which is such a strain upon me now, that a neglect of *outer* duties surely is to be pardoned me? I constantly think of you all——

> but it's impossible for me to write long letters : to-day is being mulcted me once again,——this moment I am interrupted by the Privy Councillor's lackey with a summons to attend him this morning itself :——to-morrow I shall have to set about my backward businesses at last ; so I *can* only touch in brief upon the most important points, since I've other reasons for not postponing the despatch of this letter any longer.——I shall resume this afternoon.

There, it's gone 6 in the evening before I could get back to my pen. I really shall have to look sharp about it ; so here goes for news in a nutshell.——

After my Rienzi had been given six times at raised prices and to constantly overflowing houses, it was laid on one side for a while in the midst of its triumph, to allow the singers a little rest—for this opera tries Tichatschek terribly—and to be able to go on giving it at raised prices later. Meantime my Flying Dutchman was put in rehearsal, the Devrient taking the Senta. After that rousing, dazzling and imposing opera, Rienzi, none of us had great expectations from the flieg. Holländer, and I admit I embarked on it with very great anxiety ; because a deal of imagination is needed to understand this opera, and it offers small opening for brilliant effects. It's of quite another—as many say, a new—genre, which can only very slowly break its path : all you people formed other ideas of it. Well, on the 2nd of January it was performed for the first time, and I confess I'm far prouder of the success this opera has had than of the success of Rienzi, since I had too many auxiliaries there. We gave the opera in 3 acts, so that it filled the whole bill ; after the second and third acts I was tumultuously called with the singers. The second performance came yesterday, and I had the triumph that the enthusiasm mounted even higher ; again I was called twice with the singers : the first time I made them go forward alone, but the public wouldn't rest until I had come out alone after them.

So I've brought this opera also—which arose entirely under *your* eyes—safely through, nay, perhaps founded a new genre with it. That it has pleased so, is saying a good deal, as Rienzi had raised such enormous expectations. And now the Holländer is to come out at Berlin the beginning of March.

Through the death of Rastrelli, as you'll already know, the post of Musikdirektor has become vacant here. Everybody cast eyes on me, saying I had only to apply for it, to secure the berth at once ; but it stood to reason that I would accept no subordinate appointment under Reissiger ; so I waited for people to come to me, and finally declared to Lüttichau that I could only accept a first Kapellmeister post with a salary of 1800 thaler [*ca.* £270]. I know for a fact that a competent man is much wanted here, and must have a first-class sphere of action cleared for him ; for

Reissiger has sunk to such a cypher now, that his efficiency may be rated at zero. Well, Lüttichau has just disclosed to me that he has a mind to appoint me as Kapellmeister with 1800 thlr salary, only I must serve a trial year as Musik-direktor at 1200 thlr first. Thereon I've written him, this very afternoon, that I *cannot* and shall not consent to it. What his decision will be, I know not; but it stays certain that I do not abandon my freedom except for a quite first-class engage-ment. True, I know I am thereby exposing myself to continued great worry and straits for the present ; but a man like myself oughtn't to fear anything. Even should it go slowly with the circulation of my operas—as everything does in Germany—yet their spread throughout the breadth of Germany can't fail me in the long run, for the success here has made too much sensation. Rienzi will be given next at Prague and Hamburg,—at Brunswick also in the Spring. Beyond my Dresden fee, however, I've taken nothing yet ; that will only come later. The publishers are all hanging back with their offers, doubtless waiting to see how my operas will please at other places ; for my own part, too, I do not mean to give myself away by making up to publishers ; so it all may take time.

While waiting for better things, it therefore has been of extraordinary importance to me that I finally have found—and without any seeking—the person to lend me 1000 thaler down simply on my honest looks and promise to repay the debt so soon as I shall be in good circumstances. This

person is none other than—the DEVRIENT : she
had learnt of my condition, my obligations, debts,
and entirely of her own accord has repeatedly
offered me 1000 thlr, till at last I accepted it.
It's something extraordinary,—and I avow that,
even were it not so, I honour and revere the
Devrient beyond all bounds.   She is a truly noble,
great-hearted woman.   She has taken Minna also
warmly to her heart : at Christmas she fêted us ;
Minna had really luxurious presents from her ;
whatever she could possibly wish for, she received.
I am allotting to Paris pretty nearly half the sum
lent me by the Devrient, and shall write Eduard
more in detail about it.   With the other half I
mean to try and clear myself of my old Magdeburg
debts : it will be a tough job, as the people there
are dunning me to death, and threaten to com-
promise me in my present honourable position at
any moment ; were I to pay them all they ask,
with costs and interest they would have 657 thaler
to claim.   I shan't spend a penny of the 1000
thlr on myself.—

That's pretty well how it fares with me : things
are progressing, you see, and if you come here,
dear Cecilie and Eduard, you will find us still
better, I hope.   Rienzi is to be divided into halves
[between acts ii and iii] and given on two separate
nights in future, because too much had to be
omitted on account of its length ; which is all to
be restored now, to deprive the public of nothing.
Judge by that whether the opera pleases !   At
Prague, too, they will probably give this opera in
2 nights.   Let us hope, dear Cecilie, you'll get a

sight of my operas here,—only mind you both come soon.—As to Natalie, our decision is taken : you must be so good as to bring her with you at our expense, when you will be rid of her and she can go on to her sister at Zwickau [Charlotte Tröger], where she'll be best looked after.

How are Herr and Mad. Kühne? For the love of Heaven, give them a million heartiest regards from us ; never shall we cease to remember them with emotion. But what became of those abominable beds, after all ?—Minna, who is scolding herself severely, absolutely does intend writing you ; Lord knows if all her after-fears about my operas will let her arrive at it yet! This letter must go off to-morrow morning,—lucky if she has done it by then, her writing-fever is so shockingly mild !—

Good Lord, I don't at all know where my head is ! If I kept writing of just nothing but you and yours, there'd be at least matter enough to make me begin another long letter right off. Spare me so much scribbling, and come nice and quick yourselves ; once we're together again, I trust we shall be pleased with one another, and you will convince yourselves that we haven't abated our love by a hair's breadth. All rubbish, that ! We've a puppy too, for your big bouncer [to play with], your Max. Oh, Max ! Oh, Max !

Farewell, my dear Cecilie ; beat the bees out of your cap and be sensible. Once folk have drawn so near each other's hearts as we, they don't change any more.— — I'll write to Eduard on a separate slip,—it has got so crowded here !—

Keep safe and sound,—give your Max my best kisses,—tell my friends their full share of this letter ; greet them from the bottom of my heart ; and ever hold unalterably dear Thy Brother

RICHARD W.

32. To EDUARD AVENARIUS [1]

MY DEAREST EDUARD—I'm sure you have been going through a deal of worry about me again, I left so much upon your neck, God knows ; but I really hadn't the heart to write to you again before I could ease your mind a little concerning my affairs. I am writing Cecilie fairly all I have to tell about myself, therefore merely address *you* herewith on quasi-business matters. Let me first thank you most kindly, however, for attending to the Winkler affair ; you've thereby pledged the man to me afresh, and he never stops praising myself and opera most pitifully in the old Leipziger Zeitung. So a thousand thanks !

And now to business. The Devrient has lent me 1000 thaler, to pay off as many debts as possible. My Magdeburg creditors will play a chief rôle in that ; but Paris shall be thought of also. I therefore am handing you a bill of exchange for 1500 francs. Be so good as to pay from it at once my poor brave tailor, Mr. Loizeau ; I can't deny myself the pleasure of inviting him, per the accompanying note, to come to you and fetch his money, 400 frs.

Then be so kind as to redeem my unfortunate

[1] Enclosure to No. 31.

pledges : the silver plate is in for 250 frs,—
the watch for 100.[1] How about the renewal of
the pawn-tickets ? Were you so good as to pay
all charges for me ?—If you *have* done that, you'll
also pay the fresh expenses with a joyful heart ; I
trust it won't inconvenience you, and as we are to
meet in Saxony so soon, you know, you'll have a
splendid opportunity then of accounting to me for
the last fraction and receiving all your out-of-
pockets back at once ; for I hope to be in funds
by the next time we meet.—Neither am I including
my old debt to yourself now,—I trust it's possible
for you to wait for that until you come here, when
you may be certain of recovering from me what
you helped me out of so many a fix with.—

600 frs I've marked for Kietz ; I owe him
about that much, even if it isn't more. God
grant the bare repayment of this debt may be of
use to him, of *true* use ! If Kietz is a man of
sense, he must know what he's doing ; only, it's
my opinion that *nothing* will come of him in Paris.
Do have a thorough serious talk with him : of
course he knows that I've no right to read him
lectures just because I'm sending him this money,
for he read myself none when he lent it me ;
but it's to be hoped he has not grown deaf to
good advice yet. Anyhow, I'm writing him a
couple of lines himself.—

100 fr. belong to Kietz's uncle, Mr. Fechner ;
Kietz will be so good as to pay them to him.
40 fr. belong to my shoemaker, settlement of
which Kietz will likewise take over.—

[1] Cf. R. to M. Wagner, p. 27.—Tr.

Accordingly the sum would have to be distributed as gloriously as possible in the following way :—

Kietz	600 fr.
Loizeau	400 „
my pledges	350 „
Mr. Fechner	100 „
shoemaker	40 „
interest at discretion to the highest bidders . . .	10 „
Total . .	1500 fr.

As for Natalie, my dear Eduard, please buy her what she needs most urgently—if it isn't asking too much of you ; then bring her with you when you come to Saxony, and rest assured that I shall make a point of being in the position to repay you everything at once here—travelling expenses and outlay, with what I still owe you besides. You'll keep account of it all for me ; but should it gêne you in fact, simply write me so, and I will try and manage to send you the money before you leave Paris.—Our silver and the watch you will bring with you, won't you ? At least, that would be the handiest method of getting it to us. My wife begs you to get the watch repaired at Breguet's first —where it came from ; would you be so kind as to attend to this also ? For all of which you shall float on a perfect tornado of bliss here :—we'll kill the fatted calf with a vengeance, and above all, hear my operas.

Don't be cross with me for all these fresh requests : God knows whom else I should address

H

myself to !—Be greeted a thousand-fold, and accept the assurance of the eternal gratitude and warmest friendship of Thy faithful brother-in-law

RICHARD W.

DRESDEN, 5. *January* 1843.

Cordial greetings to Vieweg, Rochow, Venedei, etc.

33. To the Same [1]

DEAREST EDUARD—I'm in great uneasiness at having no letter from either of you yet. I wrote you the 5th or 6th inst., and enclosed in my letter a bill of exchange for 1500 frs. I didn't register that letter, but merely franked it. Should it have got lost, or into the wrong hands, prompt notification would be needed on account of the bill ; but if you did receive all safely, isn't it about time that one of you gave me news of yourselves ?

I am writing on the spur of the moment, and have nothing to add to my hurried enquiry beyond the heartiest greetings to you all from Thy

RICHARD W.

DRESDEN, 30*th Jan.* 1843.

The King's ratification of my appointment as full Capellmeister will follow in a day or two.— Soon more.

---

[1] Address : " Monsieur / Edouard Avenarius / Libraire / Rue Richelieu 69 / à / PARIS."

34. To Cäcilie Avenarius[1]

DRESDEN, 8. *April* 1843.

MY DEAR CECILIE—Many and hearty thanks for the dear letter you lately rejoiced us with ; but only the letter rejoiced us, not your news in it :—so you don't mean to visit us this summer ? Upon my word, that's really odious of you! Whatever can have happened, that your decision to accompany Eduard should be abandoned in a trice ? What seemed possible 3 months ago, why can it no longer be so to-day ? Is mere money still to blame? You don't exactly mention it ; but if it's that, just let me know in what manner I can contribute toward procuring us the great pleasure of your visit. Get along with you, and do be a little light-minded ! Once you all are here, the way back will be easy to manage. Goodness gracious, it would be too silly if you didn't come too! Couldn't you all travel by diligence ? You simply need annex the coupée ; you'd have room enough for Natalie and Max, and it would be the best way of getting Natalie here at once.

Now I have dropped on that chapter, I mean to polish it off :—Can you still be in any doubt as to our intention with regard to Natalie ? I've already begged you both, you know, to advance the costs of her return as far as Leipzig :—the sooner that journey can be brought off, the better we shall like it, as we shall know you the sooner

---

[1] Address simply : " An Cécilie Avenarius " ; consequently an enclosure to another letter.

relieved of a great burden thereby, and we also cannot see the use of Natalie's continuing in Paris. Our getting her sent there [1] simply reposed on an error, since we believed we were making things much easier for the parents ; [2] our having to leave her behind us in Paris on our departure, was a case of necessity, as it facilitated our journey home ;—but now that the best and most appropriate place for Natalie has been found with her sister Charlotte, and we can well afford the expense of her return journey, it would be nonsense to think of her remaining in Paris any longer.   If Natalie has not learnt French in Paris, she may find comfort in Kietz—or myself, for that matter ; her imagining she may be of ultimate use to herself and the world by learning the French language, is a fantastic dream, the nature whereof would soon dawn on her if she would submit her *German*-written letters to a cold-blooded examiner.   Success can only bloom for Natalie in a sphere of life that—be it never so honourable and satisfactory—has nothing whatever in common with the French language.—Pack up her things as soon as possible, and if you really are not coming too, dear Cecilie, she needn't inconvenience your good husband either ; you'll simply be so good as to give her into charge of a conductor,—neither need she pass a night at Frankfort, but continue her road the same evening, and she's certain to arrive quite safe at Leipzig.

---

[1] Where *from*, we do not hear.   Had she been left behind at Riga in the early summer of 1839, under care of Minna's sister Amalie, or forwarded ahead to Dresden then ?—Tr.

[2] Not even his sisters were let into the secret, then, by this generous supporter of his wife's præ-nuptial offspring.—Tr.

Eduard will be so good as to hand her the requisite travelling-money, and may rely on receiving it back from me, together with my other debt, at our very first meeting, whether here or in Leipzig. I would forward the couple of 100 frs at once, if in the first place I thought it was needed, and in the second if I hadn't to be somewhat thrifty with disbursements *this* month, as I shall have to pay for my court-uniform in a day or two, *circa* 100 thaler. The thing is settled, then : you'll merely be so good as to let us know exactly when she will reach Leipzig, as her brother-in-law Tröger will await her there and take her on at once to Zwickau.—So we're at one upon that point, and it only remains for ourselves to express to you and Eduard our sincerest thanks for the great friendship with which you stood by us in respect of Natalie, also, in our time of need ;—God grant we may be able to reward you some day !—

Yesterday it was a year since we left Paris in a torrent of tears ; Lord, how quickly that year has slipped by, and what a quantity of things have happened to me in it ! We thought of it vividly on your birthday, for which, alas, I was unable to congratulate you in good time ; a thing I regret, as I know how much you set by outward tokens of attention. Believe me, for all that my heart is as steadfast as ever.

The 9th Apr.—It's one eternal interruption ; in this Easter-week I have also to figure a couple of times in church,—so I cannot get to any proper mustering of my thoughts. Not to forget one thing on top of another, however, I'll at once clear

up a doubt in which you seem involved concerning
our relations with the family.   Whatever makes
you think we're on bad terms ?   On the contrary,
we are on the friendliest footing ; only we see
each other very seldom, for you will be aware that
from Dresden to Leipzig is a tidy step.   In course
of the winter I went to Leipzig several times, and
we were always united heart and soul.   Minna, to
be sure, hasn't been to Leipzig yet ; but why on
earth should she go there for nothing but a visit ?
Off and on we have seen each member of the
family here, and our encounters have always been
of the friendliest description.   At the moment,
though, I can't tell you much about our family, as
I have no particular news myself.   It seems there
won't be much to do for Albert : I did so want to
get him an engagement as singing-master independent of the theatre ; and the best opening had
just presented itself through Pohlenz's death
[March 10].   They made enquiries from Leipzig
whether one couldn't recommend them a thorough
good singing-master, alike for the new Leipzig
music-school [Conservatorium] and for instruction in
general ; I promptly got Albert proposed, and
wrote to him myself, giving him every information
how to apply for the post, setting forth all the
advantages for his daughter's future also, and
entreating him to regard it as the turning-point
in his life.   He answered me with nothing but
faint-heartedness and shirking, how he feared not
being equal to the post as musician, but above all,
how he felt he couldn't live without the Theatre :
that's the misfortune, he does so hug that curs—

stage-life.   So I don't know what he's going to do.
If he'd only bring Johanna regularly out ; I have
great expectations of her, and in any case have my
eye on her for Dresden.   For that matter, though,
things are not going exactly *ill* with Albert now.—

But what is really going to become of yourselves ?   Heinrich [Brockhaus] said something to
me lately that almost looked as if there were a
chance of your returning to Germany for good :
why, that would be best of all !   What joy for us,
if there were anything serious at bottom of it !—
Lord, how obliged I am anew to your good
Eduard for his amiable pains with my affairs ; the
tale about the watch is splendid !   If he had only
omitted those dreadful receipts ; they gave his last
letter a deuced business look,—I couldn't help
heartily laughing at such punctiliousness.   But
there, I shall soon be able to express my thanks to
him by mouth.   And yourself— ?   O Cile, Cile, fie
upon you !   You mean to remain in the rue
Richelieu with your Maxel ?   Don't take it amiss
of me, but it would be abominable, first to make
one's mouth water, and then — — ! !   Just pack
your traps as well, and if you have a corner empty
in your trunk still, then pack that crazy Kietz into
it too, to drag him out of his rue Jacob at last.

I'm quite on tiptoe for your next reports ;
mind they're not too long in coming.   God bless
you, my good sister !   God bless your dear Eduard
and your darling Maxel !   May the Lord protect
you all, and bring you safely here as soon as
possible !   Amen !   To all eternity Thy faithful
brother   RICHARD W.

My dear heart's Cecilie, I cannot possibly let this letter go off without adding a few words to give you the assurance of my constant love and gratitude.   Richard has already written you everything, so nothing remains for me to tell you of our housing, family news, etc.   I am much looking forward to a real good chat with you, for I can't give up the joyful hope of being able to fold you in my arms right soon ; and as for my darling Max, I mean to smother him with so many kisses that he'll wish his horrid aunt in life eternal with a swear-word.   I have a frock in petto for him quite after your taste—ah God, were the time already here when I could squeeze you both to my breast !— I hope soon !—Do not annihilate a feeling I have carried in my heart for a year, and which has borne me up, or I could not have endured the separation from you.   Ever Thy   MINNA.

35. TO ALBERT WAGNER [1]

DEAREST BROTHER—I'm sitting down at once to reply on the main point of your letter in brief, as I fear it might get laid on the shelf otherwise, since Reissiger is starting on a month's leave of absence to-day, and I consequently shall have my hands full.   You may set your mind at rest on the principal matter, Rienzi ; the Heinefetter doesn't come here till the beginning of September, and as Tichatschek also is going away as early as the 24th inst., the project of giving my opera again

---

[1] Address : " Sr. Wohlgeboren / Herrn / ALBERT WAGNER / Sänger und Schauspieler / jetzt / in / HALLE. / Im Theater zu erfragen / frei."

here in *one* night is not to be thought of at present. You'll accordingly receive the parts so arranged still, that they agree with the full score I lent you.—The Ambassadors have nothing to sing, but should be represented in the March by supers.—So our plan of meeting for Rienzi here in May is knocked on the head; more likely I shall come to you for it.

If on your return from your brief outing—as to which I'm uncommonly glad that it did you at least so much moral good—you've tumbled into annoyances again, I haven't fared better myself, and you may console yourself with me : one disagreeable after another has befallen me. For example, an old acquaintance of mine [Apel ?] redemands from me—with interest at 5 per cent—600 thaler he lent, or rather, gave me—as tacitly assumed—8 years ago. Then a Königsberg Jew, who had come over for the [Leipzig ?] fair, called on me in Dresden and explained that I had 300 thaler to pay him. Neither is there anything decent doing in our music now, nothing but everyday fustian, etc. My only delight is a new grand piano, which is making a great sensation here ; also I am beginning to compose again, the Men's annual Singing Festival is driving me hard. As soon as Reissiger returns, I shall try and get away to Loschwitz, and commence my Tannhäuser.— Härtel sent me no invoice anent the piano ; I almost think he wants to wait for his brother's return from Rome, and then make overtures for my Rienzi ; in which case the piano would have to be reckoned as part of the fee.—Cornet has written me again ; he will be passing through here the middle of June, and wants to take the score with him ; so Hamburg will in any case be the next theatre Rienzi comes out at. The Holländer is being rehearsed in Berlin now. The Cassel people have already sent my fee for it.

Now hurry up with Johanna ; I stick to it, you know.—A Mds. Dielitz from Amsterdam was the last to sing here ; the Dutch journals declared she sang "wegschlepping"—transportingly—on the strength of which Lüttichau booked her for six star rôles at 100 thlr [each]. She appeared in Lucia, and was such a ―――― that we couldn't allow her to sing any more. She insisted on the promises made her, though, and is "slipping" 500 thlr "away."—That's how things go ; just *you* make them good with Johanna !

Kind love to wife and children. My wife sends best thanks to you all, and kindest regards.—God preserve you ! Farewell, farewell ! Thy Brother

RICHARD W.

DRESDEN, 17. *May* 1843.

[Nos. 36 and 37 of the German edition are represented by letters 4 and 5 to Minna.—TR.]

38. TO THE SAME [1]

DEAREST ALBERT—I really must answer your lugubrious letter at once. What a hash you poor

―――――――――

[1] Address : "Sr. Wohlgeboren / Herrn / Albert Wagner / Mitglied des Herzogl. Bernburgischen / Hoftheaters / zur Zeit / in / HALLE. / Im Theater zu / erfragen / frei."

people always seem to get into! Rest assured
that I, too, wish with all my heart to see you soon
delivered from these tortures, and I could despair
when I find myself withheld at every turn from
rushing in to your assistance by the considerations
I have still to observe for the present. The main
point in my eyes, though, remains Johanna; it is
becoming clearer and clearer to me that she soon
will be most welcome here. Under any condition
I abide by our bargain; but it perhaps might
happen even earlier. We're in a wretched stew,
you see, with our female singers and our Opera;
and when the Devrient leaves us, the most brilliant
portion of our repertory will be done for! And
then, the uncertainty whether the Devrient will
be here at all next winter! Lüttichau is travelling
just now; before his departure he impressed on
me to find some means of giving Rienzi even
without the Devrient. Good: my solitary chance
is to get the Wüst to sing the part of Adriano,—
we should have singers in plenty for the Irene;
but nothing will induce the Wüst to give her
part up [she did soon after], and so, with all the little
marionettes we've got, there's no other possibility
of picking out a singer to take the Adriano. If
things go on like this, and the Devrient doesn't
come this winter, Lüttichau will be in despair
about Rienzi; for it is his principal opera now,
and for a long time to come will remain so. In
that case Johanna will *have* to come here:
Heaven has endowed her with everything for
rôles like that, and I'd wager my head that the
instant Lüttichau sees her, he'll be charmed with

her,—when the rest will follow. Anyhow, I shall forward you a complete Adriano part shortly.— The sole true fear, lest Johanna might be over-worked here, loses all foundation, as she is only to sing a few, but good parts; and for that matter, no singer is worked to death here.—Keep the score till further orders, only so that I can have it at a moment's notice.—

I have been having a number of pleasant experiences.—Just fancy! from Vienna, where I know absolutely nobody, the administration of the Imp. Court-opera-house enquires if I would care to write a new opera for its next German season, and under what conditions. Isn't that fine? I replied that I had already set down my next opera, the "Tannhäuser," for Dresden, but had a second subject in reserve [cf. p. 84] which I should be glad to compose for their season 1844 to 45.—

On the 7th we had a grand festivity here, the unveiling of the monument to Friedrich August. A chant for men's voices—to be executed in the Zwinger—was ordered of me by the King; Mendelssohn had to compose the second one. My chorus, being simple, uplifting and effective, decidedly bore off the palm; whereas Mendelssohn's turned out both pompous and flat.—The King sent me best thanks and a beautiful gold snuffbox worth about 100 thaler.—

—Of the most moment to me, however, is the success of my "Flying Dutchman" at Cassel, where it was produced on the 5th inst. The letter SPOHR sent me about it is worthy of note : with the greatest warmth this gruff and inaccessible being writes me how he had the strongest predilection for my work from the first, how he had held twice the usual number of rehearsals, and rejoiced to find alike singers and orchestra shew continually increasing interest in them ; finally, that the performance had been excellent, and, in particular, he could not imagine the part of the Holländer being better sung or acted anywhere than by Biberhofer ; that the machinist (—a great point, this !—) had done his affair so well, that he was called on after the singers,—and in conclusion, that the whole opera had met with the highest and most universal approbation.—That's what I call magnificent, better than anything else ! And I'm beside myself with joy about it.—

So things are going well with me, you see, and I hope you are convinced that I'm longing to be able to say the same about yourself. Patience, it will all come right, and perhaps sooner than you think for ; whatever gives *me* a lift, may directly contribute to giving you another.—

For the last 20 days my wife has been at the baths, at Teplitz ; I shall send her your kind message.—Just before her departure we had another great delight : on my birthday, to wit, a grand serenade with coloured lanterns etc. was given me by 60 singers from the local clubs, when a poem was also presented me which they sang to a melody of Weber's.— —A thing like that is mighty touching !—

I've fairly finished my composition for the Choral Festival [*Liebesmahl der Apostel*], and promise myself a great effect with it.—You are hereby most cordially invited for the 5th and 6th July for the performance.

Best love to your good wife and children ; comfort them all with the hope of a better future, and rest assured of the most unalterable fidelity of your brother   RICHARD W.

DRESDEN, 14. *June* 1843.

[No. 39 of the German edition corresponds with letter 13 to Minna.—TR.]

40. TO CÄCILIE AVENARIUS[1]

DRESDEN, 22. *October* 1843.

MY DEAREST CECILIE—What kind of a letter do you call that you've written me? I have just received it, read it, and am quite beside myself! If it weren't for Minna's consoling me and explaining that young women in your condition are usually very mopish and moody, I should take your horrid remarks and woebegone effusions heartily ill of you.—And that in a letter which so delighted us, upon the other hand, by filling the whole gap in our late correspondence with an outpour of feeling enough to flush away all dumps that Life has power to heap!—Not a bit of it, my darling! Welcome with joy and gladness the hope of adding to your glorious Max a little equal ; and should something quite special remain over to hope, let it be the wish that the new arrival may turn out a charming little girl. Your

[1] Address : "Madame/Cécilie Avénarius/'Librairie de Brockhaus et Avenarius'/rue Richelieu, 67/à/Paris."

first confinement was your apprenticeship,—you'll
get through the second quite lightly : just look at
Ottilie,—she has learnt such a routine with it,
that she's positively ashamed when anybody asks
her if a confinement of hers went off all right.—
Myself and Minna, we haven't felt the least alarm
for you ; and why should we need to ? You're
no colossus—but, for that sort of thing, so much
the better !

Do you know what I am wishing you ? One
thing alone : to be able to return to your own
country right soon ! You've the Paris malady :
home-sickness brews in all your veins ; and that's
a malady which by all means must be soon got rid
of ! I won't exacerbate your longing by description and praise of the well-being at home,—but
it comes straight from my soul when I say, Praise
God that he let me find my fortune in my *native
land!* People like ourselves, who count so many
anniversaries whereon they have a bygone pleasure
to remember, can't long remain entirely uprooted
from the soil whence those remembrances had
sprung. Lord, my heart could break when I
think of the solitude—however magnificent—in
which you cast your glances from St Cloud across
to Bellevue; I picture myself in the inverse relation, and could almost die of sadness !—Ah, how
I hate Paris, that vast, stupendous *desert* to our
German hearts !

Well, well—the instant hope of seeing you
both transported from that desert to our home is
dashed, as I perceive from everything, and you're
chained to Paris for an untold time again ; so

nothing remains now except the hope of at least luring *yourself* on a long visit to us. Of course your fresh maternity will stand greatly in the way of that again, but let it be the task of both of you to discover means of managing that you come to us yourself, in spite of all, next summer : you will have no other problem, than how to contrive getting as far as the kingdom of Saxony,—for *there* begins my province. Once you are here—you shan't repent it, and everything shall run on wheels. This much I'll tell you : your time shall be *good*,—I won't say any more!—My God, if it could only be, if it only could be *soon ! !* I met F[ritz ?] in Leipzig,—he told me it was now decided that he *wasn't* going to Paris ;—I understood! And so I've got a thorough grudge against him : how well it would have matched my sympathies, if this man had gone to live 500 miles away from me, in Paris —where his tedium would have bored me less— and you folk had come here instead !— —

If you fulfil our wish and come to Dresden next summer, in my turn I'll come to Paris the summer after.—There's something on the cards there : the management of the Italian Opera wants a tiptop German season for next summer ; they have applied to Tichatschek already ; the whole undertaking is to be extremely solid and on an imposing scale, and of course only German operas are to be given,—above all, they've eyes on my *Rienzi.* It goes without saying, that I should come to Paris then,—how would that be, eh?— We'd kill the fatted calf for once, and have a good old romp in the bois de Meudon !—Meanwhile I must run over to *Hamburg* this winter, where *Rienzi* is to be staged with great diligence ; I've had to give my pledge to go there, all expenses paid, and conduct the first two performances.— The Berlin people, on the other hand, have dilly-dallied so long, that their opera-house has got itself burnt down ; I saw that coming. I shall not permit my operas to be given there before the new house stands erect, though they want to give the " Holländer " in the Play-house,—too small.—

Now that I am speaking of myself, I will just add that I've been unable to do any more work since the sacred composition I wrote for this year's Dresden Choral Festival ; partly my bad health, partly the smallness of my lodgings, which consisted of simply a room and a half, were to blame for it. My health is none so grand yet : hæmor-rhoidal troubles have set in acutely, my stomach is totally ruined, and the consequence is everlasting malaise and determination of blood to the head. I think of taking a thorough cure next spring, however, and hope to drive the plaguy ailment out.—As for my apartment, the evil is remedied ; we've moved into a wonderfully nice roomy suite in the Ostra-Allee, and are furnished as finely and completely as possible. Even if for this installation I have had to mortgage for some years the receipts from my operas, which of course are always on the increase, yet my salary will be enough to let me live in comfort until then ; and whatever I have bought is *for our lifetime*. Ah, what a gladdening thought that is ! You may easily imagine what my poor sorely-tried wife

I

thinks of herself now ; and with equal ease you can
conceive how happy I am to be able to offer Minna
this lasting recompense !—I only wish you two
could share our luck with us ; do make it possible !
In the meantime, just you come yourself for as
long as you like,—our luck stands open to you,—
enjoy it with us !—Everybody here is friends with
me, I believe I may say, and excepting those who
have their special cause to envy me, I really have
only to choose to whom to give the preference ; but
apart from Heine we've struck no closer intimacy
yet with anyone, for this one thought keeps
running in my head : All very well, but if you
only had your *Parisians* with you ! ! !

I heard from Hanfstängl, whom I was
delighted to meet again, that Kietz has changed
his mind and wants to stay in Paris, Hr
Neukomm had procured him orders for drawings,
and so on. So, for all his admirable qualities, the
man's past saving !—It rends my heart, to look
upon him from this distance ; whatever shall I say
to him ? *I know of nothing, can say nothing !*
His mother was here a little time ago ; I handed
her the money I owed Fr[äulein] Leplay—80 thaler
—and arranged with her to persuade the Leplay
to deposit it for Kietz, so that, when he returns to
his own country, he might find money all ready
for him to set up with. That has been done ; the
money lies waiting at Kietz' mother's,—will he
come ? *No !*— —Neither has Anders written to
me ; which is particularly annoying, inasmuch as I
do not know if he received the letter with a little
draft I sent him 6 weeks since :—that is to remain

entre nous, my dear Cecilie,—nevertheless Anders
might be given a hint just to write me, that I may
learn how I can help him further.— —

God ! if I think of the times when you knew
no greater joy yourself, good Cecilie, than to
procure help and support for me !   How whole and
pure shone forth the sterling valour of your nature !
Only believe that we never forget it and pray
Heaven the more fervently to fulfil all your wishes
for welfare and happiness.   As it is, it heartily
rejoices us that your good angel has granted you
so dear a nurse [cf. p. 120] for your approaching
days of trial,—it distresses Minna much, that she
couldn't act in that capacity herself *before*.—So
await in cheerful calm the hour that is to bless you
anew, and may this letter do its mite towards
cheering you and giving you courage and strength !
Think of nothing but the beauty of the boon
which Heaven has bestowed on you afresh, and
commit its dolour to the Providence that tempers
all things to us !   Have no fear for your health :
you are young, and will grow stronger and
stronger ; poor *Rosalie* suffered for you all, and
everything will surely go well with you since *she*
was not allowed a happy mother's joy.—So be
easy, dear child ; think of your Max, see how
bonny the boy is, and rest assured the Creator
intends that, besides that young rascal, you yet
shall bring a sweet wee girl into the world to fill
the measure of your joy !   But before all, remember that I'm to be godfather.—

I know I've not mentioned all sorts of things I
really ought to in this letter : don't set it down to

negligence,—I have no fancy for letters one can consult like a Konversations-Lexikon.[1] If I am full of one sentiment, it has to monopolise my letter ; room enough for the rest another time.— If Minna arrives at writing, well and good ; if not, don't take it ill of her : ask her to *do* what you please, she's at your call. She is as fond of you as ever you can be of her, and every line of this letter comes from her as well.—Farewell ; greet your dear ones many thousand times. Rejoice me soon with splendid news; *you are bound to be lucky!*

To our merry reunion, with boy and girl! That's got to be, so sanguinely and gladly hopes
Thy   RICHARD W.

41. TO THE SAME [2]

DRESDEN, 15. *February* 44.

DEAREST SISTER—I think it well that a brief time has elapsed between receipt of your letter and my answer thereto ; what should I not have had to write to you, if immediately after the account of your sufferings I had given vent to all the painful feelings which the sad delineation of your crippled health called up in us! You will not, cannot doubt the impression, and I have no need to protest that it was of the painfulest. The sole relief for such impressions is engrossment with the thought of help; and the impossibility of contributing to the alleviation of your sufferings, with

---

[1] Published by Brockhaus, the equivalent of our *Chambers' Encyclopedia.* —TR.

[2] Address : " Madame/Madame/CÉCILIE/AVENARIUS/pr. adr. Mr. EDOUARD AVÉNARIUS, libraire/rue Richelieu, 69/à Paris."

such a distance severing us, could only have attuned us to still greater sorrow, had we not acquired from yourself the prospect of that distance twixt us disappearing. To anyone who would not make the mischief worse by useless cries of sympathy, you see, there is nothing more welcome than the means of personally assisting in that mischief's removal ; so blessed be your doctors and advisers, dear Cecilie, who hit upon the notion of prescribing you a journey to ourselves as cure ! Good Lord, I have the highest expectations from obedience to that prescription ; so let us speak of nothing else now than your journey and your stay with us.—

To begin with : *money !*—Tut, a mere trifle ! In the first place I owe Eduard a tidy little sum for out-of-pockets, with which, when one has piled it up in solid thalers, one really can afford a start.—Good : as soon as you arrive in Dresden, Ostra-Allee No. 6, you'll find those same hard thalers all at your disposal. Then, when we've driven every fiacre in the Dresden environs to rack and ruin, had a thousand sprees, and you are quite on your pins again, we'll put our heads together as to which is better : to get the entire Königsberg family Avenarius to come here, or to travel there ourselves. I'm very much against the latter plan, as it's a beastly journey ; but if there's nothing else for it, why, you shall take your sea-bathing at Kranz. If there *is* anything else, though, we'll travel together to Hamburg, where I have business next summer, and thence enjoy sea-baths at Helgoland in the North Sea, which has a notoriously healthier briny than the

Baltic. Whatever money you require for journeys of that sort will be a simple matter ; if Eduard lent *me* money heretofore, now *he* can borrow money off me, for a change :—so that is *my* affair, and over *money* we won't waste another word. You shall enjoy yourself with us, however, and your health shall return without troubling. For my part I'm in love with Dresden, it's so very genial,—and then you should see how agreeably we're lodged ! I don't want to say too much,—but you shall be satisfied. What plans Minna's making !—I'm mum.

Now for something of moment. In any case you must come before the end of *April*, on account of our Opera. You will find the Devrient and Tichatschek both here then, and be able to get a hearing of both my operas ; whereas later, mid-May, leaves of absence are rife and there'll be no more hope of it.—How would it be if you brought Maxel with you ?—But Eduard ?—Well, I am sorry for *him*, and often prefigure the parting you'll go through in Paris, which will truly cost anguish and tears enough,—yet, who is to give little Richard [the new baby] his drink ? We'll all write to him quite diligently, and he'll be sure to delight in the good news he shall get every day of your improving health ; that shall be his comfort at home and amends for separation.—But he will have to submit, and so that's settled.— —-

A nice trick you played me with the christening of my godson ! Really, that was horribly sharp work ; and I wish you had let me know before-hand, that I might have made all manner of

arrangements.   In any case I should never have
allowed that poor devil Ernst Benedikt [Kietz] to
take my place so nakedly ; let's hope he sports
his beard still, to cover the extreme of nakedness,—
yet that's hardly sufficient at a christening.—O
Ernst Benedikt, you're a pretty chap, you !—I
hear he fancies I am owing him a mass of letters.
Letters ! as if letters were any good to him !—
Here's the right sort of letter, for him to write
me : " Sunday, the —th inst., I intend starting
from Paris ; I rely on your having a decent
lodging ready for me in Dresden ; moreover, that
you and your wife will promptly sit to me for
oil-paintings, and pay me so well for them that I
can live in decency during the long time it will
take me to regain familiarity with oils, so that
after completion of those portraits I may accept
with greater safety and good conscience the further
orders you'll procure me.   I give you my word
of honour that under these conditions I start on
Sunday the —th, provided you previously send
me a note of hand for so-and-so much that I
need."   If Kietz writes me a letter like that, he
may be sure of receiving the right answer from
me.   If he doesn't, he mustn't take it ill of me if
I consider him the best fellow in the world, but at
the same time a regular ———.   My brain reels
when I think of him !—
    And now for Marie.[1] She also has played me
a trick.   We had fancied she'd alight and stay
with *us* here ; instead of which, she comes and
pays a *call* one day, and it was as much as we

---

[1] Cäcilie's sister-in-law.

could do to make her stay to dinner. She's a dear good girl, though, and must have been a great comfort to you, my poor Cecilie, with so much sympathy, such cheerfulness and genuine amiability.—You may easily guess what we spoke about ! But she also gave me hopes for you, and relieved my mind by saying that, in spite of your great sufferings, you also had good days between, when you could even bear long drives well. To be sure, that isn't saying much, but—after your letter, which, as you remarked yourself, was written in a night of the acutest pain—every grain of comfort has importance to me. We hope the doctor who treated you here before will give your cure the right send-off.—Lord knows we should have liked to keep Marie with us a good long while !—

Ah, my dear Cecilie, only contrive to come to us right soon. I can't possibly tell you how it will relieve me, only to see you at last ; and even should you look all haggard, we'll set you up in no time : Minna is looking forward with all her soul to being able to coddle you properly.

— Farewell ! How much that wish contains ! Believe me, it is meant in all its full significance. A thousand loves from us ! Thy

RICHARD W.

42. To EDUARD AVENARIUS[1]

BEST EDUARD—Now for a couple of business lines to yourself. I'm publishing my operas, under the most advantageous conditions and

---

[1] In continuation of the preceding letter.

prospects; so my publisher, MESER of Dresden, advises me to secure my copyright for France and England against eventualities in the future, even if there isn't the smallest likelihood of them for the moment. But there's no other possibility of doing that for France, he says, save in the following manner :—Someone would have to be found in Paris to whom I could send a small number of copies of the vocal score before it had appeared in public here, and with whom I could arrange that on a certain date—to be the same as of our public intimation of appearance here—he shall announce the said score as published at his office under his ownership, no matter whether the text is German, if only we've headed it with a French title. Accordingly that someone would merely have to signify his copyright at the tribunal de commerce on the day appointed, and presumably the thing will be taken no further notice of for the present ; in a conceivable sequel, however, there would be someone at hand to declare himself owner, and from whom a transference of the copyright could be bought. But this interim ostensible owner must of course be a safe man and attached to my interest, one who wouldn't make use of the copyright himself some fine day without coming to terms with me. So please see if this will work, and whether you perhaps could take up this provisional copyright yourself ; my publisher is already attending to London in similar fashion. Anders might be the best to inform you of the special formalities for a *musical* publisher [to observe]. —I should need an answer soon.— —

The end of this month I have to go to Hamburg, to produce Rienzi there.—I was at Berlin in January, and conducted the Holländer, as perhaps you're aware.—God keep you and yours. Many greetings from us. Thy

RICHARD W.

[No. 43 in the German edition corresponds with letter 17 to Minna.—TR.]

44. To CÄCILIE AVENARIUS [addressed as 41]

DRESDEN, 28. *July* 44.

MY DEAR CECILIE—You do very right and shew true sisterly feeling, when you assume no bad reason for my remissness in writing, but quite correctly suppose I've been really too busy. People always think an hour like that is easy to squeeze out ; and yet if one reflects that a letter to friends at a distance always needs a certain rally, that this is mostly to be found in morning hours alone, and that those morning hours in my case form the only time remaining for my urgent work,—one will understand how it occurs that a man devotes one morning after another to his immediate business without fulfilling an agreeable duty, unless he has some equally immediate spur thereto.

Your last letter to myself arrived here exactly when I was away at Hamburg for the production of my Rienzi [mid-March]. It somewhat eased my mind anent your health and future, and consequently did its share toward rocking me into a certain calm in your regard ; and when on

top of that I learnt that my fondest wish, to see
you both in our propinquity ere long for ever,
was nearing its fulfilment, a feeling came over
me as if full rights must be reserved for word of
mouth. Even to-day, then, my chief reason for
writing you is just to express my great joy that
it so soon will be unneedful for us to have recourse
to pen and paper to exchange our thoughts.
Praise be to God and thanks! For the first time
I feel in good heart concerning you, for you are
re-entering the only sphere of life you can flourish
in ; I don't know how it is, but to me that Paris
life appears an exile. Good Eduard may attach
some painful thoughts to his abandonment of
Paris ; did I do otherwise ? I gave up an entire
career mapped out and striven for amid great
sufferings and sacrifices, a future of high renown
such as one believes can be won solely in Paris,
to pursue a goal which seemed to me of most
reduced proportions, but found withal my genuine
fortune—in the *home-land !* Had I had a success
in Paris such as here, of course I should have
reaped more *money* from it ; but that is all,—for
certain no more *happiness.* I have a safe and sure
appointment, not to reckon what I can earn
beyond.—So will it be with Eduard. In truth
one comes at last to count quiescence in one's
native land a piece of luck quite worth the rest.
Here you will find friends and connections
wherever you turn. Yourself—in particular—will
feel the contrast with your Paris life a boon,—
I'm judging by myself.—So, best welcome, dears ;
have trust, and lend no ear to the promptings of

petty ambition.—How should it hurt you, if
Brockhaus does give fêtes and junkets round the
corner?—you're certain to be happier than these
people with their fêtes.—

As soon as you have got a little straight in
Leipzig, you'll visit us at Dresden, won't you?
I vow you shall be pleased with how you find us;
for things are going well with us, praise God,
and as for my outer relations, I'm looking calmly
towards their constant advance. True, I have no
children, and probably shall never get one; but
God knows, when I picture the anxiety and dread
for Minna I should live in, with a hope of that
sort, such luck does not appear at all desirable!—
And then, your last experiences, poor Cäcilie,—
are they quite adapted to display the unruffled
happiness of having children? My poor little
godson! What offence did he commit, dear
Heaven, that life's sufferings should so beset him
already?—Our mother was here in Dresden, on
her way from Teplitz, the very day your letter
came; she had already told us of little Richard's
accident, which wrung from us deep sighs,—dear
God, what cares you have! But you reassure
us now to this extent, that you merely say you
feared awhile the infant would remain blind of
one eye; which leads us to conclude, on the
other hand, you have hope that the worst of the
mischief will dissipate. Anyhow, we shall soon
be able to convince ourselves; within a month,
God willing! How happy I shall be, too, to
convince myself that your own health in particular,
whose bad condition made us very sad by no

means long ago, is firmly re-established ! *Fritz*
gave Mother very glowing accounts of your
appearance, and so relieved us greatly. Once you
all are here, at the big family congress in Saxony,
you'll flourish more than ever.

With myself it still is work-time, and very
tiresome at that just now. For the last 5 months
I've had to lay aside my new opera, the composition whereof I had only just begun, I'm so very
busy with the unfortunately too procrastinated
publication of my two older operas. It has been
a chaos of work, and, in spite of all diligence,
the vocal score of *Rienzi*—which by all means is
terribly bulky, and as big as 3 ordinary operas—
will only appear by the middle of August, and the
Holländer a few weeks later. I therefore propose
taking a holiday from the latter half of August
on, to go into the country yet, perhaps to Pillnitz,
where I mean to finish my new opera.—You
might be of great help to me then with it ; do
visit us there, that charming spot is bound to do
yourself a world of good.—

Please tell Eduard I've abandoned the notion
of securing the copyright of my operas for France,
since the thing's too great a bother ; and then,
if Eduard's leaving Paris, to whom could I commit
the trust ? For London I have a publisher of
the first standing, Beale, who will make it his
particular concern to get my operas mounted at
an English theatre there.—

Enough of that : in a month you'll be here ;
then tongues will be untied. Till then I've
nothing more to wish you, beyond—at any rate

a comprehensive wish—a *right prosperous* journey! It will much fatigue you in the singular, but conduct to a truly pleasant goal. It will be the last journey of its kind for both of you ; keep safe and sound till then. We are expecting you with open arms and gladsome hearts ; may our Wiedersehen be as joyful as our last parting in Paris was sorrowful!—Remember me to my old friends, whom I heartily pity your being unable to bring with you. Salute and kiss thy Eduard and dear youngsters with all the fervour of our hearts, and come all of you right happily to Your

RICHARD W.

Na, don't you think Minna's rejoicing?— The Albert's are very well ; he doesn't know I'm writing you. Johanna is getting on capitally ; the day before yesterday she sang the Irene in my Rienzi, and beat all her predecessors in this part. Lord, how they must be feeling now!

45. TO THE SAME[1]

MY DEAR CECILIE — Hearty welcome to Germany! With husband and children, be hailed from my and Minna's deepest soul! It was a feeling grown quite unfamiliar to us and rewakened to life, that warmed us on receiving news from both of you again at such close quarters. How it afflicts me, not to be able to address our welcome to you by word of mouth! To keep writing still,

---

[1] Address : "Madame/CECILIE AVENARIUS/bei Herrn Friedrich Brockhaus/in/Leipzig./frei."

is quite unbearable ; and yet it's clean impossible
to get away from here at present for so much as a
day, since the approaching arrival of Weber's ashes,
and after that a new opera of Marschner's [*Adolf
von Nassau*] which I want to bring out by New
Year, prevent my thinking of even the briefest
removal from Dresden. I'm obliged to begin by
unloading my vexation thereat, ere I can regain
breath to express our great joy and relief at the
final return of you both to the beloved homeland.

   As a fact, we were a little uneasy about yourself
and the postponement of your journey to this very
late season ; so much the better to hear that everything has gone off well. Your head is buzzing,
you don't know where you are, seem as if in a
dream, and all is flickering before your eyes ?
Quite so : we know all about that from experience ;
it's like being laid under a spell, a transportation
of that sort from Paris to Leipzig or Dresden.
Believe me, though, one becomes another person
in time, and—precious soon tumbles in love with
one's country again. Your having found neither
lodgings nor anything awaiting you, honestly sets
me in amazement ! The Deuce ! Whatever can
our kindred have been thinking of ? Or was it
your own desire to see to everything yourselves ?
Be that as it may, if you're only in good health, a
rest will taste the better for it afterwards. But
just you let that happen very soon, that we may
taste some of it also : I mean, that you may soon
come and see us yourself. That I shall visit you
both as soon as ever I can get away, is self-
understood ; but we shan't be truly happy till you

come to us in *our* home, where I cannot but say we're living very pleasantly. Moreover, our number has become a large one through Albert and his family, and our company couldn't be more united and congenial. In short, you shall enjoy yourself at our place.

And now for the immediate : what about that rendezvous at Cläre's? Minna is going to Chemnitz, for the christening, after the Christmas holidays ; will you be going there too? In that case it would be simplest if you came back with Minna to Dresden and brought at least big Maxel with you straight away. You shall remain with us as long as ever you like, and then I—who shall be able to take a run from here by then, I trust—will personally conduct you home to Leipzig, where I may hope to make my young godson's acquaintance at last too. The plan works out quite nicely of itself, you see : Eduard will meantime get your household into order, whilst my godson no doubt can be taken good care of at one of our relatives', for instance at Ottilie's, as perhaps his being too young might somewhat gêne you.—My ideas, you see, are reckoned for a real protracted Wiedersehen ; don't bring my hopes and plans to nought.

On the sure assumption that in one way or the other we shall meet and have a good long talk soon, I pass by all enquiries and communications for the present, and keep returning to this plea instead : " Do make it possible to come and pay ourselves a visit soon ! "

Once more : be *vastly* welcome,—that's what

we Dresden kin all positively halloo to the pair of
you ! Come and convince yourselves *how* we all
mean it soon. I greet and kiss you both a
thousand times on behalf of all the Wagners in
the Ostra-Allee. Thy

RICHARD W.

DRESDEN, 12. *Dec.* 44.

46. TO THE SAME[1]

DRESDEN, 9. *January* 45.

DEAREST CECILIE—Minna meant to write you
this time, but I see she won't arrive at that to-day,
and in order that you may get at least a quick
answer to your dear letter received the day before
yesterday I am taking Minna's place again ; for
the ceremony with which she always sets about the
writing of two lines is something past belief. So
excuse her, and don't do her the injustice of
arguing to her sentiments from her dread of pen
and ink ; indeed she is unchangeably your truest,
most devoted friend.—And now to business :—

You might have assumed with greater certainty,
dear child, that we should do all we could to get
and chain you to us for as long as possible. Just
come and welcome with *both* your youngsters, and
in God's name bring the *bonne* as well—if you
think that needful when I tell you that Natalie is
with us at present, on her first visit in fact, and
might easily supply the place of bonne to your
little ones. If you'd rather trust the bonne's

---

[1] Address : " Ihro / Wohlgeboren / Madame / CECILIE AVENARIUS / Insel-
Strasse No. 5 / LEIPZIG / frei."

K

services though, just bring her with you too ; only first hear the accommodation our flat has to offer, which I submit to your judgment herewith. In our abode we have : No. 1, a study for me ; No. 2, a so-called salon, which, with my everlasting callers, is bound to stay free ; No. 3, Minna's parlour, which forms living-, dining-room, etc., in one ; No. 4, a bedroom for the pair of us, and No. 5, a ditto for visitors, which at the same time is a sort of wardrobe. This No. 5 will be placed at your disposal with a good bed for yourself, a bed for Max, and a little sofa on which a very comfortable crib can be made up for Richard. I'm afraid the bonne, if you still intend bringing her, would have to sleep in an attic, though it's quite a respectable one ; she shall find her bed all ready there.—

That's the look-out : if you approve, just give us 2 days' notice of your coming, and whether with or without bonne. But in any case be certain that we cannot control our impatience, and you simply will give us the greater delight the sooner you arrive. That I shall thereby be able to make closer acquaintance at once with my godson, than I could have on a flying trip to Leipzig, only heightens my rejoicing in our Wiedersehen.

What else should I write you at present, with such an expectation? Merely the repetition of our most instant prayer : Come, come as quickly as humanly possible ! ! That's what all of us cry to you from the bottom-most depths of our hearts. So to a *very* swift reunion ! Thy

RICHARD W.

Minna begs you, for your own convenience, to bring the children's bedding with you.

47. To Eduard Avenarius [1]

DRESDEN, 16. *May* 1845.

DEAREST EDUARD—Devil take it! For the last hour I've been hunting for the letter from Paris in which you cast up the account, at my request, of what I owe you,—and cannot find it. Nor have I kept in my head the exact total; so I must beg you to name it once more, as for the life of me I can't remember how much over 100 thaler it was. I will send you the money at once then, and spare no apology for the long delay.

As I shall thus be writing you again a few days hence, now merely the needful in brief.—Moreover, I shall shortly be paying both of you a visit in person.

Adieu for the meantime. Best love to *Cile*, the children, and all the rest! Thy RICHARD W.

DRESDEN, 16. *May* 45.

48. To Albert Wagner [2]

MARIENBAD, 4. *August* 1845.

DEAREST BROTHER—Best thanks for your letter and communications, which I won't answer any further here, partly because I shall be able to have another chat with you so soon, partly because I'm only allowed [by the doctor] to spend quite a

---

[1] Address: "Herrn/EDUARD AVENARIUS/Brockhaus & Avenarius/in/Leipzig." Post-mark: "Dresden, 16 May 45."
[2] Address: "Herrn/ALBERT WAGNER/Ostra-Alice 23, DRESDEN/frei."

short time upon writing. Saturday the 9th we leave here, to travel back by easy stages ; we think of making little stops at Eger, Carlsbad, Teplitz—Aussig, and reaching home by steamer Friday afternoon the 15th at latest. Unfortunately I can't make out for certain here yet, whether the steamer from Prague really comes on a Friday ; if not, I shall return as early as *Thursday* the 14th. So I have to bore you with a big request, namely that you will give our Amalia the needful instructions to set our domicile in order. The joiner will, or rather, must have finished by then :—there is no hurry about my wife's work-table, which needn't be put right just yet, whilst the piano no doubt only requires a little rubbing up, by no means French-polishing ; on the other hand, please draw the men's attention to the clock-consol, which is all cracked. In any case we may reasonably ask the lazy joiner to have completed his job by the beginning of next week, when the maid must make it her duty to have all the rooms ready for our return by Thursday the 14th ; if we don't reach home on Thursday, it will be Friday, as I said before. You might, perhaps, tell Röckel I shall be able to take over Church duty on Saturday the 15th [really 16th] in any event.—

So in 4 days' time we shall have finished our cure, upon which we shall have spent five whole weeks ! The indications point to a good result with me and Minna, who, as usual, have kept as aloof as possible from acquaintances one's pestered with wherever one goes, and never strayed far from our forests and hills. My brain refused to

take a rest, however, and so I finished yesterday
the writing down of a very complete and detailed
plan for *Lohengrin* which gives me great delight,
nay, I frankly confess it, fills me with complacent
pride. You know the fear that overtook me
so often of finding no other subject to equal
Tannhäuser in warmth and individuality,—but the
more I made myself familiar with my new matter,
the more I penetrated its idea, the richer, more
abounding did its pith reveal itself, and swell to so
ample a flower that I feel lucky indeed to possess
it. My invention and modelling have the lion's
share in this creation : the old German poem
which has handed this high-poetic legend down to
us is the most threadbare and mawkish of all its
class, and I consider myself very fortunate to have
yielded to the fascination of rescuing this almost
unrecognisable legend from the rubble of its poor,
prosaic treatment by the ancient poet, and restored
it through my own invention and remoulding to
its native worth.—Apart from that, moreover,
what a successful opera-book it makes ! Effective,
attractive, imposing and affecting in its every part!
—Johanna's rôle in it [Elsa]—which is very considerable and strictly the principal—is bound to
be the most ravishing and harrowing thing in all
the world.—Enough : when the heart is full, etc.

Give Heine 75 regards from me, and my very
best thanks for his letter ; tell him I shall write
Liszt direct from here to Bonn, and am very much
in accord with the Weber plan.[1]—God only grant

---

[1] See letter 2 to Liszt, of the following day, *re* " a worthy monument to
be erected in Dresden."—TR.

that the wish, or rather, the irresistible impulse to begin my new opera may not seize me so soon as this winter, that I may devote a thoroughly clear head to the affairs of our Royal Saxon Opera! I have many sweeping reforms in mind.

But I didn't mean, and don't dare, to cover more than this fresh page ; so for the finish ! You are all doing very right to make the Mama as cosy as possible, and we shall be only too glad if our means can contribute towards it. Best love to her, if she is with you still!—O Hanns, your time is drawing near :[1] it would be the *worst* result of the long pause in your appearance—if you had learnt nothing mean-time ! Bear that in mind, and be willing and diligent,—perhaps I'll bring you something too.—

Na, best love to you all from me and Minna, and above all rest assured we're looking forward *heartily* to seeing you again ! Be in your best spirits, and don't spoil the good temper I am hoping to bring with me. Adieu ! Fare well until then—and 50 to 60 years after ! All of yours,

RICHARD W.

[No. 49 in the German corresponds with letter 19 to Minna.—TR.]

50. To EDUARD AVENARIUS [2]

MY DEAR EDUARD—Kind love, and may you have plenty of Christmas-boxes !—Here come I

---

[1] Johanna Wagner [and her 'creation' of the rôle of Elisabeth].
[2] Address : " Herrn / Eduard Avenarius / Inselstrasse No. 7 / LEIPZIG. / frei."

with a favour to ask for my friend HEINE, of whom Heinrich [Brockhaus] perhaps has spoken to you already in a certain regard. Heine, who has translated many, many volumes from the French, is wanting work, and seeks it through myself of Brockhaus und Avenarius. Heinrich told me it often happened that you were in need of a good translator,—as only the other day with some Memoirs, I don't remember whose ; he promised me to think of Heine when similar cases arose. Well, a case just occurs to Heine himself in which you might think of him : he fancies that the book of Vaulabelle advertised per enclosed [1]—with which you're sure to be acquainted, as its third volume's appearance has made a great sensation in France already—ought to form a good catch in Germany as well, between the works of Thiers and Louis Blanc. Should your firm be of the same opinion, Heine would like you to entrust him with the translation as quickly as possible.

I accordingly pass on his offer and request, personally adding for my own part the heartiest petition to yourself to try and think of *Heine* anyhow in future cases ; he is a most deserving friend of mine, unceasing in his efforts to oblige and serve me whenever and howsoever he possibly can. Moreover, it is very essential for him to earn something besides his salary off and on. So, if my pleading has any power, I am convinced you will remember Heine for my sake as far as possible, perhaps even in the case adduced. I meant to

[1] Achille de Vaulabelle : "Cent jours—1814/1815. Chute de l'Empire, histoire des deux Restaurations etc." (Perrotin, 41 rue Fontaine-Molière).

have spoken to you about it at Leipzig,—but you know how things slide in that hubbub !—

Last Friday [19th] we had a very fine performance of Tannhäuser again [the seventh] ; after each of the last two acts the singers were called, and after them *myself*.—

I expect we shall see one another a little longer the end of February, if I come to Leipzig for the production of my " flieg. Holländer " [not given there till seventeen years later].—Fare splendidly well until then, and also thereafter ! Remembrances—you know to whom, wife and children above all, from me and Minna. Adieu. Thy

RICHARD WAGNER.

DRESDEN, 23. *Dec.* 1845.

(Close upon Christmas, worse luck ! !)

51. TO THE SAME[1]

DEAREST EDUARD—A question and request. Albert is bothering me from Paris to send a few copies of my operas, to put them on sale at Franck's perhaps ; not so much to make a profit, as to give my friends and Paris musicians in general the opportunity of becoming acquainted with my things. Therefore I had already determined to send off a parcel to you through Meser, taking advantage of your former kind consent to forward things like that to Paris. But Meser

---

[1] Address : " Herrn / Eduard Avenarius / Brockhaus & Avenarius / in / LEIPZIG./frei."—Dresden post-mark, " 27. May 46 " ; Leipzig post-mark " Town-post, 28. May." Note by the recipient : " Answ. 28. v."

now says he heard at Leipzig from the Berlin Schlesinger that printed music has to pay a duty of over 100 per cent at the French frontier; so I would beg yourself, as one familiar with all these ins and outs, I'm sure, to let me know if that's really the case, or if your people have any means of defeating this wicked French law. Should you corroborate the necessity of submitting to this enormous tax, naturally we shall take a little time to reflect, though I should be loth to have my music remain unknown to the Parisians on this account.

Cannot you visit us at Gross-Graupe? It's glorious here in the country! Is Cecilie still going to the seaside? Goodbye; many kind remembrances from Minna. Thy

RICHARD WAGNER.

Letters for me should simply be addressed to "Dresden."

21 [?] *May* 1846.

52. TO HIS MOTHER [1]

MY DEAR MOTHER—It is so long since I congratulated you upon your birthday, that it does me real good to be able to observe the proper day at last —so often overlooked by me, alas, in the hurry of business—to tell you how profoundly it rejoices me to know you're near us yet in soul and body, be able still to squeeze your hand from time to time, and

[1] Address: "An/Madame/J. GEYER/Salomons-Strasse No. 6/LEIPZIG./ frei."

recall together with and through yourself my youth
you once cherished and shielded. Only in the realisation that you abide with us yet, can your children
still distinctly feel themselves one family. Whom
life has blown hither and thither, to knit fresh
bonds of kindred here and there,—when they think
of you, their dear old Mother who has formed no
other ties upon this earth than those which knit
her to her children, they all are one again, thy
bairns!—God grant this boon may be vouchsafed
us long, long yet ; and may God preserve you
long in full possession of your faculties, that to
your life's end you may reap the only joy you can
upon this earth,—the joy of a sympathetic onlooker
at your children's prospering !

When I feel so driven or withheld, continually
struggling, seldom gaining full success, often the
prey of dejection at my failures,—nearly always
quivering from rough contact with the outer
world, which alas so seldom, hardly ever, answers
to one's inner wish,—then nothing save a draught
of *Nature* can revive me. Often as I have cast
myself with tears and bitter cries into her arms,
she always has consoled and raised me up by shewing how imaginary are all the sorrows that torment
us. If we aim too high, then Nature lovingly
reminds us we are really only bits of her, her
outgrowths like these trees, these plants, that
unfurl from the bud, shoot up and sun themselves,
drink in the strengthening air, and neither wither
nor decay till they have shed the seed to put forth
buds and plants anew, and so the once-created
lives its ceaseless links of renovated youth. When

I feel my single self so integral a part of Nature, how utterly all idle egoism melts; and if I then would fain extend my hand to all good men, how much the rather must I long for that dear Mother from whose womb I sprang, and who is withering while I—bloom! How it makes one smile at those curious errors and perversities of our human Society, racking its brains for new-fangled devices, whereby these lovely ties of Nature so often get entangled, rent and torn!

Dear Motherkin, whatever strange occurrences have stepped between us, how swiftly all that is effaced! Just as when I steal from out the city's fumes into a leafy dale, stretch my full length on the turf, feast my eyes on the tapering tree-trunks, and list to some sweet woodbird's song until a tear rolls down my cheek unchecked for very happiness, —so do I feel when out through all the jungle of cross-purposes I reach my hand toward thee and cry : May God preserve thee, dear old Mother,— and when at last He takes thee from me, may he do it right gently and softly! Of Death 'twill be no question : *we* shall continue thy life for thee, and an ampler, manyer-sided life than thine could e'er have been. Thank God, then, who so richly blessed thy body!—

Minna, to whose memory I owe my recollection of your birthday this time, sends greetings and congratulations with all her heart. Farewell, good little Mother mine! Thy son

RICHARD.

DRESDEN, 19. *Sept.* 1846.

53. To Cäcilie Avenarius[1]

Dearest Cecilie—That's sensible of you, to mean to come to us for once ; had you done that long ago, many a foolish doubt would have never arisen in you, or been easily demolished. I don't write letters willingly, Minna hardly at all ; a visit to Leipzig has never yet been able to afford us great attraction : and so we haven't seen each other for a long time,—which is the whole mischief.

Whoever may have thought me cold and without interest in him, would understand me if he knew how frightfully I've been besieged by constant cares about myself,—disappointment, ill-humour, form terrible drags. If you had only paid us, as said, one other and longer visit, we should have told one another our troubles, and after that —remained the same old friends ; and that's what's still to be.—

So you are coming, and will alight at our place, —that is right, and a matter of course.

I am well or ill—as you please ! No doubt I shan't get truly well again before I get true peace of mind. At present I'm a trifle better,—as you will see for yourself. Minna is looking forward joyfully to your arrival. Love to Eduard and children. Farewell and come *soon !* Thy brother

RICHARD.

Dresden, 14. *Dec.* 47.

[To make the family history a little more complete, I interpolate a letter from ALBERT Wagner to his daughter

---

[1] Address : "An/Frau/Cecilie Avenarius/Inselstrasse No. 14/Leipzig./ bez."

Franziska, subsequently married to the subject of Sieg-
mund von Hausegger's " *Alexander Ritter* " (Marquardt
& Co., Berlin), from which monograph I derive it.—TR.]

DRESDEN, the 18*th January* 1848.

MY SWEET FRÄNZELE—Everybody, even the maid,
has gone to the theatre to hear the "Weisse Frau " [*Dame
blanche*], which Johanna is singing in ; so I am left quite
alone in the house, since I contracted a bad cold at Leipzig
that has presented me with a severe cough and catarrh,
joined with a little fever to-day. What better can I do,
then, my dear child, than have a talk with you ? Everything is so nice and quiet round me, and I can indulge
in my thoughts undisturbed.

First, then, for that chief sad occurrence, the death of
our dear Grandmother. I had no time to write to you
from Leipzig, but was truly sorry that you hadn't been
to see her again ; on the very day you passed through
Leipzig [en route for an acting engagement ?] she took to her
death-bed. She had spent the Sunday with her daughters,
and seemed in fairly good health. Monday she suffered
from a little indigestion, took her food very late, and
caught a chill through standing at the open window
either during or after it ; in short, she kept her bed on
Tuesday, but without being actually ill. On Wednesday
she was not so well, on Thursday better ; at least, Julius
and the maid hadn't the smallest alarm, though my sisters
declare that the peculiar hovering of her eyes made themselves and the doctor rather anxious. Julius, however,
being better acquainted with Mother's infirmities, wasn't
at all alarmed, and therefore didn't write to us till Saturday
the 8th, when her illness seemed growing more serious.
Then he wrote to myself. Sunday the 9th I received
his registered letter while still abed, and though I wasn't
expecting so sudden an end, I determined to set out for
Leipzig at once, to get another glimpse of my old mother
who so long had been standing on the brink of the grave.
I started at half past 12. Arrived at Leipzig, I pulled

up at mother's, to enquire at least how she was doing.   I
rang, but the bell made no sound, and nobody came.
Then I asked the porter's wife, who told me *all was over*
and Hanne had gone out for a moment.—I drove straight
on to Ottilie's, where I found Julius and the whole family
assembled in grief.   There I heard the account of her
last hours, as above and what follows :—

It was precisely on that Saturday her condition grew
worse, and although there was no positive pain, the worst
was already to fear for her.   Nevertheless she was cheerful
and composed, and towards evening, surrounded by her
daughters, whom she frequently called her "good angels
of girls," she had a regular vision, and after a silent prayer
she said, " O how bright and beauteous everything around
me is !   What glorious apparitions," and so on,—for, as
she told them upon recovering her senses, none but the
purest, loveliest figures had appeared to her : "Don't
think my departure is grieving me," she said, "I am
fully prepared.   Ah, what a happy time I have had, and
how happy I am now, surrounded by my good children !
What have I done to deserve it ? "—Enough : she made
a perfectly beautiful speech to her children.—That was
at 8 in the evening.   Then she grew somewhat more
restless, and was a little delirious, but only for moments :
" Hanne, please dress me ; don't you see, Büsner (the
porter at Fritz's, who hanged himself) is waiting for
me ? "—Then lucid again.

True, once or twice in the night she said : "Julius, I
am in great pain," or " I'm very agitated,"—but always
calmed down soon after.   Toward 4 in the morning she
began to drop asleep, and Julius, quite exulting that
sleep would restore her—as she had neither had sleep nor
appetite for several nights—lay down on his bed in his
clothes about 5, giving orders to wake him at once
[should need be].   Mother slept on quite beautifully and
peacefully, however, right into the day ; so Julius sat
down to his writing-table at half past 8, to attend to
business matters.   Ottilie had passed the night there.

Luise also came about 8, as did the Avenariuses, and Julius began to fume at the risk of their disturbing Mother. Then in comes the maid about half past 9, and says to the women-folk: "O dear! she was sleeping so soundly; and now she's just drawn one deep breath, and I can hear nothing more."—Avenarius went in, came out again to Julius, and told him she was gone.—

So ended my good Mother's life, and all say: Whomever God loves, may He give them such an easy, beautiful, and elevating death as hers! She had slumbered peaceably across, and as if this death were also meant not to have the least thing repellent about it, even an hour before her burial—not until when did we let them screw the coffin down—there wasn't the faintest odour from her body, and one might tranquilly have sat for hours beside it. Moreover, death had beautified her; the skin had blanched, the wrinkles smoothed, and the noble brow shewed forth in all its beauty; merely the mouth had fallen in for lack of teeth.—Julius—who loses not only a mother, but his life-companion in a sense—was quite beside himself, though he controlled his emotion as well as he could. That Sunday I went home with him, and we slept in the green bedroom—the first from the parlour door. Mother lay in the blue middle one, and so I was wall to wall with her the whole night through; fondly thinking of her, I fell asleep—a little upset and uneasy, but without the smallest dread. Next morning, while I appeared to be sleeping, I heard poor Julius sob aloud, and then I saw how deeply it affected him. He was so used to living with Mother, and though they had their little tiffs, he knew he should find her whenever he came in, he had a parent's roof above his head; now the poor fellow is left all alone,—and so many recollections throng on him, recalling Mother's love and harrowing his heart. He repeatedly told me that of late she had asked more and more anxiously: "Hasn't my son returned yet?—When ever will he come home?" etc.; whilst a few days before her illness she followed him to the parlour door as he was going out, and suddenly fell weeping on his neck : " Eh, Motherkin, what's up with you ? " said Julius. " Ah, dear Julius, every time you go out I feel as if I never should see you again."—All sorts of expressions like that, plainly shewing she had harboured a presentiment of her death for some time, recur to his memory now, and fill him with affectionate sorrow.

Myself I've paid her brimming toll of tears of love, for she was a good mother who lived for nothing save her children, for no other pleasures in the world ; and even during these last six to eight years, when she became more senile, she really lived in mental commune with her children and her grandchildren as she sat alone with her thoughts in her room. In earlier days she was a bright and active woman, by no means un-gifted ; her sense of beauty in Art and Nature, and her correct judgment, surprised me oft. In addition to which, she was of a truly high religiousness, simple, and without any hypocrisy or cant. She didn't go to church, but the sublimities of Nature, the grandeur in the highest intellectual works of Man, had a profoundly religious effect on her that amply compensated her for church-observances, and gave her a knowledge of God. Thus her death was a cheerful supreme surrender of her soul to God, even though no priest attended her.—Peace to her ashes ! her memory stays fresh and fair in all our hearts, and—perhaps we shall meet hereafter. God grant myself and all of us as beautiful a death !

For that matter, if she could have looked down and seen the tokens of esteem and love which people paid her, she would certainly have been glad. Her coffin bore ten wreaths and three fine palms, sent by various people, and no one omitted to follow her ; even Schletter said, " If you hadn't invited me, I should have begged to be allowed to follow her ; for I consider myself a little bit one of the family."

After my sending notice to reach Dresden on Tuesday of the day of interment, Richard arrived in

Leipzig Tuesday evening ; since my letter, which had told him Mother looked so beautiful in death, induced him to see her once more. He was greatly affected, and quite the old Richard again, who was so fond of his mother, you know, in days of yore.—I saw Mother first on the Monday morning, while she was still lying, or half sitting, in bed exactly as alive, and it was quite my good old little Mother. For the coffin afterwards they dressed her in her black gown, white stomacher and favourite little brooch, a white cap with white satin ribbon, and placed a bunch of flowers in her hand. Melei had sent another bouquet with a tiny poem, apparently composed for the occasion ; we laid that on her lap. On Wednesday the 12th the hearse started at half past 10 in the morning—followed by five carriages and sixteen persons.—Marbach had kindly given us up the grave reserved for him by side of Rosalie's,—he can go on top of Rosalie ; and I was very glad of it, for Mother, Rosalie and old Aunt Wagner now lie all close together. I kept my eyes on the coffin until it was covered, and salt tears of love and mourning flowed into her grave.—I trudged there again the next day through deep snow, and it was marvellously beautiful to see the pretty flowers and sprays and ribbons glistening amid its fresh thick flakes. Then I bade farewell to her ; but many a time, as often as I go [to Leipzig], shall I stand again by the united graves of those beloved ! — —

. . . . . .

Hold me dear and write me prettily. With love and care, Thy aff. Father   A. WAGNER.

54. TO EDUARD AVENARIUS [1]

DEAR EDUARD—I enclose an essay of mine, which probably will not be wholly unwelcome to

---

[1] Address : " Herrn / EDUARD AVENARIUS / Buchhändler / in / Leipzig. / Paid."

you [*Vaterlandsverein* address] ; at least, its idea is that of making for a combination of parties such as you appear to me to have likewise had in view with your recent proposal of a "monarchical republic." If you can make any use of my essay, please do. Best love to Cecilie, and hold me dear, Thy

RICHARD WAGNER.

DRESDEN, 15. *June* 1848.

55. TO EDUARD AND CÄCILIE AVENARIUS [1]

DEAR EDUARD, DEAR CECILIE—Minna, Kläre and I have only just seen in the newspaper the loss befallen you. You may readily conceive what a shock it gave us. Will it lighten your grief in any degree, to know that we sincerely share it with you? At any rate be certain that we do.

But might we not contribute something besides to your fortifying? Would Cecilie, for instance, let herself be moved to come to us *at once* with *Max* and *Richard*, and stay awhile with us in Dresden? A change of air and scene is always beneficial in a case like that,—perhaps through its very distraction. We should be heartily pleased if Cecilie vouchsafed our prayer and came to us right quickly. As Klärchen is here as well now, she'd find herself en famille.—

We shall look for Cecilie's arrival.

Sincere remembrances, and declaration of our saddest and most sorrowing sympathy. Thy

RICHARD WAGNER.

DRESDEN, 4. *Sept.* 48.

---

[1] Address : " Herrn / Eduard   Avenarius / Buchhändler / Marienstr. / Leipzig / Immediate."

56. To Cäcilie Avenarius

DEAR CECILIE—I have taken over the job of writing to you this time : Minna had more faith in my style, than her own, to offer you our joint felicitations on your birthday [26th] with all becomingness ; but as I write, she is baking a *baba* posterity shall sing the praise of, albeit it's meant for no one save yourself. My better half, who is trying to become of more use to the world every day, has devoted herself with uncommon success to the pastrycook's craft—as you will have gathered from the Christmas cakes you never got ; whilst I am applying myself body and soul to the improvement of my hand by Latin characters—as you likewise will see. Thus we hope to make our way in the world with aplomb, come what may ; meanwhile we're combining the aforesaid noblest of our faculties for the preparation of an agreeable birthday greeting to you from afar. May we thus be near you bodily (with the *baba*) and spiritually (with my characters) on the day which saw you come into the world some years ago ! If the world has vexed you now and then since that day's repetition, even to-day I can wish you no better preventive of further vexation than to become thoroughly reconciled with this world by getting quite well. All is won, when one wins one's life itself and holds it stoutly : no pleasure, no enjoyment can be yours except through life ; and to live happily, means to be sound of limb,—for without a healthy body there's no healthy mind ;

and the activity which delights us since it's that we gladly exercise, is the only joy in life, not possessions which merely flatter, never bless us. The admirable man you have for husband will know how to make his abilities tell under any circumstances ; even should he be annoyed by obstacles upon his path at times, he'll conquer them. And yourself, you know quite plainly what you have to do ; you cannot hesitate an instant as to what you wish and want : only one thing can impede you in it,— bodily ill-health. So, if we wish you settled health to-day, we're mainly wishing you the power and forethought to take the utmost care to strengthen your enfeebled body ; come and see us this Spring, and we'll give you an object-lesson how to set about it. In the meantime gain strength from the *baba*, of which I've the highest opinion without having made its acquaintance ; and cheer yourself up with my precepts, as to which I at least can assure you that the conviction of their soundness is fortifying me more and more every day to bid defiance to all reverses with a cheerful mind : for it's the worst of all tactics, to give way to the enemy ; and one does that when one doesn't oppose to him an inner force which nothing in this world can conquer.

At Weimar my Tannhäuser has just [Feb. 16] had a success unexampled there, as verified to me by all accounts. The Hereditary Grand Duke has almost implored me to visit him in May ; and though I don't make much bones of the whole Grand-ducal kettle of fish, his invitation quite squares with a wish of my own to make a little tour in

Thuringia and the Harz about that time. Should this occasion conduct me through Leipzig, perhaps I shall bring Minna with me, and then you could return with her direct to Dresden : i.e. if the world hasn't tumbled in by then ; for our noble princes one and all seem doing all they can to make it tumble.

Now goodbye for to-day! Be healthy—and then you'll be gay. Give your offspring my very best compliments ; put your husband in light heart, and tell him he's to hold me dear.

Vivat hoch! we cry—Peps barks and Papo whistles to it. Thy   RICHARD.

DRESDEN, 25. *Feb.* 49.

[The Dresden " May days " intervene, with Wagner's flight from Germany to commence an exile destined to be prolonged over a decad.—Tr.]

57. To EDUARD AVENARIUS [1]

DEAREST EDUARD—It's nearly a month since I took leave of my wife, and not the smallest news of her has reached me yet. I wrote her a letter from Zurich, addressed to Mad. Portius in Dresden,—I wrote her two letters from Paris, care of yourself in Leipzig,[2]—and not a word bears witness to me that Minna's still alive!—My anxiety is boundless : why don't I receive a sign of my wife's existence from anywhere?—No longer can I contain myself in bare expectancy, and

---

[1] Address : " Herrn / EDUARD AVENARIUS / Buchhändler / Marienstrasse No. 2 / Leipzig. / ALLEMAGNE."
[2] These letters are not preserved.

though I buoy myself with the hope of perhaps getting a letter again from her in a day or two, I am compelled to put an end to my terribly-haunted impatience through an urgent enquiry of you : What is the matter with my wife ? what do you know of her ? why on earth doesn't she write to me ?

I have fled from Paris and the repulsiveness of a stay there quite useless to me for the present ; the cholera was raging when I left. Before my departure I wrote to Minna, and told her my resolve to settle down with her in Zurich for the time being ; let us hope she'll yield to my entreaty and decide on rejoining me there. Every arrangement is made, upon my side ; a fixed annuity, which Liszt is now extracting me from various quarters, will in any case ensure us peaceful living at a pretty spot. From there I shall attend to my Paris affairs, the profits to be expected from which in a favourable event I shall then devote without deduction to clearing off the debts I left behind in Dresden.

But my present agony is great ; I curse every day that slips by without news of my wife.—O, do write me this instant and solve the enigma.

A thousand thanks to you all for your sympathy. Kindest love to Cecilie, and remembrances to all my people, with best thanks for their interest. Farewell, dearest friend, hold me dear. Thy   RICHARD WAGNER.

REUIL
Laferté sous Jouarre
département Seine-et-Marne   (18. *June* 1849.)
(MR. BELLONI).

58. To sister Clara Wolfram [1]

ZURICH, 1. *December* 1849.

DEAR KLÄRE—Don't be vexed at your lateness in getting a letter from us. Minna wanted to be the first to write, and I also thought it would be more agreeable to you to learn from *her* how we are faring ; but there, it always was an effort to her, and I'm glad to relieve her, especially when she begins urging me herself.

In the first place I want to thank you both most heartily again for your concern about me, and for the help you vouchsafed me at that difficult time [his flight last May]. Above all I am indebted in my deepest soul to your good husband, who mothered me so admirably ; I confess that my departure in such circumstances set me greatly in need of support, and it was a stroke of luck to have someone of the stamp of your husband at my side. But although I rate my moral obligation to him far higher than the pecuniary ones I incurred at the same time, I feel that the latter in particular ought to have made me write him long ago, or rather, to the pair of you. Forgive its not having happened. Anyhow, I believe I've no need to assure you both I'm grateful for your kindness ; whilst I equally assume that I don't need to swear to you that I'm in no position yet to liquidate my debt. Excuse me, all the same, for not having mentioned this matter before.

I would rather Minna had written you about

[1] From the copy in the *Tägl. Rundschau* of Feb. 13, 1906.

our life here, as I can't help thinking you'd place more trust in her account than in mine ; but I reserve the right of getting her to read my letter through and ratify its contents—so far as concerns matters of fact.

You people seem to think it very disagreeable for us to be living at Zurich : for my own part, I know no place in Europe at the moment where I'd rather stay. The solitary choice I had was between here and Paris, and however seriously I may be contemplating my eventual appearance with an opera in Paris, my knowledge of local conditions makes me certain that two or three years might elapse before an actual performance of a work of mine there could be dreamt of ; whilst it is highly questionable whether, under existing conditions, such a thing would be possible at all. Between the ordering or acceptance of an opera — which I doubtless should soon have obtained—and its actual production in Paris, there lies a mighty gulf, only to be filled by money or bridged with the aid of intrigue. But neither have I money, nor am I a dab at intrigue : those belong to the excellent Meyerbeer, before whom every honourable artist in Paris has laid down arms long since ; among them I know many good men who have declared to me, in Paris, they hadn't the remotest expectation of appearing at the Grand Opera while that rich intriguer Meyerbeer held sway. You good people entirely overlook the reigning good-for-nothingness in all our public artistic affairs. My having stood so lonely from of old with my enthusiastic efforts for true

art, that I could nowhere succeed in bringing my
works to bear victoriously on the despicable ruling
fashion ; even where I best was able to produce
them — namely Dresden — my having attained
nothing beyond fleeting sensations, forgotten
again the next morning, or supplanted by any
successor evoked in a quite contrary mode ; that
I accordingly was using myself up with nothing
to shew for it, and through keeping faith with my
artistic convictions I simply estranged the whole
modern egoistic world of craftsmen from me more
and more, saw myself abandoned to every mean
trick without a defender, and drew upon me
nothing but distress in return for my total endeavour,—all this you people pay no heed to, or,
if you heed it, think so light of it that you fail to
see why I don't tranquilly continue writing operas,
—a job you're kind enough to think I understand
so well. You don't reflect how I must feel with a
work like my " Lohengrin " lying finished two years
without having been able to present it even at
Dresden,—where my last before it had success and
brought the institution honour ; you only wonder
why I can't keep writing operas and leave all
other things around me out of count. But I at
any rate have had to do what you aren't doing :
to meditate upon the cause and connexion of
circumstances that now make honest zealous effort
altogether fruitless, be it in Art or wherever you
please. To meditate upon this, means to rebel
against the whole concatenation ; and the stronger
my artistic enthusiasm, the sincerer and more
imperious is my feeling of revolt against the

vulgarity, philistinism, effrontery and contempt-
ibleness in our whole blessed round of circumstances. Of far more weight than writing operas,
and fresh supplies of operas which no one cares
a rap for, do I now hold it to express myself
in public on our art-conditions ; and I am doing
it by addressing my words to *thinking artists.*
Whoever's an artist and able to think, he understands me ; let our hacks of the pen and the rest
pull me to pieces, it troubles me not, for that is a
matter of course since it's *them* I'm attacking.
Enough of that : it was the discussion of my
relations with Paris that brought it up.

To resume : if I by no means drop Paris out
of my future reckoning, still there is nothing for
me to do now in Paris itself, as I neither can
intrigue nor have any money to fling about ;
work, on the other hand, even for Paris, I can do
anywhere better than there. At Zurich I had lit
on a friend of my youth [1] through whom I quickly
won a little circle of very dear and steadfast friends
(all Switzers) ; with my detestation of big cities,
and considering the beauty of Zurich's emplace-
ment, under such circumstances I made up my
mind to reside here. The fact of German refugees
abiding here could not deter me : firstly, because
I've no such philistine dislike of them as seems to
rule in precious Saxony,—and secondly, because I
stand in no manner of relations with them. None
of them did I know at all well personally, neither
have I seen occasion to pick up any closer acquaintance with them here. All the rumours that have

[1] Alexander Müller.

reached you about my keeping company with
Saxon, or any other race of refugees, are false, and
invented by Saxon asses. I am living in complete
retirement, as has been my habit all along, and my
society consists in a few Zurichers—as a fact, of
high standing—who, despite the recentness of our
acquaintance, have proved themselves better and
more actively sympathetic friends than all the
Dresden connoisseurs who praised my works so
often. The rumours anent the degree of my share
in the Dresden uprising, with which people appear
to be pestering you, are not much better than
those anent my Zurich haunts. For Minna's sake
I've taken steps in Dresden now to get the desig-
nation "for common offences" withdrawn from
my warrant of arrest : I almost repent it, since I
might just as well have sat quiet under even this
low trick the Dresden courts have played on me ;
but Minna found it a relief, as said, and so I did
it gladly. Nevertheless it's still possible that it
will be refused me.—

My wish would be, to be able to resume artistic
work without disturbance ; I am brimful of hope
for the future, and in that hope find strength and
relish for the best within my power to achieve.
To be able to stay quietly here or near by—
preferably forgotten, to regarded, by the world
outside—and work up all the manifold artistic
subjects I have in my head, is my greatest desire ;
I have taken due steps to attain it, and hope they
won't be altogether unsuccessful. Probably I
shall go to Paris the beginning of next year, to
produce something at the Conservatoire ; at the

same time I shall try and come to a complete agreement with my poet [French librettist].

On the whole that's all I have to tell you. How Minna is taking it, you no doubt will soon guess ; that she doesn't completely concur with me or my aims and proposals, lies as much in the thing's nature, as in the heterogeneous natures of the two of us. How many of you will there be, who quite concur with me ? I do not entertain much hope of it. There's so strong and ineluctable a force within my soul, however, that I should only be truly unhappy if I had to turn it from its natural course for any *outer* considerations ; on the contrary, I'm quite cheerful if I can obey it, be it even amid the most varied privations and trials. The only thing to cast me down is just my concern for my wife, without whom I shouldn't care to live ; that the knowledge of her necessity to me is imbuing her with strength to suffer all with me, notwithstanding her inner resentment, is what lifts her so high in my heart ; and my love towards her is the single bond that still holds me in touch with a world upon which I should turn my back entirely if I followed my utter loathing of it. May my efforts succeed in arranging our life as endurably as possible. Meanwhile Minna is bearing her position with fortitude and—as always—with immense activity ; moreover, a little feminine society is already forming for her.

I intended writing to our Leipzig kinsfolk also, but really shouldn't have much else to tell them than the present letter contains ; so I will beg you to forward them these lines to read—perhaps first

to Cecilie or Hermann. Give them all my kind
love : please let them be convinced I am heartily
fond of them, however different our views may be
on many things ; neither must they think ill of
me if my nature and tenets should annoy them in
many respects.—
Will you kindly forward the enclosed letter to
Wigand of Leipzig? It touches a question of fee
[*Art-work of the Future*], in reply to which I am expecting some money I feel sure you won't grudge me.

From yourself, dear sister, we're expecting news
right soon about your family and everything doing
in it. I hope you all are well.—Renewed thanks
for your last anxious letter and your sympathy in
general. Best love to the husband and children ;
farewell, think as well of me as you can, and
remain fond of Thy brother   RICHARD.

59. To his Niece Franziska Wagner

DEAR FRÄNZE—Your letter gave me true and
great delight, but don't suppose it was because you
praised me so ; no, it was because I feel that it
expresses in the most natural manner, and perhaps
quite unconsciously, that inner discontent without
which no one now can be a genuine human being.
It is the first time I have made your true acquaintance : that Dresden comedian-mart had raised a
wall between us ; I always deemed you serious
and thoughtful, and yet I never knew distinctly
how I stood with you in such surroundings. So
it delights me to see this development in the good
side of your nature.

I am mistrustful of everybody concerned with the Theatre of to-day, and feel about actors as the Police-court with men : whom it looks on as rogues till confronted with the cryingest proofs to the contrary. How many of you arrive at so much as remarking that you're strictly thrown together with a thorough pack of vagabonds ; how far fewer escape from that slough to pure artistry ! Your whole family has really only got the first length ; reach the second yourself, and I'll bid you hearty welcome. No one knows better than I, that the performer is the actual artist ; what would I not give to have been the impersonator of my own heroes ! How happy, happy I should be ! My whole art is nothing but a weft of yearning thought, eternal wish and inability; for ability means making actual, progressing from conception and aim to deed and reality. But that actuality is in the hands of the Comedian world nowadays, where high wages, fine dresses and newspaper puffs are the principal objects. Rescue yourself from it as well as you can ; but above all shun no griefs nor disagreeables, for at that price alone can we now be men and artists : the soft-shelled stays slave and comedian. Do not blench at the bitterest gall in the cup ; to a sound nature it gives strength and self-confidence, and finally a proud disdain of all that's vulgar, a cheerful mind and true felicity.

I will give you one more counsel for your happiness. Should you find a man you can't help loving, love him with your fullest heart and soul, —and send God and the world to the Devil for what they may say ! This world can give you nothing but vexation, yourself alone that love which passes everything, and without which all besides is empty, null and dead.—Never let false humility arise in you : where it abides, there lurks false pride. Never trim your course to base demands, but resist them with all the loftiness whereof you're capable in your affection for the high. Play the rebel wherever you can,—never swerve an inch from your conviction ; and where'er you can't conquer, just laugh and be cheerful.—I can give you no better advice, for I have learnt for myself that I was unhappy for only so long as I wasn't *thorough*, but made an impossible attempt to mingle fire and water, good and bad. To-day —however much I have to suffer, whatever poignant griefs I feel, I suffer in reality no more : I look death in the face at each instant, and thereby recover my liking for life ; for I can be cheerful and proud now — in my contempt for any life without true substance.

Much has happened with me ; it is impossible for me to relate you that just yet. I am going far away now, and shall long be alone ; I cannot do otherwise.[1]—You will hear of me through Karl [Ritter] ; write me through him if things are going as you wish. Farewell and hold me dear. I do not say, Be happy, but, Be strong and keep faith with yourself, no matter if it leads to outward happiness or the reverse ! Farewell. Thy

RICHARD W.

4. *June* 1850.

---

[1] See the project of Oriental travel (soon abandoned) in letter 37 to Minna of a month previously.—TR.

60. To his Brother-in-law Prof. Hermann Brockhaus [1]

Dear Hermann—Many thanks for your letter and the news you give me in it. I am sorry you should have taken such trouble with a thing whose fruitlessness I could but be convinced of in advance. But I'm sorrier still to learn that my Dresden catastrophe affected Ottilie so painfully, as you inform me. I should almost like to ease her mind about it. To me my old Dresden appointment had long been a torture I should sooner or later have had to cut short—even without political occurrences—if I meant to preserve, or rather, to save myself as sane and self-respecting man and artist. I regret nothing except my not having been previously in the position to depart in perfect peace from a relation which—for all its outer certainty—must have brought about my inner ruin. Never in all my life have I felt so blithe and happy as that summer of 1849 in glorious Switzerland ; I confess that even my grave concern about my wife was powerless to quell the feeling of relief that took lasting possession of me when I had hewn a Gordian knot asunder and got completely at one with myself. In my Dresden appointment I was the most uncertain, undecided person, quieted from without only when I played the hypocrite, impotent from within whenever I declared the truth. All that's at end, and no

<hr />

[1] Address : " Herrn / Professor Dr. Hermann Brockhaus / in / Leipzig." No Zurich post-mark ; Dresden post-mark (the letter evidently having been enclosed in some other for there) : " 11. Febr. 51 " ; Leipzig ditto, " 12. Febr."

concern for livelihood can disturb my inner harmony any more. I know that with the best that I can do—and must do, since I can—I can't earn money, but only love, and that from those who understand me since they want to. So I'm without a care for money too, since I know that love is caring for me.—

So let good Ottilie and all the rest of you be reassured about me and take it that a great stroke of luck—yes, the greatest possible to man—has come my way ; a piece of luck which, as it certainly cannot be weighed in the hand, can only be marred for me through those nearest me not understanding it. Even a glance at *that* world which makes my art-endeavours for the public so fruitless at present, can only repel me in passing, for I know that beneath it a new world is astir in the which, happy man, I am living already.—

So—be satisfied with how I'm faring.

One more request, dear Hermann. Please ask Heinrich [Brockhaus] from me to keep the said library together exactly as transferred to him. Presumably it will be taken off his hands again ere long through reimbursement of the sum he lent me ; so he would oblige me if he'd look upon the books as nothing but a pledge, not payment. I thank him for his kind offer to lend me single books therefrom.—

I can quite understand no doctor understanding Ottilie's condition. The fact that in her case the blood is at work on the nerves, and good air, rational diet and *water* would completely restore her, — is certainly no concern of our Doctores

M

Medicinæ. Let Ottilie come to Switzerland this spring, and we'll soon put her health to rights. Hearty greetings from me to the "individuals"—get healthy, all of you, and quit that idiotic Leipzig. What would you say to a professorship at Zurich?—Farewell, dear Hermann, and keep good to me! Thy   RICHARD WAGNER.

ZURICH, 2. *Febr.* 51.
(ENGE.)

Please wish Cecilie best luck from us both ; I'll write to her next time, for certain.

61. To EDUARD AVENARIUS [1]

DEAR EDUARD—You, too, will no doubt have had news of me lately through Hermann, who I hope passed on to Cecilie my greetings and good wishes. I still have no news of her confinement ; has it taken place yet, and did it go off all right?

Presuming you already know whatever there's to know about us, also that Cecilie in particular isn't angry at my having left an earlier letter of hers unanswered—it was precisely the time when my head was so terribly filled up with Minna—I make straight for a request which you mustn't take ill of me.

Two or three weeks back I addressed myself to J. J. Weber with the offer of a manuscript that will make a fairly stout book, 4 to 5 hundred pages small octavo, under the title " Oper und Drama."

---

[1] Address : " Herrn/Buchhändler/EDUARD AVENARIUS/in/Leipzig." No Zurich post-mark (consequently an enclosure in some other letter) ; Leipzig post-mark, " Town-post, 17 Mr."

I came to offer it to Weber because I knew he has published a good many studies of the sort—and with success, so it seems ; further, because Wigand makes all manner of excuses when he's asked to pay for anything. Since I certainly must look out for money also in the present instance—always a ticklish point between relations,—moreover, as I do not know your line of publishing at all, but am bound to think the character of my manuscript might make it difficult to obtain the consent of your partner—Mendelssohn,—I didn't want to embarrass *you* by any offer to yourself ; and with that, as I fancy, you won't be displeased.

But I'm so completely ignorant of all the book-trade's etiquette, and so absolutely unacquainted with anyone to whom I could apply about it, that you must forgive me if I beg of you at least to lend a helping hand through your advice. If you do not think it unprofessional, I would ask you in the first place to enquire of Weber on my behalf whether he'd care to have dealings with me. The manuscript is now in the care of " königl. Kammer-musikus Theodor Uhlig, Poliergasse No. 2, in Dresden," who has been instructed by me to hand it over on your demand or Weber's. So, if Weber doesn't tumble to it, you would much oblige me if you gave me definite advice whom else I might approach. I quite understand that, as book-dealer yourself, you can't intervene in this matter direct ; so I merely beg you to let me know the needful steps to dispose of such a manuscript to the best advantage. For nearness sake you perhaps might place yourself in communication with *Uhlig* in Dresden at once, and empower him to take such steps and give such orders as you may deem advisable, but couldn't execute *yourself* in my name. Uhlig is discreet and sensible.—

Now, don't be cross with me for coming down on you with such a hash. If I felt compelled to write a book like that, and am bound to try and launch it on the world as profitably as possible, I am equally obliged to look around for somebody to help me,—and God forbid your taking it amiss of me for stumbling on yourself.—

I'm very eager for particulars about your household ; Hermann merely wrote me that you were pleased with your business affairs. So far, so good ; but let us know at once how Cecilie is doing, and what sort of increase you've had to your family. Couldn't you manage to pay us a visit in Switzerland ? It really isn't farther than to Königsberg, whilst the environs are indisputably more beautiful even than at Maraunen.

—We are leading a peaceful and fairly endurable life here, in a small circle of good Swiss friends. Minna has become quite at home here, and so have I.—If all goes well, I shall fall to on another big dramatic composition this spring : Siegfrieds Tod.—

Now—don't be cross with me, and give me your support in the matter aforesaid—providing you can.—Best love from both of us to Cecilie and the children ; farewell and stay fond of Thy

RICHARD W.

ENGE. bei ZÜRICH,
10. *March* 1851.

62. To the Same

Dear Eduard—Weber writes me that he will print my manuscript if I'm satisfied with a fee of 100 Rth. [*circa* £15] ; so I ask whether you advise me to accept the offer—failing better prospects ? If you believe I shan't get more, I beg you to convey the enclosed letter to Weber. In that letter I accept his offer, *i.e.* for an edition of 500 copies, but naturally reserve the bargaining for another fee in the conceivable event of a second edition. I should be glad of your information how I ought to provide for such an event.—But I still have to thank you cordially for what you've already attended to.

We heard of Cecilie's successful accouchement through Cläre, who writes that it went off very well and your family has been enriched with a boy. Minna believed you'd have liked a little girl this time ; however, I suppose a boy may be also put up with, and am sure there are many who heartily envy you. For our part we congratulate with all our heart, and testify our great joy in particular at hearing of Cecilie's good state of health.

And now we are hoping to receive news from herself soon ; or is she still cross with me ? And myself—am I ever to hear of you ?

Farewell, and accept my best thanks for your brotherly painstaking. Thy

RICHARD WAGNER.

ENGE. ZURICH,
7. *April* 51.

63. To the Same

Dear Eduard—I'm merely writing you in brief, directly after receipt of your letter, because I want to get the pending business polished off at once.

You've much delighted me by the interest you have devoted to this affair as well ; I hardly expected you would take it up like that. Before everything else, though :—as I gather that it will cost you no vanquishing of God knows what scruples to publish a book of mine, and you thereby relieve me in the most brotherly fashion of all the ceremonies of a formal offer to you,—naturally it is self-understood that I accept your expressed preparedness to publish with all my heart, and I'd a thousand times rather have to do with you in this affair than with Herr J. J. Weber.—So, acting on your own representations, I have written Weber the enclosed, thanking him for his favour, but saying I would try for better terms elsewhere, of the granting whereof I have prospect, and I therefore request him to deliver you the manuscript.

Now be so good as to grant me whatever conditions you can ; let the book be got up handsomely, and—appear soon. I should have liked to attend to the proof-reading,—I've had too much bad luck with printer's errors heretofore.

Apropos, I suppose it won't be disagreeable to you that I have allowed a small fragment of the book to be printed already, in the form of 3 articles

for the Deutsche Monatsschrift[1] under the title
" On Modern dramatic poetry " ("from a larger
essay of the author's to be published shortly "). I
fancy that sort of thing can only do good, as it
rouses and attracts attention,—I hope you'll think
so too. I am getting no fee for it.—For that
matter, I do not expect to grow fat through my
literary activity.—In exchange, I'm now proceeding
to a labour that ought to bring me in a lot, namely
the composition of my "Siegfried" [*S. Tod*]; for
which, however, I shall also never draw a halfpenny ! !—That's how I'm pulling through, you
see. But I'm to sing the *Fides* [*Prophète*] shortly
in Berlin.—

Well, as we now are positively entering on
" business " correspondence, and consequently shall
have frequent occasion to write to each other, I
reserve all other news to-day. Moreover, Cecilie
is soon to hear more. For to-day, please salute
her as heartily as possible from me and Minna ;
her letter gave us great delight, which we shall
do our best to return. God preserve you the
" colossal wet-nurse," and build up your new little
boy on her chaste bosom. Cecilie's tidings cheered
me nicely about the pair of you ; why—things are
going quite well, it appears.

So—enormous love to wife and child. Shortly
much more.

Farewell, and please don't leave me in the lurch
—*re* Weber. (You'll see the book will go well in
the end—I have tokens of that—and in fact the

[1] The first appeared in the March number, 1851, second and third not
till the May.—Tʀ.

most immediate future. But more about that, too, another time.) Adieu ! Thy

RICHARD W.

ENGE.
ZURICH, 15. *April* 51.

You'll forward the letter to Weber by *town-post*, won't you ?

64. TO THE SAME[1]

DEAR EDUARD—Weber has just written me that, anticipating my consent to his terms, he had already placed my manuscript in the hands of the printer, and therefore would suffer loss by my non-acceptance. He now offers me 20 louis d'or at once, and another 20 l. d'or when the edition of 500 copies is sold out.—To my mind it would almost be a trifle shabby to throw him over now, and under the circumstances I am sure you'd advise me, yourself, not to tread on his corns any farther ; so I am letting Weber keep the manuscript.

After the overtures from your side, I'm therefore left with nothing but the regret that I didn't offer myself to you from the first ; though I hope you will not overlook that it was nothing save a certain sense of delicacy that withheld me. Anyhow I am sorry now, not to be having to do with yourself ; the business part of it would have acquired quite a genial flavour. Nevertheless you certainly have not missed a gold mine ; I cannot

[1] Address : " Herrn / Eduard Avenarius / Buchhändler / in / LEIPZIG." No post-mark.

deny for a moment that undertakings of this sort
are more a matter of good-will than speculation.—
There I go again, having to write you post-
haste ; I must still stay in Cecilie's debt for further
communications.—Give her best love from me and
Minna, though ; we are doing quite tolerably.
I'm setting to at the musical composition of my
Siegfried [*S. Tod*] now.—
Farewell, then, and hold me dear. Thy

RICHARD W.

ENGE. ZÜRICH, 3. *May* 51.

Once again : *Best thanks !*

65. TO HIS NIECE, CLARA BROCKHAUS [1]

ALBISBRUNN BEI HAUSEN
Canton ZÜRICH.

MY DEAR CLÄRCHEN—I have long been
intending to write you for once in a way, but
reserved it for the first day I should feel in a
thorough good humour. I almost fancy that's
the case to-day ; so you shall really hear a word
from me now, as I've heard so much good of
yourself. The other day I sent you and Ottchen [her
sister Ottilie] my love through your aunt Portius ;
then came a letter from your aunt Cläre, telling
me of your valorous love for myself. See, that
set me all aflame and afire ! I court the affection
of nobody, and leave people to think what they
like of me ; but anyone who therefore thought
me cold and insensible, would have nicely deceived

---

[1] Third daughter of Friedrich and Luise Brockhaus.

himself. If but a finger of true unconditional love is held out to me from anywhere, I snatch at the whole hand as possessed, draw the whole mortal to me by it if I can, and give him, an' it may be, just such a thorough hearty kiss as I should like to give yourself to-day. That is the way with us madmen, you see, who don't care a fig for fame, honour, or riches ; we're fonder of a merry child like you, with whole heart and clear head, than of anything the wise and prudent run after with care and trouble, agony and sweat, as if *they* really were the mad.—So you stick up for me?—Eh, but that's fine ; and in return you shall some day be with me in Paradise. Do you know where that Paradise is ? Ask your heart and your blithe tingling veins ; they will tell you it better than I !

Look here, dear Clärchen : you said the first thing you would do when independent, would be to come and see us here? Do you know how you may gain your independence mighty soon? Take my advice : give father and mother no peace till they send you away. If it makes them concerned, why, pull your nimble wits together and shew your parents that, if you want to come to me, you're meaning nothing very dreadful by them : on the contrary, perhaps your first true good, to fly off as dove twixt them and me. They surely don't consider me a rascal, and maybe you'll even bring about their also finding pleasure in me ; and does a pleasure to be won, then, weigh so precious little in this dreary, joyless world?—Only set to work the right way, and you'll quickly succeed.

When you do come, however, you must arrange
to come quite safe and well protected ; and for
that I can advise you nothing better than to get
yourself accompanied by the prudent Ottchen. If
Ottchen is with you, your parents will know you're
as safe as in Abraham's bosom ; the lynx-eyed,
sapient monitor, who nearly got the length of a
good mention from Fräulein Eule,—my ! *she'll*
take care of and protect you. And I must further
assure you that I'm very fond of Ottchen, and
should be positively delighted if she came as well.
Give her a kiss from me at once, to go on with.—
There, that's settled !—

You both shall find quite good accommodation
in our house, even if a trifle skimpy ; Minna
knows how to manage, you're well aware,—it
takes more than that to put her in a fix. Next
summer we shall probably go into the country, on
the Zurich lake, where it really isn't much worse
than at Prossen [the B's country-seat]. Nor shall you
suffer hunger at my place ; goodness knows how
it comes, but it never comes to that with me !

Just one thing further, Clärchen ; I heard of
your father's accident ; if he has ever done or
wished me good, I will repay him with a piece of
advice I think no small beer of, for I give it with
entire conviction of its excellence. Let your
father go to a *Hydropathic institute,* take a complete
water-cure under *intelligent* guidance, above all
shrink from no expenditure of time or patience,
and I prophesy he'll gradually get *perfectly* well ;
yes, probably even recover his lost eye.—I give
your mother just the same advice ; in fact I give

it everyone whose well-being I have at heart. Above everything, flee from all medicine-men : they systematically poison and ruin you. In that I speak alike from theoretic knowledge and practical experience ; for I write you to-day from a hydro at which I've been taking a cure for five weeks ; I am sure of recovering from a most troublesome ailment, namely a digestion ruined by excessive mental application coupled with wrong diet and medical quack-salvery, with resulting derangement of the nerves. Your father's condition is simpler to deal with, even should the treatment cost much time.—Follow my advice.— Now farewell, my dear girl. Above all, write to me soon : I shall be staying three more weeks here ; then I return to *Zeltweg, Hottingen, Zürich.* Remember me to your people, and assure them I wish them all the best of everything. Forgive my horrid scrawl, and hold me as dear as you possibly can. Thy

RICHARD WAGNER.

23. *October* 1851.

66. To EDUARD AVENARIUS [1]

DEAR EDUARD——I really must follow up my all too hasty lines of yesterday with something more detailed to-day. Perhaps a copy of the Preface to my " Three Opera-poems " [*Communication etc.*] will already be in your hands by the time this letter reaches you, and you will know

---

[1] Address : " Herrn./EDUARD AVENARIUS/(F. Avenarius & Mendelssohn)/ Buchhändler/in/Leipzig./frei." The " hasty lines " above referred to are not preserved.

what's the matter. So nothing now beyond a closer account of the situation, that a solution may quickly be found.

As Härtels had undertaken the publication of the music of Lohengrin, I necessarily had to give them the refusal of the projected edition of my "three opera-poems," since a part thereof, the text of Lohengrin, belonged to them already. The "Communication to my Friends," which I am setting in front of that edition as preface—and, you may easily understand, was my principal object—certainly appeared to me little adapted for Härtel's jog-trot lists ; consequently I wrote them at the very time of sending, that they needn't feel at all obliged to publish it, but in case it didn't suit them, they had only to tell me so candidly, and I would look out for another publisher. They simply replied by acceptance, and the despatch of a volunteered fee of 100 gulden [*ca* £10]. Now they confess that they hadn't read my manuscript, and, after making its contents' acquaintance, feel placed in the impossibility of allowing the book to appear with their imprimatur.

That was the reason why I addressed myself to you yesterday. Reading Härtel's letter through again, however, I find that it is less their personal sentiment, than a thorough alarm lest the book should be confiscated and process served on themselves, that constitutes the ground of their refusal. So I've written them (and that letter will reach Leipzig together with this to yourself) saying that, should such be the case, and they be governed by nothing save a reasonable fear of confiscation,

I am prepared to alter or tone down the most hazardous passages. As the very last thing I dreamed of with this book was a political demonstration so entirely out of season, I could make them this concession without demeaning myself in any way ; so if they are satisfied with it, and the changes can be easily effected, I am perfectly willing.

Out of respect for them, I had to make them the offer above. Nevertheless, I now believe they're less concerned for a few modifications of the sort, than to be rid of the whole business ; for I certainly can't alter so much and so radically as to give the book a wholly different colour, namely a colour to suit their taste as apprehensive bourgeois with perhaps a streak of piety. Wherefore I return to yourself, and entreat you to examine very carefully whether there really is such serious ground for fearing confiscation in the present case ; in truth, I can't conceive it ! Could any State authority view this edition of three opera-poems [*Fl. Holl.*, *Tannh.* and *Loh.*], no matter if a bold word be breathed therein from time to time, as a political pamphlet ? What else do I say, then, than has repeatedly been said with much more emphasis—and still is being—in the domain of the newer philosophy ? If I touch upon my Dresden fortunes, it is simply to give a truthful picture of the march of my artistic development ; but nothing whatever occurs in the sense or tone of provocation. I am bound to deem it quite impossible that this writing should afford cause for suppression, even if it should give

offence here and there.   I hope, nay—I strongly
presume that you also are of my opinion and
recognise in Härtel's fear the whole paltry timidity
of these good people, who would rather not have
anything at all to do with such a thing.

Accordingly, I hereby declare that I should
like best of all to see my Preface appear *unaltered*,
as I should really be able to change very little,
and moreover, even the slightest amendment must
lead to abominable pottering, expense and delay.
If you or—in case you don't care to—another
publisher will undertake to bring out the book
just as it is, I give unconditional preference to
such a course.   I hope *you* will do it and venture
something *with your brother-in-law* for once :
that's what I should like best, and it would give
me great joy.   If, however, you're too much
hampered by your partner (my sole consideration
here), it has just struck me that perhaps *J. J.
Weber* might be sounded *before* Wigand ; for, in a
sense, this book is the completion of that now
appearing with him [*Op. & Dr.*].   Moreover,
his imprimatur is in smaller disrepute with the
authorities than that of Wigand, who therefore
would have to be regarded only as a last resource.
As for the question of cost, I again declare my
readiness to refund the fee in case of need, as I
fortunately am able to just now.—So, please me by
putting the thing in rapid order, and with your
firm if possible.

I should have liked to indulge in a little
"family " chat, only my water-cure forbids me,
after this fairly long effusion.   But be sure you

shall soon have a report in writing such as I gave
you by mouth through Uhlig a short while back.
Once more, best love to wife and child ; farewell,
and hold me as dear as you all can. Thy

RICHARD WAGNER.

ALBISBRUNN, near Hausen.
    Canton ZÜRICH.
        31. *October* 1851.

P.S.—I add this to tell you I'm this moment
withdrawing from the post the said letter to
Härtels [1]—with the proposal for changes ; it might
merely complicate the negotiation anew. So
they'll get no word at all from me direct, but
simply through yourself. Take the matter entirely
into your own hands, and — remembering my
wishes—proceed as you think best.   R. W.

67. TO THE SAME [2]

DEAR EDUARD—Did you get my two letters
or not? The absence of any answer makes me
uneasy, as so very, very much depends—for reasons
I will tell you of—upon the *hastening* of my book's
appearance.

If you have received no letter from me yet at
all, please go to Härtels and announce yourself
as—publisher of the "Three Opera-poems." If
it must be, however, make haste and forward me

---

[1] He sent them another, however, three days later, followed by a
correspondence on this matter extending to the end of the year ; see *Richard
Wagner's Briefwechsel mit Breitkopf & Härtel,* published by that firm early
1911.—TR.

[2] Address : " Herrn/Eduard Avenarius/Verlagsbuchhändler/in/LEIPZIG."

the sheet in question with the passage to be altered, to clear the matter up. Farewell. Thy
RICHARD WAGNER.

11. *Nov.* 51,
ALBISBRUNN
near Hausen, Canton ZÜRICH.

68. TO THE SAME [1]

DEAR EDUARD—Best and heartiest thanks for your brotherly attention to the Härtel affair ; imagine its only now striking these people to send me the passages they jib at !—From the enclosed you'll perceive that I've complaisantly omitted everything the least bit risky ; which for the most part was the more difficult, as the space had to be filled again with pretty well the same number of words. A few minutiæ I have left unaltered ; they are of a nature which could only alarm ——s of the first water : hoping Härtels will have forgotten all about them, I am not even returning those leaves (if only for weight of my letter). Should the Härtels, however, insist on alteration of these trifles also—which is scarcely conceivable— I think you had better put an end to the whole business by relieving them of the publication ; they've angered me enough already with this disgraceful delay. But I fancy they'll listen to reason, especially if you will take the trouble to drum it into them ; and if they then let go all further fuss, please also back me up in getting them to *hurry* the appearance at last.

[1] Address : " Herrn / EDUARD AVENARIUS / (Avenarius & Mendelssohn / Verlagsbuchhändler)/in/LEIPZIG./frei."

N

Above all, my dear Eduard, don't be cross at the impudence with which I'm making you my —forced—negotiator in such a boggle. Indeed I regret very much that it didn't occur to me right from the beginning to deal with no one but yourself ; though you certainly lose nothing by that, you are having almost as much of a pother now as if you at least were interested as my publisher. So—forgive me, and accept my heartiest thanks once more for your amiable pains.——

If you would thoroughly oblige me, though, please let me know at once how your approaching final conference with Härtels goes off, and what prospects I have of my book's speedy appearance.—— Farewell and hold me dear.   Thy

RICHARD W.

ALBISBRUNN, 22. *Nov.* 51.

I shall be at Zurich again from to-morrow. Address :

ZELTWEG,
    ZÜRICH.

69. TO HIS NIECE FRANZISKA WAGNER

ZURICH (ZELTWEG), 21. *March* 52.

DEAR FRÄNZE—I want to make a good shot at your birthday, that my felicitations may reach you betimes ; so please accept them before anything else.

Your letter delighted me the more, as I had long been expecting one, and its being so behind-hand inspired me with all sort of doubts in your regard as well.   I began to think I must couple you with Johanna, who has already advanced in

her filial obedience to the point of completely
ignoring me. At or near Frankfort last summer
she met on his return journey from here the
Dresden musician Uhlig, who by the most rigid
economy had made it possible to visit me in
Switzerland ; he talked to her about me, and she
was overcome with shame and a fancy to take that
short journey herself : her mother held her back.
I wrote to her myself once, and further had her
reminded that a letter from *herself* would give me
great delight. But it seems to be painful to your
mother and father, and a dangerous precedent, for
Johanna to concern herself with me : a fear that
involves the whole consciousness of their attitude
towards me ; and the prickings of conscience are
always disturbing. I should like them, nevertheless, to know the wrong they do me if they fear my
ever importuning them : toward those who feel
alike with me I am responsive and frank as a child ;
toward such, however, as do not understand me,
and don't want to, I'm quite abominably proud.
At present I am living solely on the friendship of
the Ritter family, which had assisted me before
and has now ensured my livelihood through a fixed
annuity ; from such intimate helpers I can accept
anything without a wince, whereas I'm so squeamish
toward others that I once returned even Hermann
Brockhaus a sum of money sent me. If your
parents only knew how easy they might feel about
me in this regard, perhaps they no longer would
prevent Johanna from corresponding with me.
But what really horrifies me, is Johanna's having
been able to bring *herself* to leave me out of touch !

I don't give much for males now, and nothing surprises me in them, the egoistic philistines ; but the heart of a young woman !—It's dreadful. Perhaps, however, she is to be excused by the tinsel surrounding her.—Don't urge her to write to me ; nothing but the spontaneous, the unforced, can give me joy.

With yourself it is different, and I hope it isn't merely the unpretentiousness of your position, that has preserved your healthy feeling ; your good angel—so it seems to me—is your very sense of self-reliance, your self-respect and respect for your own independence. Thus the dramatic artist appears to me to distinguish herself in your person from the operatic singer ; with the latter the mechanical breaking-in of the throat to modern claptrap seems to extend to head and heart. The force of drill is extraordinary : do not we see how the soldier can be turned into a mere marching and shooting machine ? With you, on the contrary, it surely has needed an evolving from out of your own inner self ; a good actress is bound to feel, she cannot simply copy feeling. Thus in my own case—as you know—mere "singers" have never contented me ; I want sound actors who can sing, and so long as I do not find them, the representation of my works will remain a mere shadow.

That leads me direct from yourself to the Schwerin production of Tannhäuser. It gave me real pleasure through bearing witness to that self-sacrificing zeal I'm able to arouse in individuals. That the multitude leaves me indifferent, you'll

find perfectly natural ; I know that *it* can't grasp
what I am driving at.   In the happiest event, our
public and our cognoscenti do not feel that through
the medium of the artwork a human soul is telling
them its joys and sorrows ; in one of us they
always see only the artist whose business it is to
set something before them and reap honour and
fame in return (to say nothing of—money) ; and
after duly applauding him, they leave the house to
become the selfsame callous scamps in life again
they were before.   I know I am speaking to the
winds with my artworks ; my only holdfast is the
individual in whom I can see that through my art
I have preached to his conscience, stung him up to
free himself from lies and hypocrisy, and made
him thus a fellow-combatant against the good-for-
nothing reign of " worldly wisdom."

I'm greatly pleased at the development of your
artistic talent ; so far as art can ever compensate
us for a lack of life, 'twill make you happy.   I
should very much like to see you some day, but
that no doubt will never be the case unless you
come and visit us ; I shall *never* return to
Germany, even were I 100 times pardoned.   So
think out a plan for your coming to us.—Minna's
doing well ; she amuses herself much more than in
Dresden, has female friends and entertainment.
I'm always suffering from my nerves, and probably
shall not last out much longer ; still, I do want
to complete my Siegfried dramas first.   When
Spring comes, I shall get back to work.—So farewell, good Fränze ; kind thanks for your letter,
and write again soon to Thy   RICHARD W.

Peps is still alive and kicking, and squats on the back of my chair as of yore. Papo—died a year ago ; it was terrible, and never have I wept so much, as for that dear little animal.—Minna sends kind love ; you greatly delighted *her*, too, with your letter. Karl Ritter went to Dresden about New Year ; his health isn't good.

70. To the Same

DEAR FRÄNZE—Couldn't you manage to give me precise information *whether* Johanna has concluded a contract with Paris already, whether it is with the " Grand Opera " or the Italian Opera, and *when* she starts on that contract?—Then, in case she hasn't definitely signed yet, please tell me if you think you could persuade her to insist upon getting a clause inserted in the contract to be concluded with Paris, according to which she would stipulate for her appearing in Tannhäuser also under certain circumstances?—

The case is this. Through the blundering of Meyerbeer, who lately hired a certain herd of scribblers there to pull me to pieces, I've suddenly become renowned in Paris, or at least an interesting figure. So it has now been insinuated to me from there to give my consent to an effort to get me the order to write an opera for Paris. I refuse to hear of such a thing, chiefly because I won't " set " other people's " texts," and least of all in the French language ; but I should have less to object to their getting Tannhäuser well translated and given at the Grand Opera, provided I were

guaranteed a *good performance*. The latter is at
any rate possible, with *Roger* as Tannhäuser,
and Johanna ; Roger would be the Tannhäuser I
should like best in all the world, certainly far
preferable to that . . . Tichatschek. The possibility of a very good performance is my first
attraction with it ; then the prospect of a terrible,
but serious and out-and-out successful fight with
Meyerbeer excites my—call it malice ; added to
which, engrossment with the preparations for an
immediate and interesting production might be
very beneficial to my health, which, in my present
situation, is marching at the double to its utter
ruin.

Well, that's an affair Johanna can give the
crucial turn to, if she only springs into the lists for
me with *energy*, and completely emancipates herself
from her dependent position toward Meyerbeer
(Paris). Tell me, as said, what hopes you have
of it.——

Give Herr Stocks my kind regards, and say I
would have answered his letter before this if I
hadn't to spare myself greatly, and letter-writing
didn't tire me excessively. His already thinking of
Lohengrin for Schwerin almost frightened me ;
though I shouldn't have the heart to refuse him as
soon as I learnt that the Schweriners not only
meant to quit the beaten track quâ intent, but also
with the execution, and made no bones, for instance,
of a cor anglais, bass clarinet and third bassoon,
beyond the ordinary strength of their orchestra.
These are trifles, but where even *they* arouse demur,
I'm justly nervous anent the bigger matter.

And now, I should much like to see *you* on the
stage, all accounts of your acting so whet my
curiosity ; where and *when* would that be possible?
Farewell for to-day.   Best love from me and
Minna.   Thy

+ + + Richard Wagner.

Zurich, 28. *Sept.* 52.

I'm also sending you " sous bande " a brochure
[*Perf. of Tannh.?*] which I would beg you to hand
to Herr Stocks.—
Don't tell a creature of the Paris project; nobody
must get wind of it.

71. To the Same

(Zurich, *October* 13, 1852.)

My dear Fränze—Kind thanks for your
letter !   The part that pleased me most of all was
your intending to pay me a visit ; if you mean it
in regular earnest, you will give us great joy, and
on our side we hope to be able to offer you here
what will make you not repent your sacrifice.
Accommodation you'll find with us, right enough :
a famous divan stands in gear for your slumbers.
But our country will soon make you open your
eyes, I assure you ; nor shall you hear a single
word with us of " art."—
Don't bother yourself any more about the
subject of my last enquiry ; I'm not so in earnest
with Paris, and whether anything comes of it, or
not, is fairly indifferent to me *in itself*.   For God's
sake do not think I'm hankering after fame and

honour ; if I ever have my eye on anything in
respect of my operas, it is only the chance of a
good representation, purely for the artistic interest
of the thing.   Your father, to be sure, has other
things in his eye with Johanna, which you have so
far forgotten that yourself you can speak of his
taking thought for nothing save his children's
"welfare."   Albert wrote to me unasked the other
day about her Paris contract, and said it bore on
Meyerbeer alone: my whole heart went into the
grief I expressed to him that even Johanna, who
stands so near *to me*, should have also had to job
herself to that rapacious Jew ; she might easily
have found a nobler object for her youthful
powers, than to lay them on the altar of that bag
of bones !   If Hans is really so fond of me, can
it give her any satisfaction to be positively betray-
ing me, in a sense ?   Eh—but that "welfare" !
Another pile of money, another dollop of celebrity :
isn't *that* it ?   Get along with you all and your
"welfare" !   No doubt Johanna hasn't quite
enough yet, and couldn't she attain the height of
fame if she gave her service to a *worthy* cause?—
Surely it would have been of great value to me,
had "Lohengrin" been given in Berlin the following winter ; everything points to it : but Johanna
—for whom I wrote my Elsa—is staining herself
black, and bringing Meyerbeer's Africaine into
the world—all for the sake of her "welfare."
Who knows if *I* shall live out the next twelve-
month ?   and I should so have liked not to let
Lohengrin be given anywhere else *before* Berlin !
Enough of what distresses, wounds, and hurts

me just as if my sweetheart proved unfaithful
to me !——

I was much pleased by Johanna's portrait and
your letter with it. I told her so at once, and she
answered me with a long letter yesterday. Good
Lord, I always liked her, and my huff was directed
to something quite other than herself and character.
I shall write her again presently, and try how
much influence I still can exert upon her and her
parents with the "practical eye." If I could only
win her altogether to true art, and set her up as an
exception before the twopenny prima donnas of
our day ! I told them you were coming to me,
and added that I'd drag nobody besides here by
the hair who didn't mean to come. I also believe
that an Alpine excursion would do more for
Johanna's real "welfare," than all that cursed
voice-hawking to the ends of the earth ; unfortunately, I'm not the only one who thinks so !

But just you come yourself, and be assured
that you're administering a true cordial to me with
your attachment. I can't bear the [present breed
of] males, and should like to have nothing to do
with them : no one is worthy his salt, who can't
really be loved by a woman ; but the stupid asses
cannot even love now ; if they've talent left, they
fuddle it, but as a rule they're content with cigar-
smoking. The only people I look to for anything
still are the women, if only there were more of it !
No one has courage,——all are played out.——Now,
you do better ; I've hope of you ! Write me
again some day, and don't be too saving ; I shall
be earning a million soon, and will share it with

you! For the rest, beware of " doing well " ; and if things go badly with you, remember your eternally ill-faring Uncle and Opera-maker

RICHARD W.

Why shouldn't you give greetings to Stocks? Minna is cooking, and greets.

72. TO SISTER LUISE BROCKHAUS

DEAR LUISE—Many thanks for your kind letter, which came as rather a surprise to me. Its effect on me was the more impressive, as the mood that led you to it seemed a doleful one in all regards. I have no very clear idea of your present situation, but guess that you have ground enough to be remembering the unfortunate with predilection. I should be unable to convey to you exactly what I mean by that, as too many links between us are things of the past to me, and the only ones present rather pertain to indefinite feeling, than to consciousness. So I find myself compelled in my answer to speak of almost nothing but myself; and indeed what you particularly ask about, is how things are going with me.

A year ago I wrote to your Clärchen. I was at a hydropath's then, with the idea of becoming a physically healthy being out and out. At the back of my wish lay a health that should make it possible to rid myself completely of the torment of my life, namely of Art; it was a last forlorn struggle for happiness, for true joy in a worthy life, such as can only be vouchsafed to the consciously sound. That I had deceived myself about my condition, at any rate was soon to grow clear to me,—my life is worn bare, and without having ever enjoyed it, I now can merely eke it out, and that with Art ; but how desperate is my position with *my* art towards our public art-life, will only be realised by those who can gauge the extent to which Art has to replace for me a life full of unfulfilled yearning. How shallow, on the contrary, is the estimate of those who point me to a perhaps to be attained renown! My burning need of love, unslaked in life, I pour into my art ; and in the happiest event I have to find myself taken for an energetic reformer of—Opera! Thus I rush from one dissatisfaction to another, and in the mournful quest my health slides deeper and still deeper down the descent from which nothing —no cure in the world can preserve me. My nerves are already quite worn to a thread ; perchance some turning in my outer life may stave off death a few years yet : but that could only apply to death itself, it can no longer arrest my decline. —In a nutshell, that is all I can tell you about me.

The Dresden reviving of Tannhäuser [Oct. 26] left me fairly indifferent : as to the chief affair (the rôle of Tannhäuser), I know the representation there is a most miserable failure; the fact of odds and ends attracting people can't content me.

To that Dresden in general I can only think back with a shudder ; no man ever put forth his whole soul with fuller breast, than I did there,— and on what walls of leather did my cry continually impinge! Now I have lived to hear myself

upbraided with "ingratitude" towards the King :
as if the uselessness of all my sacrifices of my life
and my artistic powers in exchange for an appointment there, or for "favours" flung pell-mell to
every vagabond, had been my own fault, and not
the fault of those absurd conditions I attacked at
last, made furious!—Enough of that.—

Give my kindest love to your Marianne, with
heartiest felicitations. Will you not all come and
see us some day, then, in our beautiful Switzerland ?
How my heart yearns to have Clärchen and
Ottchen once more at our table ! Give them all
my best love, and wish your husband, too, pros-
perity. My wife joins heartfeltly in all these
greetings and good wishes. But yourself, dear
Luise, above all I beg you'll write me soon again,
and stay fond of Thy brother   RICHARD.

ZURICH, 11. *Nov.* 52.

I have nearly got through with my Nibelungen
poems : whether I shall carry out the music for
them too, I must make entirely dependent on my
feeling well : if my situation doesn't radically
change, I despair of that. Probably I shall let the
poems appear before long [in print.]

73. To sister Cäcilie Avenarius

ZURICH, 30. *Dec.* 1852.

DEAR CECILIE—I intended writing yesterday,
for you to receive my letter on New Year's day,
but was unwell and couldn't get to it ; so my
felicitations will arrive a day too late.

You may be sure your letter gave me great and hearty joy ; I had been almost expecting to have news from you long before, and accordingly supposed you had taken something amiss in my last. So much the better !——Whenever you return to me like that, it instinctively reminds me of our youthful days, when we two were really the ones who belonged most to each other ; not a memory comes back to me from those old times without your being woven in it.——No doubt it's the same with yourself, and as one always regards youth as the happier period, so the disagreeables of the present may make you also long for him who was the nearest to you then.   That scene upon the bank at Loschwitz with my boots, Humann etc., still has its little revival with me from time to time ; if we hadn't put the key in that pumpkin [see *Life of W.* i, 79-80] everything would have gone off much better then, don't you agree ?——

All that has changed for the worse now.   With my passionate longing for utterance, I am living amid surroundings that drive me inward more and more ; no one has greater need to unbosom his whole store sans reserve, and to none is less re-given than to me : my output stands in no proportion to my intake.   I'm incredibly poor in agreeable impressions ; I always have to feed on nothing save myself.   It is a peculiar misfortune for me that I've almost none but philistines for friends, and they often cleave to me with an affection that, since it doesn't strictly apply to my true nature, can only be returned by myself with a certain lack of candour.   On the whole it's the male ones that grate on me most, and I still derive pleasant impressions the soonest from women. What dreadful nonsense it is, that men should keep company with no one but men, and women with women ; the whole human race must go to ground in the end through such perversity. If only the women, though, were not also, for the most part, so ruined already ! Nowadays the men are all born philistines, and through them the women become so. That's flat !—

So I am leading a sort of dog's life here. None of the illusions about friends to which I lend myself so readily will hold water for long ; at last the effort of illusion pains me, and perforce I let things stand in their unvarnished truth just as they are. Thus I continue in the same old solitude ; but I shall succumb in the end to this want of victuals for my heart. My nerves are all out of order, and after repeated attempts at a radical cure I have lost my last hope of recovery ; the utmost I can do now, is to gain rest and as much comfort as needful to help me hold out. My work is all that keeps me going, but the nerves of my brain are already so ruined, that I can never devote more than two hours a day to it ; and even those I can only accomplish by lying down for another two after my work and trying to sleep a bit ; if sleep doesn't come, that day is done for. In this way I have now completed my big Nibelungen poem ; if zest is afforded me from without, I shall start on its music next Spring.

My operas are being given at various places now, as you are aware ; nothing much is like to come of it, and I don't reckon at all on a wide circulation. Moreover, it's too disgusting to have anything to do with this tag-rag of Theatre-directors and Capellmeisters. You have heard something on that head from Steche [his Leipzig lawyer], then? I haven't had a letter from him lately; Mad. Steche's lines would much delight me.

Don't be vexed with me for having dished your concert hearing of the "Tannhäuser" overture; what you wrote me thereanent decided me to send prompt word to David [leader of Gewandhaus orch.] that I did *not* desire that performance. I want to have nothing to do with this pack of l—, I meant to say, of Leipzig musicants; I don't comport with them, and they therefore shouldn't fash themselves about me, for I know how that fashing turns out!—So—you save your thaler. [See *Life*, iii, 372-8.]

There, the sheet is drawing to an end, and I, poor beast, cannot do more at one sitting; so make the best of this jeremiad.—Should things ever thrive with me (pecuniarily), I hereby invite you and all your chicks to Switzerland at *my* expense : that's a bargain.—Best regards to husband Eduard from myself, with all the children.— Minna's wrapping New Year's gifts; Peps is snoring; and I—send love and thanks to you with all my heart. Farewell. Thy   RICHARD.

They've gammoned you a bit, with that villa. Two years ago we occupied a pig-stye in the country by the lake, which my friends facetiously dubbed " Villa Rienzi " ; maybe that's the charming villa !—

Minna declares she'll turn furious if I do not deliver her greetings to you and yours ; please furnish me with a receipt for them soon.

74. To the Same[1]

DEAR ——, *I hereby most cordially invite you to a reading of my lately-completed dramatic poem : " Der Ring des Nibelungen," whose several parts I propose to recite on four consecutive evenings (namely, 16th, 17th, 18th and 19th inst.) IN THE LOWER HALL OF THE DÉPENDANCE OF THE HÔTEL DE BAUR, commencing at 6 o'clock on each occasion.*

I should also be very glad to see any other gentleman or lady at these recitals whom, anticipating their friendly interest in the subject, you care to bring me uninvited. RICHARD WAGNER.

ZURICH, 12. *February* 1853.

I must say you're a pretty lot !—

So there was no special occasion to drop me a line ! Do you think, then, those two or three cuttings (which I might have got from anywhere) are sufficient to give me a notion of how my Tannhäuser turned out at Leipzig ?—You relatives are just the people to depend on, to get taken in ! For all that, I remain Thy loving brother

RICHARD.

14. *Febr.* 53.

---

[1] Address : " An/Frau/CECILIE AVENARIUS/Windmühlenstrasse/Leipzig./ fr.". The upper portion of the page is occupied by the formal printed invitation, below which comes the written note.

75. To niece Franziska Wagner (no date)

Dear Fränze—Do you think you could be so good as to remind Herr Stocks that upon every account I should very much like a word from him concerning " Lohengrin " ?

My consent to this opera's production went off to him a long time back, and I haven't yet had an answer about it. In any case it's of moment to me to ascertain how things stand with the matter. You owe me a letter ; won't you write soon to Thy
Uncle Richard ?

76. To Cäcilie Avenarius

Dear Sister—How gladly would I write long letters to yourself, the Steche, and the Riese; but I cannot contrive it ! I've an abominably extensive correspondence now, and so many letters to write, that it gives me a positive horror. Added to which, my countless minor labours constantly prevent my getting to a longed-for big ; ill-humour, chagrin, lassitude,— disgust, does each its part towards making me thoroughly sick of my life : I haven't a single joy.

I oughtn't to have told you that just now, though ; for, were I to be understood as if the letters from you all had given me no joy, I should be done an injustice. All the same—there's something in it—: *writing*, that odious having *to write !* Seeing—hearing—and speaking : there you have what would suit me, and bring me true joy. I should like to be under your roof,—then

all would go right ; even your own reproofs anent
my "egoism" would soon go to the right-about,
and you'd see there can't be any question of such
rubbish here.—But what can I write to you ?
Nothing else than that I hate all " writing," don't
want to write, but to speak and hear.

To-day I'm merely writing to yourself in haste,
after receiving your last lines. Fräulein Riese is
so anxious for my new poem : I am sending it.
There'll be " writing " enough for you all there ;
read it with gumption and it will tell you more
than ever I could write in letters.—I was fool enough
to send a copy to that . . . Brendel : Frau Steche
should borrow it off him at once ; I'm convinced
he hasn't read it yet. Put your heads together and
tell me how you like it.—

However, that isn't to say I shan't answer the
letters of all of you yet ; indeed they so went to
my heart, and so entirely bestowed on me the
genuine boon—of sympathy—that I can't think of
just pouching them this way ! ! Give my kindest
regards to that pair of dear ladies to-day ; come
all three of you to Switzerland this summer (when
Liszt is coming !)—and you shall be content with
me. Isn't Frau Riese a friend of Emilie Ritter's?
Money is bound to be getable,—if need be, I'll contribute toward it. The beginning of May I mean
to give my local friends something of mine to hear :
a grand musical performance of suitable pieces from
my last three operas. If it can be made to fit in,
perhaps I shall read my new poem as well.—

What sort of heroism was that of yours, to go
to Weimar ? Others have dared it before you ;

don't make such a fuss of it—or I shall bring the
" big bogey " [see *Life of W.*, i. 78].

Ach ! you're all crazy, and I am crazy, and—!

Just all of you wait till *I* present my things to
you ; you shall have a fit of the creeps then, I
promise you !

Adieu ; enough of nonsense. Every limb of
me is itching with impatience that I cannot—*talk*
with you. Farewell. Remembrances to all. Thy

R. W.

9. *March* [1853].

77. To FRANZISKA WAGNER

Well, how goes it, Fränze ? Are you coming,
after all, or weren't you really in earnest ? For
what you advanced about " Papa " wanting to
take you with them to " Paris in the Spring "
seemed a wee bit strange to me, as I had heard
nothing whatever of the Paris expedition commencing so soon as all that. If that was nothing
but flummery, then prove me further that your
entire plan of visiting me wasn't merely a fire of
straw, or I shan't believe you any more !—We
have moved into a larger abode now, in the same
house, and are most luxuriously equipped ; two
beds stand in waiting for guests.

The 18th, 20th and 22nd May I have a grand
performance of compositions of mine. I shan't
send you my new poem : if you come, you shall
receive it here ; and if you don't come, you won't
get it at all !—

Very kindest remembrances to Herr Stocks,

who has given me great delight again ; whenever
I receive a letter from him, I know that something
good is coming. I send him my best and heartiest
thanks once again.

One item more. People who don't come to see
me before *the end of June*, will not catch me at all.
July I go to baths in Graubünden, and end of
August to Italy. The beginning of *June*, too,
comes *Liszt*.

Now you know quite enough. Let us hear
from you soon, and be sure that your visit will
be giving Minna great pleasure as well. Adieu,
Fränze. Thy illustrious Uncle   R. W.

ZURICH, 17. *Apr.* 53.

78. To His niece Clara Brockhaus

(ZURICH, *June* 1853)

MY DEAR CLARA—Many thanks for your letter.
I didn't answer it at once, as I have had so much
to do of late with the music-performances of which
you'll have read, and finally was so greatly fatigued
by the exertion, that I was obliged to keep everything else off my neck for a while. After a little
repose I am setting to work to pay off letter debts,
and your name shall figure in my very first list.
To be sure, I haven't much to tell you ; in my
home and life there comes a flood-tide now and
then, but otherwise the rule is ebb. Had you
been here for my last birthday, though, you'd have
enjoyed yourself ; the music-performances gave
even myself great delight, and an affection was
shewn me on all sides that was bound to go

straight to my heart. O why, indeed, were *you* not there? Your parents couldn't do anything more sensible, than to pack you off to me some day. We are living in a very pretty, roomy flat now, where you would find quite comfortable quarters all the year round. As you're so burning for music and song, perhaps I might be of some use to you, and we could learn many a thing together. For my own part, I'm so longing for some young creature near me ; my possessing no children is a subject of grievous lament to me now. You, dear child, might be of great importance to me, perhaps determining all my future life ; and truly, I should thank you for it !—So I've been pondering how to set about kidnapping you from your parental home some day, at any rate for a while ; mightn't they be got to consent to your paying me a visit, if they could feel certain you'd come to no manner of harm here ? I rather fancy they'll be reasonable, and it would be a mere question of *how* you were to make the journey. And that we'd precious soon discover. I believe *Franziska* will be visiting me shortly ; probably somebody else would come with her, and you could join their party without any danger. How would it be, again, if your mother were to make a détour into Switzerland for once ? It couldn't hurt her in any way, and surely she might put up with us for a while ; when she could leave you behind. Have a good straight talk with her !

When you were here with me, we'd do a lot . . . (6 *lines cut away for the sake of the signature on their back*) . . . but if I am to understand you are

wishing to embark on a " carrière " as " singer,"
I almost think we should agree, after closer scrutiny,
that in the present condition of our public art (and
particularly our theatrical) the satisfaction of that
wish would be certain not to make you happy.
On the other hand—in my opinion—if you were
thoroughly equipped for it, you certainly might
practise art, and be of use to it, without entering a
profession which merely derives its name from art,
but not its title. We would have many a debate on
that, and I feel sure I should succeed in shewing
you the road to satisfaction of your wish without
your therefore having to enter the *profession* of
Singer. . . .

*(Lines cut off, as said: viz. greetings, date and
signature.)*

(Postscript on the margin :)
Perhaps Karl Ritter will bring you this letter.
Receive him kindly ; he belongs to the family to
whom alone I owe my present independence !

79. To Cäcilie Avenarius

That really is an 'orrible tale, dear Cecilie,
enough to give me the shivers,—but don't you let
a single hair turn grey on its account. I suppose
some spy supported here by Royal Saxony, not
knowing what news to report to his bread-givers,
let himself be stuffed with something, and in his
turn has stuffed up the Saxon police. I've *no idea*
of trespassing across the German frontier ; on the

contrary, I propose moving farther and farther
from it for this summer, as far as the Mediterranean Sea. So give your police my best compliments, and tell them they should put their cash
to better use than getting portraits made of me ;
further, that I hope they've made me look quite
handsome, I am wearing my hair long at present,
and have superb arched eyebrows [see *Life*, iv, 98 and
115].—

As a fact, the affair was very comic to me.
Someone was arguing with me the evening before
I got your letter, and bet a good round sum that
nobody would interfere with me if I went to
Germany straight off : the order would certainly
be issued from high quarters everywhere to ignore
my presence, and so on. I couldn't agree, and
maintained the contrary. What a joke it will be
now, to clap your letter under my friend's nose !—
I am starting this evening with Minna for
Interlaken and the Bernese Oberland ; thereafter
I shall be expecting Liszt here by the middle of
July. Why the Devil don't you accept, then, if
he's so determined to bring you ? Are you waiting for a special instigation from myself as well ?
Too ridiculous !—Mathilde Schiffner knows better ;
she is coming entirely of her own sweet will, in
mid-July, to pay Minna a visit and play ducks and
drakes with her morsel of savings. That's what
I call being human—though it's rather giddy to
expose oneself to the seductions of a journey all
alone !—
I'm very grateful for your last letters ; only,

don't be cross with me if I didn't answer quite at once. I have an appallingly extensive correspondence now, and am extremely averse to writing. Further, I've felt very tired of late from my music-performances. The latter were splendid, however—nay, divine ; I received the purest and finest impressions, and they have remained with me. Believe me, not a soul of you knows my music unless I present it myself ; my latest discovery !—

Best compliments to the Steche and Riese ; they aren't to be angry if I've written to neither again yet, but let them be sure their letters gave me great delight.—Years hence I contemplate producing all my works complete here—the future ones as well : how, and with what means, must still be my secret,—when I hope to see you all here. But—the Saxon police will not catch me,— they may wager their truncheons on that ; my longing for the precious fatherland is far too faint.—

Farewell ; love to Eduard and the children— from me and Minna. Thy RICHARD.

ZURICH,
20. *June* 1853.

80. TO CLARA BROCKHAUS (—*address not preserved*)

DEAR CHILD—As you wish it, I'm briefly answering your anxious lines at once ; for which accept my warmest thanks.

What may be at the back of the latest tom-foolery that scared you all so,—whether a local

spy duped the Saxon police, or what not—the
Lord alone knows ! So much is certain : I hadn't
the remotest idea of going to Germany, but may
contentedly leave the bad performances of my
operas there to proceed without my presence. On
the contrary, I wrote you a little time back that I
thought of going to Graubünden for baths soon,
and then taking a trip to the Mediterranean (Nice,
Genoa, etc.). And that brings me to my last
letter, which you do not mention at all. I sent it
to Karl Ritter at Dresden, who was to bear it you
by hand ; presumably he hasn't done so. I will
remind him to-day to let you have that letter,
which you *must answer, whatever you do*.

Unfortunately I can't spare you any more time
to-day. Liszt is on a visit to me, and we're having
a fine game of it, a perfect riot of delightful confi-
dences, whilst every hour has its feast. You might
just as well have been here too !—

Hoping this scrap will have reassured you and
yours, I send them all my kindest love, and to
yourself my hearty thanks for your affection, which
gives me great joy. Drop a line again soon to
Thy   RICHARD W.

ZURICH,
4. *July* 1853.

81. TO CÄCILIE AVENARIUS

DEAR COUNCILLORESS—What a chapter of
accidents !—Frau Steche's letter and album arrived
here while I was taking a cure at St. Moritz—
Graubünden ; on my return to Zurich I found
them both among a mass of other parcels that

couldn't be sent after me to the baths for fear of
robbing me of all repose and relaxation. I only
stayed a little while at Zurich ere going on to
Italy ; before which I had to polish off a crowd of
applications and consignments, with the greatest
repugnance, including the writing to unsuccessful
composers on the works I'm so lucky as to receive
from them now by the dozen ; and then, my
other correspondence ! I always prefer getting
through with such bothers as quickly as possible,
—so a great clearance had to be made before
I could think of the album-leaf for Fr. Steche.
In the end, I was half seated in the diligence
when that leaf began to prick my conscience ;
luckily something occurred to me—the swan's
song omitted from Lohengrin—and I inscribed it
post-haste [see *Life of W.*, ii, 156]. Fr. Steche
was to have had a *letter* from Italy, where I
promised myself a thorough good idling and
therefore meant writing to *many* I had merely
disposed of in brief,—to whom did I not intend
to write !—but alas, the humour for it never came :
I fell sick at Genoa, and after fighting with the
decision 4 days, at last made for home at full
speed. Arrived here, I learn that *your* letter is
actually en route for Genoa ; whence it has only
just returned to-day.

May the above explain much—to yourself and
to others. To-day I'm therefore simply writing
to set matters straight. If Brendel *hasn't* read
[the *Ring* aloud] yet, neither is he to ; I never
wished to have this manuscript made known, and
it can't belong to anyone except myself as yet.

Let it be divulged to *as few other people as possible;* it would only lead to tiresome misunderstandings.—

Minna is by no means " getting stout and fat " just now ; on the contrary, she is so thoroughly unwell, that her condition fills me with concern and care. Anyhow, I must spare her as much as I can, and allow her a rest ; so I am trying to cocker her,—as the poor thing but deserves. At the moment she's away at Baden on a cure (4 leagues from here) ; I visit her daily, which keeps me on the constant move. So excuse me if I'm only writing on tiptoe.

For the rest, don't lament over me so ! Julius did very wisely, not to shew you my letter. Adieu. Greet left and right. Thy

RICHARD.

ZURICH,
15. *Sept.* 1853.

82. TO EDUARD AVENARIUS

DEAR EDUARD, MOST HONOURABLE TOWN-COUNCILLOR !—You know I never come to *you* except " on business " ; so don't start growling if I blurt it out straight off !

Here goes :

" It is absolutely necessary to have a new drain laid in the Petersstrasse—"

No, you must get that sort of petition presented to you by the ratepayers.

Let's have another try :—

Out of the solidest correction-house in Saxony I received the other day a five-sheet letter from my former colleague, königl. Musikdirector

Röckel. Among other things, he is under the delusion that I stand in relation with " book-dealers," and consequently begs me to obtain him orders, in particular for translations from the English. At present he's translating a book by the American philosopher EMERSON—I believe—for O. Wigand, but fears the latter won't be able to keep him occupied enough in future. Well, it occurs to me that you're the only man I can approach ; for J. J. Weber, after all, is nearer Wigand than to me.[1] I therefore beseech you to give the poor prisoner an order, if you possibly can, and if it comports with your business. You can do it direct, if you address your letter to the Governor of the penitentiary ; otherwise *I* might act as go-between myself.

So much for business,—now I've nothing further to do, than to send you hearty good wishes, and to Frau Stadträthin into the bargain.

I am going to Basle next week, for a rendez-vous with various Karlsruhe-Musical-Festivallers who want to pay me their respects ; whence I shall go on with Liszt to Paris for a week. If you have any commissions for there, let me know. Adieu !
Thy   RICHARD W.
    ZURICH,
  28. *Sept.* 1853.

83. TO CÄCILIE AVENARIUS

But have you lost all your knowledge of me, dear Cecilie, can you interpret my nature so little, that you misunderstand my mostly jocular, but

---

[1] The meaning here is obscure : "denn J. J. Weber liegt doch Wigand näher als mir."—TR.

always *intimate* brusqueness so entirely as appears to be the case when you declare I've pained you once again with my last letter? To whom shall one behave sans gêne, then, if not even to one's brothers and sisters?—Be ashamed of your suscepti- bility,—and let us hear no more of that fresh piece of rudeness!—

This moment I've written a note to the Steche, which you no doubt will attend to? The other billet please consign to your town-post; Herr Steche will explain it to you.—

I stayed on in Paris with Minna another week after Liszt's departure. Kietz and Anders were flourishing. Of course we kept quite to ourselves, and all the gossip in the papers about my Paris doings was pure nonsense.—

I compose of a morning now, and only occasion- ally write letters in the afternoon, etc. ; when I never feel up to it, though. For the rest, I am living here as if in the country, completely retired. I have plenty of fame now, it seems ; as for money, it's so-so : I never have any,—just like me.—

Minna's condition of health gives me great concern ; she is falling away, of a sudden, and getting so thin as to frighten me.—Natalie is to come back and relieve her of housekeeping ; there's nothing else for it, she fags herself so. Best thanks for seeing to the letter.

Was *Eduard* able to do anything for R(öckel) in Waldh(eim)? Best regards to him.

I'm wanting to coach up *Peps* for Lohengrin ; anyway better than Widemann [Leipzig ?], of whom I hear shocking accounts !—

This is a terrible scrawl ; what you can't read, you must guess at ! Write again soon. Adieu, dear sister. Thy RICHARD.

ZURICH,
22. *Dec.* 53.

84. TO CLARA BROCKHAUS

MY DEAR CLÄRCHEN—Many thanks for your kind letter ; it was a thorough treat to me. My mind had been much occupied with you again of late ; your coming-out at Leipzig afforded the occasion. I was delighted that people found fault with your singing too passionately (or what was it?). If you intend to be a concert-singer, and want letters patent for it, you must trim your sails another way, whatever you do, and take a pattern from the Mayer, that beau idéal of Leipzig taste in song. No doubt you'll have learnt how they murdered my Lohengrin there ; of such are the joys my dear fatherland gives me. However, I already have abandoned Lohengrin as well ; they may do with it as they like !—

With the Nibelungen it will be another story ; I am not writing those for the theatre, but—for ourselves ! All the same, I shall produce them ; that is the sole and final life-task I have set myself. I shall build my own stage for them, and train my own performers : how many years it may take me, is quite immaterial if I only attain it some day. After the production I shall fling myself and score upon Brünnhilde's pyre, that all may burn away.—

But what are you really going to do with your voice ? If you want to become my Brünnhilde, tell your father he must let you loose in two years' time ; I hope to have finished the whole music by then, and then my man-hunt will commence. It would be grand to find yourself !—

I have been diligent since I got back from Paris. I cannot take to anything but work now ; I benumb myself with it, and smother up my wretched life. Since November the " Rheingold " has been begun and ended, all but the instrumenting I'm at work on still. In the summer I shall compose the " Walküre " ; spring of next year, it will be the turn of " Young Siegfried " ; so that by the summer of the year after next I expect to have got through with " Siegfried's Death " as well. Then you will come — at latest — won't you ?—

What's that sage Ottchen doing ? Not consulting Fräulein Eule, is she ?—But where do you really live now ? You never send me an address. I am having another shot at Prossen.

How are Father and Mother ? I heard they were tired of their country place ; why don't they try a Swiss trip, for a change ?

To tell the truth—'tis yourself I sorely lack ; a greater joy could not befall me, than your coming to me soon. Your aunt, too, would be highly delighted ; she is heartily fond of you. Of course I can't blame your father for not wanting to part with you ; but he should come too !—

Dear child, farewell. Greet your people, and give Ottchen a kiss. Now let me hear again

soon :—hear ?—unfortunately all I can mean by
it, is to see something in writing !

Adieu, accept my thanks once more, and remember me ever with love !—Thy

RICHARD W.

ZURICH,
12. *March* 54.

85. TO EDUARD AVENARIUS

(ZURICH, 3. (?) *July* 1854).[1]

DEAR EDUARD—Do see if you can't shew me
a truly great favour !

I am in a very painful, though transient,
pecuniary fix. Not till the late summer or autumn
can I reckon with certainty on fairish receipts,
whilst sundry pressing debts (unpaid accounts) are
now becoming such a bugbear to me, that I'm
almost ashamed to go out ; added to which, I
have endorsed a bill or two myself—to assist those
concerned,—so that I *must* find money to go on
with. My only local friend who has always helped
me out of straits of this kind [J. Sulzer] is so deeply
involved in the railways just now, that he cannot
lay hands on a farthing of cash. *Liszt*, who
previously has helped me from without, is in a
great quandary himself. As I had to write to
Brendel a little while ago, I begged him to see
if there weren't one to be found among all my
admirers who would lend me a *thousand thaler on
note of hand* for 4 or 5 months ;—he, also, has

---

[1] Undated, and envelope not preserved. Recipient's endorsement,
" 1854, 3. July."

P

hideously delayed his answer, and writes me at last to-day that he knows of none, unless it were *Härtels*, or if you could pull it off through *Mendelssohn* [E. A.'s partner ; see p. 163].

So, it really being nothing but a question of assistance in a passing fix, I end by giving my related chest a thump, and turning to yourself with a plea for intervention. If it could be done through your associé, undoubtedly I should like that best ; since Härtels—as I think I incidentally informed you—have shewn themselves petty and shy on a similar occasion (I offered to sell them my copyright in my operas). I will give a formal *note of hand* for the end of this year—as said—if that may be ; but should it facilitate realisation, I could also make it out for 4, or even 3 months, as my harvest-time will come then. I'm sure the bill will land me in no difficulty, since enquiries for my operas are already pouring in, and without the least exaggeration I may compute my coming autumn takings at a couple of thousand thaler. To set your private mind at ease, however, I may tell you that in the worst event, of my not having amassed the whole sum by the term of expiry, I could count with certainty on the assistance of another friend [O. Wesendonck], who would be only too happy—I know it—to oblige me like this. He is away for a few months now,—and—to tell the truth—I should not care to demean myself— as it would be, a little—in the eyes of this family, unless in the *direst* extremity. Sapienti sat !—

So just see, you good Stadtrath, if you're able to help me. Promptitude—as I have shewn you

—is essential. I'm off to Sitten for the Music-feast, but shall be back here in a week.—

Minna is at her whey-cure already on the Lake of Lucerne. The weather also, which you ruined for us with your trip to Glarus, has turned fine again to-day at last.—How did the whole outing agree with you?—

Best love to Cecilie, remember ; I hope to get a leisure hour en route, to answer her last dear letter.

I've been industrious again ; the " Walküre " is commenced !—

Adieu ! Send good news soon to Thy

R. W.

86. To the Same

DEAREST BROTHER-IN-LAW—Please do not be cross with me for leaving your kind letter so long without an answer.—I regret my having been so gauche as to bother you with a money-affair I might have easily guessed that you could only feel disquietude about, not be able to procure assistance in. Brendel's injudicious hint was to blame for it. Don't let the matter grieve you any more ; even if things aren't going altogether as I wish, especially as I'm getting remarkably fewer orders this autumn than I believed I might hope for—perhaps on account of " bad times "—that is absolutely not to give you any care yourself. There'll always be a screw loose with me, you see : if I were thoroughly happy—I should need hardly any money at all ; but like this, I keep oscillating between an often quite eccentric craving for the sweets of life and—loathing of life itself; whilst as artist and man, on the other hand, I become more and more incapable of making the smallest concessions to the wage-paying world of to-day. Let us drop that ! !—

It amused me, all the same, to have this opportunity of feeling the pulse of the enthusiasm I've aroused; it remained sheer impossible to beat up 1000 thr from that enthusiasm for a couple of months.—However, we'll drop that, as said; 'twould be inexplicable, were it otherwise !

My wife has just started. She is going to *Zwickau* first, where she has given her parents rendez-vous at the house of other relatives ; thence she will visit Cläre at Chemnitz, and go on to a lady friend in Berlin [Alwine Frommann] for a brief time, paying yourselves a tiny visit first at Leipzig. You might let her know in a fortnight, say at Chemnitz, whether she'll catch you and Cecilie.—

Minna must tell you how we have got on [since you left].—That *Gastrophie* book has become her inseparable ; she has taken it on her journey. Sulzer declares that Vaerst [its author] doesn't understand an atom of his subject, and is nothing but a gas-bag.—

I am working like mad, to get my Nibelungen finished for next Easter fair ; of course you know I'm writing them for the Polish Jews and sideshows.—

Farewell. Don't be cross with me again.

Despise me, if it must be, but—hold me dear as Thy brother-in-law   R. W.

     Best love to Cecilie ! !

     ZURICH, 2. *Sept.* 1854.

[For almost another four years, *i.e.* down to Wagner's removal from Zurich, the only " Family " letter as yet discoverable is the following to a favourite niece.—TR.]

87. TO CLARA BROCKHAUS[1]

     ZURICH, 28. *Jan.* 57.

MY DEAR CLÄRCHEN—You see, I haven't forgotten you! Let that be enough for you, and forgive my not having answered your letter so long. Anyone who had a good look into my life, would rather wonder at my having any relish left for this and that from time to time. I never have true rest : either great excitement during work, or great, prolonged exhaustion following it. In between I am seldom in the mood for a letter, and still seldomer have anything agreeable to relate. I wanted to write you in a thoroughly good hour, but my conscience warns me not to be too expectant of it any longer, and before all else to rid you of the possible idea that I purposely refrained from writing you.

Above all, accept my hearty congratulations on your betrothal. Naturally I couldn't help smiling

---

[1] A fragment. The letter originally consisted of a double leaf of octavo, folded in three. From this the bottom third of the second leaf, containing the signature, has first been cut away with scissors, and then the whole remainder of that leaf torn off,—manifestly for the benefit of autograph-collecting friends.

at the shade of timidity with which you announced
your betrothed to me as Officer. Do you folk
really think me such a mass of prejudice, that a
man's profession could bias me against him?
Then I must tell you that, oddly enough, I have
met most outspoken enthusiasts for my operas in
the Officer calling, and at Dresden in particular I
always had very staunch friends among the officers
of the Guards. From that you will see that even
personal vanity must have stripped me of my prejudice. But, putting that aside—all I wish to be
convinced, is that you have made your choice with
all your heart : if that is so, as you assure me, then
commence your young wedlock and welcome, and
be assured, on my side, of my best wishes. In
which case my wife sends gratulation also from a
brimming heart.

(Conclusion missing.)

[For the events between this letter and the next, with
the final departure from Zurich, see *Life of Wagner*, vol.
vi, and the "Minna" and "Mathilde" volumes.—Tr.]

88. To sister Clara Wolfram

GENEVA, 20. *August* 58.

My dear Cläre.—I promised you further
particulars as to the causes of the critical step you
see me now engaged in. I therefore tell you what
is needful to enable you to counter any other
gossip ; toward which, however, I'm most indifferent myself.

What has supported, comforted, and above all

strengthened me since six years past to endure by
Minna's side despite the enormous differences in
our characters and dispositions, is the affection of
that young gentlewoman who at first and for long
drew near me diffidently, hesitant and shy, but
then with more and more decided confidence. As
there never could be any question of union between
us, our deep attachment took that wistful character
which holds all coarse and vulgar things aloof, and
discerns its only source of gladness in the other's
welfare. Since the period of our very first
acquaintance she had nursed the most unremitting
and sensitive care for me, and courageously obtained
from her husband whatever might lighten my life.
. . .[1] And this love, which had remained un-
uttered by a syllable between us, was at last to
cast aside its veil when I wrote the poem of my
Tristan, just a year ago, and gave it to her. Then
for the first time did she lose her self-command,
and declare to me she e'en must die!

Reflect, dear sister, what this love must have
meant to me, after a life of toil and suffering,
sacrifice and tumult, such as mine! Yet we
recognised forthwith that no union could ever be
thought of between us, and were resigned ; abjur-
ing every selfish wish, we suffered and endured,
but—loved!—

My wife seemed to grasp the situation with
shrewd feminine instinct. True, she often acted

[1] The passage here omitted from the German edition, equal to about a
whole page, will be found *in loco* in my Introduction to the "*Mathilde
Wesendonck*" volume of the master's letters. Personally I see no reason for
suppressing it—in fact, the contrary—but in deference to my friend Herr
Glasenapp (who presumably complies with Wahnfried wishes) I follow his
example in the present place.—Tr.

jealously, deriding and running down ; yet she tolerated our intercourse, which upon its side never contravened morality, but was simply aimed at being in each other's company. So I assumed Minna to be sensible enough to comprehend that there was strictly nothing here for her to fear, as no union was to be dreamt of between us, and therefore that forbearance was her best and most advisable policy. Well, I had to learn that I must have deceived myself in that ; tittle-tattle came to my ears, and finally she so far lost her senses as to intercept a letter from me—and break it open. That letter itself, had she been in any position to understand it, might really have afforded her the fullest reassurance she could wish ; for our resignation formed *its* theme as well. But she went by nothing save its familiar expressions, and lost her head. She came to me raving, and thereby compelled me to explain to her with quiet firmness how things stood, that she had brought misfortune on herself by opening such a letter, and if she didn't know how to control herself, we two must part. We came to agreement on that point, I calmly, she passionately. The next day, however, I felt sorry for her. I went to her, and said : " Minna, you're very poorly ; get well first, and let us have another talk about it then." We hit on the plan of a cure for her, and she seemed to quiet down. The day of departure approaching, she insisted on speaking to the Wesendonck first : I stoutly forbade it. My whole object was to make her gradually acquainted with the character of my relations to that lady, thus convincing her

that there was nothing at all to fear for the continuance of our wedded life, wherefore she had
only to behave wisely, sensibly and nobly, renounce
all foolish vengeance and avoid any manner of
fuss. At last she promised me this. But it gave
her no peace : behind my back she went across,
notwithstanding, and — doubtless without even
realising it — she insulted the gentle soul most
grossly. So, after Minna's telling her, " Were I
an ordinary woman, I should take this letter to
your husband," nothing remained for the Wesendonck—conscious of never having kept a secret
from her husband (which a woman like Minna, of
course, can't comprehend !)—but to inform him at
once of this scene and its cause.

Herewith the nicety and purity of our relations
had been invaded in a coarse and vulgar way, and
many a thing must change. Not till quite late
could I succeed in proving to my fair friend that
the very loftiness and unselfishness of such relations
as subsisted between ourselves must make them
forever incapable of explanation to a nature like
my wife's ; for I was met by her grave reproach,
that I had omitted this, whereas she had always
had her husband for a confidant.

Whoever can fathom what I've suffered since
(it was the middle of April then), will comprehend
how I feel in the end, now that I have to recognise
that the most unceasing efforts to preserve those
troubled relations have borne no fruit at all. For
three months I had Minna tended at the health-
resort with every care ; to pacify her, at last I
broke off all association with our neighbours during

that period ; careful only for her health, I tried
everything possible to bring her to reason and
recognition of what beseemed her and her time of
life : all in vain ! She abides by the most ludicrous
fancies, declares herself injured, and, scarce allayed
a little, the old fury soon bursts forth afresh.
Since a month back, when Minna returned—while
we had guests in the house—it had to come to a
final decision. The two women so close together,
was impossible any longer ; for neither could the
Wesendonck forget that, in return for her supreme
self-sacrifice and most delicate regard for me, she
had been met upon my side, through my wife, so
coarsely and insultingly. Moreover, people had
begun to talk. Enough : the most unheard-of
scenes and tortures never ceased for me, and out
of consideration as much for the one as the other,
I finally had to determine to give up the pretty
asylum once provided me with such tender affection.
Now I require rest and the completest seclusion,
for the grief I have to weary down is great.—

Minna is incapable of comprehending what an
unhappy wedlock ours has always been ; she
pictures the whole past as something other than
it was, and if I've found relief, distraction and
oblivion in my art, she even may believe I never
needed them. Enough : I have made up my
mind on all that ; no longer can I tolerate this
eternal bickering and mistrust around me, if I'm
to have any heart left to fulfil my life-task.
Anybody who has watched me closely, must have
been surprised from of old at my patience, my
kindness, nay, weakness ; and if I'm now con-

demned by superficial judges, I've grown insensible
to such a thing. Never has Minna had a finer
opportunity of shewing herself more worthy to be
my wife, than now, when it was a matter of pre-
serving the highest and dearest to me : it lay in
her own hands to prove if she verily loved me,
but she doesn't even understand what true love is,
and her fury sweeps down all restraint!—

However, I excuse her by her illness ; not
but that even this might have assumed a milder
character, had her own been gentler. Moreover,
the many tribulations she has suffered with me,
over which my inner genius (which I have never,
alas, been able to impart to her) has lightly borne
myself, move me to considerateness towards her ;
I fain would give her as little pain as possible, for,
when all's told, I'm very sorry for her. Only, I
feel incapable henceforward of abiding by her side ;
neither can I be of any good to herself by it : I
shall always be incomprehensible and an object of
suspicion to her. Therefore—divided ; but in all
kindness and love! I would not have her shamed ;
merely, I wish her to recognise in time, herself,
that it is better if we do not see each other much
again. For the present I leave her the prospect of
my rejoining her in Germany, when the amnesty
arrives,—which also was the reason she was to
take all our furniture and things with her ; though
I mean to bind myself to nothing, but let everything depend upon my future mood. So please
adhere to it, yourself, that the present is only to be
a passing separation. Whatever you can do to
make her calm and reasonable, I beg you not to

leave undone, for—as said—she really is unfortunate ; she would have been happier with a lesser man. And so take pity on her with myself; I shall thank you for it from my heart, dear sister !—

I shall wait here in Geneva a bit till I can go on to Italy, where I think of passing the winter, presumably in Venice ; the solitude and removal from all torturing company are reviving me somewhat already. It was a sheer impossibility to think of work of late ; once I recover the mood to go on composing' my Tristan, I shall consider myself saved. Indeed I must attempt to help myself that way ; I ask nothing of the world, except to leave me leisure for the works that are to belong to it hereafter : may it therefore also judge me mildly!—

The contents of this letter, dear Cläre, you are welcome to use for explanations wherever needful ; in general, however, I naturally shouldn't care for much talk about what has taken place. Only the very fewest, you see, will *understand* the case here ; for that, one needs to know the parties well.

Now farewell, dear sister, and hearty thanks once more for your discreet enquiry, which I have answered, as you see, in confidence. Treat Minna indulgently, but also let her gradually become aware what she is doing with me.—Thy brother

RICHARD W.

89. To Cäcilie Avenarius

VENICE, 28. *Jan.* 59.

Let me assure you, dear Cecilie, even without your letter of to-day I should shortly have written you ; my not having answered you a year ago has been a constant load upon my conscience, and that not merely as a debt. I'm living so boundlessly alone, that I hardly live on aught save ties of fantasy and recollection now ; yet, however wide that circle's compass, you have often risen up therein. Only the other day I was intending to enquire for your address ; so much the better to have obtained it from yourself. Best thanks for to-day's information ; I had learnt nothing of the Berlin Lohengrin [première Jan. 23] beyond what a telegram of Bülow's told me, [namely, that] it had turned out tolerably and been well received. The first point, and whether it would satisfy me, I will leave in abeyance ; as things are standing with me now, the second matters most to me, for my only further interest in life is bound up with takings of this sort (I always get the best returns from the worst productions !). My works are doomed to give me joy for only just so long as I'm at work on them ; once finished, I have nothing but worry with them, and the sole redeeming feature is their supplying the means for fresh work by making life possible to me.

Father Geyer's face lies constantly before me now upon my writing-table. A Zurich acquaintance, who is also a friend of Hermann Br[ockhaus]'s sons, on a journey to Leipzig obtained me a most successful, particularly skilful photograph of the portrait, and surprised and touched me very much with it on his return. It is one of the extremely few things I took with me on my departure from Zurich. Thus it forms a link through which I feel connected with the world; whereas the feeling of detachment and solitariness is otherwise preponderant. I wrote to Ottilie and thanked her ; [1] she never answered me. Some time ago I had need of a book published by Brockhaus, but it was too expensive for me to buy. So I wrote to Hermann, gave him my news, and begged him to obtain me this book—as if for himself—were it only on loan.[1] He, too, has not replied to me ; which really ought to have been done, at least by Yes or No, to a request.

The more pleased am I, that you haven't let yourself be deterred by my silence. Your previous letter came at a terrible time of suffering. The true source of the untold griefs and sorrows that rained on me last year lies in my wife's sad state of health. However insensately and passionately she behaved in the most delicate situations, I cannot after all be really wroth with her for that. Everyone suffers in his own way, and she suffers in—hers ; but she is suffering, and did suffer most acutely. Only think of a heart continually beating as never with an ordinary person save in instant peril of death ; and added to it almost total sleeplessness for a whole year ! It isn't possible to make anyone who suffers such agonies responsible for what is done in semi-mania. Yet it had at last become unbearable for us to be together. To be able to go on existing, I was obliged to draw a fresh supply of strength from solitude ; and Minna, too, I knew that change and possible diversion must do her good. As a

---

[1] Neither of these letters is preserved.

fact, she seems fairly progressing at Dresden ;
though I learn, to my sorrow, that she has come
very much under the influence of backbiters again.
Now that, myself, I've recovered some peace and
composure, I am resolved to treat her always with
that kind indulgence she needs so urgently if her
condition, which essentially is governed by the
mind, is to be improved to some extent. Her life
is so entirely laid in my hand, that, just as I
might swiftly deal her death, of course I can only
stretch it forth to tend her.

I shall not arrive at writing Clara yet awhile ;
what I should have to discuss with her, exhausts
me too much. Please write to her yourself, though,
not to read my last lecture amiss. I thought I
recognised from Minna's letters at the time she
was with Cläre that, with the best intention—and,
I almost believe, the shrewdest insight—the latter
was trying to exert a certain active influence on
her regarding her relations with myself. To
some extent my letter from Geneva had authorised
her to. But everything that can or could affect
me had to be entirely left out of account by myself
in the end, when I came to dwell on nothing but
the anguished woman's pitiful condition, particularly with her awful complaint. It seemed to me
as if everyone she approached must feel the same,
and I therefore begged Cläre completely to shun
every topic that might agitate Minna afresh.
Perhaps that offended her. If she will reflect,
however, that all's too late here, and it can merely
be a wholly profitless and bootless cruelty, to
bring Minna to a sense of her true relation to me,

I comfort myself with the thought that she [Clara] is bound to agree that, the *one* course being quite impossible, it is better to keep the possible other alone in view : namely, to wheedle the unhappy one, and help her thus to bear the remnant of an inevitably wan and trying life in peace. That is exactly what I myself am determined to ; for the solitary weal I still can taste is that of—dealing others as little woe as possible. Who stands the very nearest to me, thereby knows how to help herself ; my greatest care accordingly is for her who understands me so little.—

As to the future shaping of my outward life I can tell you next to nothing yet, though I heartily thank you for your interest in it. I scarce can hope for pardoning by the King of Saxony ; yet it is not impossible that a combination of several German princes friendly to me may succeed in getting me the German Bund's restricted leave to stay in certain of its States—with the exception of Saxony. That is bound to be decided this year. Meanwhile it's settled that my new work, "Tristan und Isolde," is to have its first performance in September at Carlsruhe. I think of passing next winter with Minna again. Where—will much depend upon the condition of her health ; in any case I shall have to try and find a particularly mild southern climate for her. But all that is quite in the clouds. Paris I abominate ; Venice suits me well enough for the present. Here I am living as if out of the world, between sky and sea, in great retirement. Unfortunately I have often been ill, though not dangerously, yet

most depressingly. I think of staying here till
June.—

Occasion serving, please ask Eduard if he
would give himself the trouble of considering, and
—if it isn't too much to him—reporting to me
how I best might bring my poem of the " Nibe-
lungen-Ring " successfully before the public. I
can't help fancying that this poem ought to draw
and hold attention purely for itself, as literature ;
but even the outward get-up should be directed to
that, and the way in which Härtels regard and
handle such a thing—as mere appurtenance to an
article in their musical catalogue—I never shall
approve of. Do beg Eduard about it !—

I have an interruption this instant, and must
conclude.

Farewell, my good sister ; remember me, and
send me news more often. If I do not answer at
once, don't think it indifference. I am always in
sorrow, but mostly for others, and any tinge of
bitterness decreases in me more and more.

It has done me good to have a moment's chat
with you. Give your husband and children my
hearty greetings, and rest assured of my continual
sympathy and love. Thy brother

RICHARD.

90. To Clara Wolfram

LUCERNE, 7. *April* 59.

Best thanks for your letter, dear Cläre. Don't
be cross with me, if I write but little in reply.
You would hardly believe the size my correspond-

ence has gradually increased to, and how chary I often must be of words, not to have to break off work entirely.

Now for it! First as regards that allowance to Julius, you're really taking too much trouble. Once and for all, I will pay the 5 louis d'or annually; if I'm able, it shall also be more. I should prefer not sending it before the end of summer, as my takings improve towards autumn. So, never another word on that!—

In the next place, I hope you understood me well enough, not to take offence at my begging you last autumn to avoid every subject with Minna that might excite her? At that time she was writing me with greater and greater heat and passion, so that I was bound to assume there was far too much discussion with her of that ticklish point. Of course I might have known it would be difficult, in fact impossible to elude her, and in my request to you there wasn't the faintest reproach; yet I felt I couldn't do enough to ensure a tranquillising influence on her all round. A heart like hers, that absolutely refuses to come to a rest, is a dreadful affliction; I was deeply grieved for her, and as I saw plainer and plainer that it was sheer impossible to work through reason on her reason, I recognised that there was only one choice—either to treat her with considerate cajolery, always evading, simply soothing, ignoring all that issued from her,—or frankly and definitely to abandon her to her misery. It is a matter of course that I could only choose the former. So far as anyway possible to me, I have treated her in all my letters according to this principle, now seriously, anon with jest ; and the effect has seemed proving of gradual benefit to her. I am not letting her go short of money, ample money for a really pleasant life, and have just supplied her again with enough to lead a life of truly elegant comfort the whole summer through. God only grant that all this, with the summer cure at Schandau, may have so radically improving an effect on her, that she may make it possible for me to re-entrust my home to her this autumn without having to fear that fresh relapses into her old condition should rob us both of any further hope !

As for myself, this solitude is doing me a world of good. True, I have often been unwell, but it has never weighed upon my spirit. Within me is the fairest, deepest calm. What confers it on me, and makes its maintenance possible, is the noblest and most touching experience of all my life : here everything is high upraised above the common ; incredible sacrifice, but peace profound. I live still, to complete my works,—for that alone ; and for that, towards that, I am helped.—Sufficient intimation !—

I expect to write my third act here ; I am in capital mood for it.—Farewell, dear Cläre ; be thanked for your sisterly love, and ever count on my reciprocation. Thy brother   RICHARD.

(SCHWEIZERHOF.)

[September of that year Richard Wagner removes to Paris, where he is rejoined by Minna mid-November and they live together till the summer of 1861.—Tr.]

91. To Eduard Avenarius

Paris, 10. *May* 1860.

Dearest Eduard—I've a big petition for you. —I want my Nibelungen pieces to appear very soon—in fact, at once—as poem. The first piece, das Rheingold, will shortly be coming out in the vocal score, and I want to lay the entire poem before the public simultaneously. I haven't the smallest intention, however, of letting this poem appear at the music-publisher's (this time Schott of Mainz) ; like my earlier ones, it would reach little else than musicians, as " opera-text," and be only regarded as such ; whereas I scarcely need impress on you, who know this poem, how idiotic a point de départ that would be. Consequently I'm on the look out for a firm whose very name would give the book its due importance, and can't help thinking Cotta is the most appropriate for that ; so I require someone who would offer Cotta my poem with the needful weight of recommendation. An author of repute would seem to me the best ; but I stand on closer terms with none. Therefore, as I hear you're still a sort of dealer in books, and anyhow you retain old connections completely denied to myself, I most cordially beg you to take this matter in hand.

My business views in its regard are—tentatively —as follows :—

I expect of this poem a widespread and popular success with the reading public also, particularly in course of time. That success is bound to be both heightened and made most enduring by eventual

performances of the single pieces at the theatres.
I have granted the music-publisher the right—
for the present with Rheingold—to print the
pieces *separately* (in cheap editions) without any
stage-directions, as text-books for the theatre-goer;
but I have specifically reserved to myself the
issuing of the whole poem in one, and it is this
I now offer the book-man I have my eye on.
Methinks the work should rouse great interest at
its very first appearance ; then, when the vocal
score of Rheingold gets among the public,
musicians too will feel a want to make the *whole*
poem's acquaintance. The same want will repeat
itself still more strongly with Rheingold's actual
production ; and so on with every subsequent
production of the successive single parts, which I
have resigned myself, as you see, to bring out
separately and one by one. So there'll be quite
an unusual sequence of good openings for the
poem's publisher.—For a commencement, I believe
I ought to stand out for an edition of 2000 copies,
at somewhere about 2 thaler net per copy (handsomely got up). My fee for this edition would
have to be on the customary scale ; then fresh
stipulations, no doubt, for every new edition.

Now see, dearest Eduard, what you can contrive for me. The thing's a little pressing now,
as I've let a deal of time slip by, and the vocal
score of Rheingold is being already engraved.

I daresay you would meantime lend the
publisher, to have a look at, the copy I once
committed to the hands of you and Cecilie. As
soon as he makes up his mind, I will rapidly revise

the manuscript once more, and send it from here to be printed.

For the rest, dearest friend, excuse any lengthier news from me. I shouldn't know where to begin, and my relations have swollen to such an excess now, particularly through my distance from Germany, that, what with correspondence etc., I hardly ever get a moment to myself. Merely this much : negotiations with Dresden regarding my return to Germany are now proceeding under very favourable auspices. Tannhäuser will be given at the Grand Opera here (by command); which—without my knowledge—I owe to Princess Metternich. Everything stands at my disposal, in consequence ; only I have no money yet, but on the contrary, have had to shell out terribly.

Much hearty love to Cecilie. Minna is doing quite passably.

Farewell, and be good to me ! Thy

RICHARD W.

16 RUE NEWTON,
    CHAMPS ELYSÉES.

92. TO THE SAME

PARIS, 6. *June* 1860.

DEAREST BROTHER-IN-LAW—Best thanks for your careful and obliging answer. I have followed your advice since, and applied to Cotta direct : he has declined, alleging war-funk. I foresaw it, though not precisely the war-funk. Believe me, it isn't laziness, if I beg you afresh to take this matter up for me. Even my despatching the book from here is attended with fatal difficulties :

I haven't had my copy back from Cotta yet ; it may have got lost—and is *the last* I possess.

So—whether you prefer J. Weber or a Berlin publisher, I beg you to regard yourself as invested with my fullest authority to bring the thing off. Do reflect how unversed I am in book-trade matters. For instance, you tell me I had better make a definite demand at once : yes, but what ? I only look for what's reasonable and proportional ; but how the Devil should I know what that is ? If I ask for this or that specific sum, it's certain not to be agreed to, and I shall be told : " For such and such reasons, that cannot be done ; and for such and such others, we could only offer you so-and-so." Mere useless delay.

Consequently—if you otherwise have time— please arrange all this for me yourself ; just because I don't understand it, you see, I'm applying to someone who does. Surely that's quite natural. Moreover, I must beg you temporarily to let the prospective publisher see the copy I once committed to your hands ; if the thing comes off, I will revise my own copy (in case I recover it) and then despatch it to the printer.—

You write me, you're in an awkward position for a transaction of this sort, being in the book-trade yourself ? What of that ?—God bless me, if you're really still associated with the Leipzig business—and care to have a finger in this pie— just fire away, like a good fellow, without any more fuss !—I had a symbolic effect in mind with " Cotta " ; but I fancy the thing will quite stand on its own legs without.—So, exactly as you consider good and reasonable—I've told you *my* ideas of the business already—only I cannot agree to an issue of the pieces *singly*, as I had to allow the musical publisher of the separate " operas " to have the *textbooks* printed singly.

Now let me soon hear something charming: I need it badly !—

Best love to Cecilie ; her lines delighted me. Her not having arrived at hunting up her brother in his exile once in 11 years is a little suspicious ; letting one hear a word by 3 to 4 years' fits and starts cannot at all make up for that. Moreover, I fancy I sent her a fairly sufficient account of myself from Venice, beyond which there truly isn't much more now to say : I am committing the folly of still clinging to life, and it serves me quite right if things are going with me right miserably. And so they will, until they go no longer and folk say, Ach, Herr Jesus ! We know all about that. In the meantime it often amuses me to hear myself complimented, or envied for my " higher art-life." Banker Kaskel once told me : " Look at you, Herr Wagner, and the good time you have ! You write a new opera, and coin a mint of money with it. But we poor fellows have trouble enough to keep our finances in order ; nobody gives *us* a penny."

Ah, it really is a perfect joy !—

Well, I am hoping to be able to send Minna off to the baths at Ems. Probably I shall have to stick on here, myself. Farewell, and give me good news soon ; also take hugely big thanks from Thy   RICHARD W.

93. To Cäcilie Avenarius

" Cile ! Cile !
    There's a big bogey in your bed ! " [1]
Take my word for that !
You misunderstood my joking tone the other
day [p. 232 ?]; at least there wasn't an atom of
bitterness in my irony.   But whence, child, should
one keep drawing the right supply of humour ?
The only comfort I can give you in reply to your
mournful accounts of your own life, is : Console
yourself with mine ! !—If that is not enough for
you, then lay to heart that answer of the Princess's
in *Tasso :* " Who, then, is happy ? "
But there are various points I can't quite
comprehend.   I can understand association with
your brothers-in-law being unavoidable by your
husband, out of regards he must pay ; but I can't
help wondering at your inability to withdraw your
private self from such encounters.   Brothers-in-
law of that sort ought really to be unable to inflict
their presence on yourself, unless some weakness
on your husband's part permits.   I think you
should always conform to your husband, and if
things are right between you two, you mustn't
mind the rest ; hear my advice, however :—
Consider nothing but your children : how glad
I should be if I had children for my wife !—Cares
which they occasion you should never count ; in
those cares resides the gist of your existence.   For
the rest, seek as much time as you possibly can for

---

[1] See page 196 above.

good reading. Believe me, the company of living people invariably costs more than it brings in ; one always loses by it—for the most part. The book of a noble spirit, on the contrary, is the most precious of friends one can have : there all conflicting interests are silent, the voice of a departed victor speaks us peace. — Abundant leisure for good reading is the single boon for which one cannot strive enough ; 'tis the chief of fortune's favours when a man can taste it in full measure.—

Touching your health, too, be consoled with mine. My nerves are so terribly sensitive, they are always vibrating, either engendering the acme of pleasure or the deepest depression and pain. The feeling of pleasure arrives quite uncommonly seldom, of course ; only ensuing, with myself, on very striking inner processes, or sometimes through a sudden favourable change in the weather. But all that is very rare, and excessively fleeting ; the feeling of pain, anxiety, prostration, harassment, is the *constantly* abiding state. Some 10 years since, this undeniable observation worried me intensely ; in the end, I have learnt to submit. It cannot be helped, and even may let one grow old (a lesson for yourself as well) ; nay, there is actually a prospect of its diminishing with age : the most passionate natures have often first learnt comfort in old age. Toward that one's moral fortitude must much assist : in other words—one must compose oneself. A whole night's profound sleep is the heavenliest blessing I know ; I often take a deal of pains preparing it. 'Tis my only physic. We require naught save rest ; but how hard it comes to one of *us* to get it ! Yet there's many a thing one can acquire : I am regularly training myself not to flare up at every trifle ; one can effect a deal in that way, and I've often been able to praise myself already. And one does such a lot of good by it, not only to oneself, but to others ! God, how many needless upsets in the house might I not have spared myself and wife ! I really do spare her a number of times now, and in very important matters.—

Enough of sermonising. — My—so-called— amnesty at all events has given you more joy than me. True, I now may tread the German Bund's domains again—with exception of that mighty kingdom, Saxony—for the sake of representations of my works ; but those representations themselves, the only object here in view, are certain to give me more trouble and annoyance of every kind than any satisfaction I shall reap. That stands beyond all doubt ; and yet it remains my chief goal and sole life-task, without which I shouldn't at all know why to bear this senseless life. If the case had befallen me a year ago, I certainly should not have come to Paris, and have saved much money and unrest ; upon the other hand, it's only Paris, with the eminent acquaintances I've made here, that has helped me to it. For the present I must stay on here till the production of Tannhäuser, which will take place by command of the Emperor—true enough,—in fact it was the Princess Metternich, without my knowing any-thing about it, who obtained me that command.

Owing to that turn of the cards I'm in an unpre-
cedentedly favourable position for this undertaking ;
the entire establishment of the Opera will stand
at my disposal, I am master and only need to ask
for what I want. From all which I expect at any
rate to draw the profit, that the representation
will be the best this opera has ever had.—It will
come off toward the end of this year, and I then
think of producing my Tristan in Germany with
all despatch—but where ? ?—

Your husband, the ex- or present book-dealer,
E. Avenarius, is a perfect enigma to me ! As he
didn't answer me at all, I thought he hadn't
received my last letter, in which I begged him to
find me a publisher for my "Ring des Nibelungen" ;
and now I hear through yourself that he had it all
right. What *am* I to expect of Germany, if my
own brother-in-law treats me so shabbily ! Give
him a dressing, I beg of you, and stir him up
to answer me and fulfil my prayer if possible.
Otherwise I shall disinherit him !—And now, good
Cile, let your cure do you good ; pluck up heart
and practise repose, but true repose ! And take
my thanks for your loyalty. Farewell ; make the
best of this, and keep good to me. Thy

RICHARD.

94. TO EDUARD AVENARIUS

SODEN, 13. *August* (1860).

BEST BROTHER-IN-LAW—The date [address ?]
will tell you everything. The women have made
a nice mess of it, and the slowness of you both in

writing to and fro has not improved things ; if Cecilie had only set out at once! I got here yesterday, and must return to Paris Saturday ; Thursday and Friday I shall be at Baden-Baden : I say no more. Minna did wrong not to tell you I was coming so soon.—

But I am writing post-haste, on the point of embarking for Frankfort. I preserve incognito everywhere. The idea of my going to conduct my operas at Wiesbaden straight off could have occurred to nobody but a fabricator of canards.—I should have liked to write you about the publishing affair more at my leisure, but will rush through the pith of it. I would have accepted a contract on the basis of dividing the profits, only how on earth could I make sure of my not being cheated, unless the publisher were a special friend of mine? Everyone refuses to believe in the honesty of book-dealers in the matter of editions and such-like. Myself I've had no good experiences as yet in that regard. Härtels were also to share the profits from *Lohengrin* with me ; the pianoforte scores of that opera have been selling throughout all Europe and America for years, and even yet it hasn't brought Härtels — — — enough profit for them to have had aught to divide with me ! ! On what such firms subsist, how the Härtels keep up house and pay for their garments, remains a mystery, if nothing is yielded by such undertakings even at the end of 10 years.—What might reassure me, would be its only being a matter of a small edition of 500 copies for the present : but on the one side I consider so small an edition unpractical, because—through its getting sent out, of course, to no one but musikdirectors and other musicians—it won't fall into the proper hands ; on the other, are you prepared to guarantee that Weber won't reprint without informing me, in case a large demand should actually arise, or in fact won't have more copies printed in the first place ? In this way I'm afraid I shall *never* draw a halfpenny from my Nibelungen poem either ! —I'd accept these or similar conditions [however], if *you* would bring the work out ; just think it over. Relieve me of my scruples, for indeed I've good reason to place small faith in publishers, etc. ; only reflect that for the publishing of Rienzi, Fliegender Holländer and Tannhäuser, I'm still—in debt ! ! Is my mistrust, then, not highly justified ?—

Please don't let it irk you to give me further information, and—if possible—to obtain me a certainty, at least for *the future*.

I suppose it's no use thinking any longer of a Rhine rendezvous this time ; but I expect you'll both be coming to Paris for the production of Tannhäuser. That will be something remarkable in any case, and certainly the *best* performance of this opera there has been as yet.—

Love to Cecilie, and thanks for your own kind congratulations.

Minna sends very best love ; the cure has done her *a lot* of good.—

And so—farewell ! ! Thy   RICHARD.

95. To sister Luise Brockhaus

(Undated, end of March 1861*)*

Dear Luise—Here is the report I once promised to Fritz ; I have finished it amid a thousand interruptions.[1] It mayn't be a very fine model of style ; neither has the manuscript, which I couldn't possibly write out again, perhaps proved excessively legible. As it is intended for printing —in the Illustrirte, I suppose—and compositors generally make a very good job of bad writing, perhaps you people would do better not to read the report till it lies before you in type. Ottilie [her daughter], however, may have an eagle eye, and find her way through this manuscript with the same energy as formerly at Vachette ; so a preliminary reading may be left to *her* ingenuity.—

For the rest, I should have nothing material wherewith to supplement that article, unless it were a few stronger remarks on the weak spots in the representation, which formed my true real torment in the whole affair. To think of my having to submit to its being conducted by a musical sergeant (as Herwegh calls him in a Zurich paper) ! My sufferings *before* the production, which unfortunately I couldn't even prevent, were far greater than those *after* it. To tell the truth, I am glad to have been stopped by the Jockeyclub from bringing my work to an

---

[1] Clearly this is the account of the *Tannhäuser* fiasco, dated " Paris, 27. March, 1861," originally appearing in F. Brockhaus's *Deutsche Allg. Ztg*, April 7, and now included in *Ges. Schr.* vi ; cf. *Prose Works*, iii.—Tr.

actual hearing ; myself I should have been unable to hear it out !

What really galls me, is my having let myself be caught in such a trap once more, after long years of resignation ; and I can console myself with nothing but the resolution that such a thing shall not occur again.

For that matter, I have by no means lost my temper with the Parisians : they're a light-minded lot, and pick up any silly talk one foists on them ; when it comes to the point, though, they are as impressionable for the good as ever, and take up the cudgels to one's heart's content for whatever pleases them.—All I'm amazed at, is the obtuseness of my high protectors in Germany, who never give a thought to the indignity of an artist of my seriousness strictly remaining exposed to all the chances of an adventurer's life. Which of them will offer me a respectable den for my person, a fit atelier for my art?—O do not let this "German depth and fervour" mount too high into our brains !—Down to the present I don't at all feel like abandoning Paris yet ; when Ottilie has reached the tail-end of my report (the corner of the Boulevard and Rue Montmartre), please take the hint supplied there in real earnest.[1]

In the meantime I'm astonished at my health ; it seems as if I were to be preserved for many another storm.—

Again I thank you warmly, best Luise, for your previous letter ; what touched me in particular, were your exhortations in my wife's

[1] To this "hint" we have no present clue.

behalf. To be sure, she is much to be pitied; but, Lord knows how, she too is holding out. How dearly I should like to be able to offer her a peaceful habitation where she wouldn't have me too incessantly at her elbow; I never ought to come to her till stress and annoyance are past for the while: as now, for instance, when in spite of all the wretchedness of my position I almost feel on velvet after the thrashing received.

Clärchen wrote me quite kindly and almost repentantly; no doubt she has excused my inability to answer her as yet, and will also be indulgent if it doesn't come to that awhile. Please tell her, though, she rejoiced me much.

My fate will probably not let me off a thorough atonement with Dresden; methinks I shall perhaps have to subject myself to a political whitewash there next autumn. Let's hope they'll then be gracious. Really, I can think of no suitable place of residence for my wife apart from Dresden.

For the moment I'm utterly project-less. Attempt what I may, I know I shall derive more care and trouble from it, than delight. Doubtless 'twere best if I could vanish wholly from the world; but that's so hard.—

Farewell now. Remember me most kindly to Fritz and the children, and rest assured of my sincerest thanks for your sisterly interest. Thy brother   RICHARD.

[After retiring from Paris the end of July 1861, and passing all the late summer and autumn at Vienna in futile endeavours to bring out his *Tristan* there, Wagner returns to Paris in December, where he devotes about six

R

weeks to the poem of *Die Meistersinger*.   Minna and he
have already parted, practically for good ; see his letters
to her.—Tr.]

96. To Cäcilie Avenarius

19 Quai Voltaire, Paris, 7. *January* 62.

Dear Cile—I write you a mere couple of lines
at once, lest it mightn't come off again later ;
better a little and swift !—

If you only knew what a strange feeling it gives
me, to perceive from your letter how infinitely
little you good people know of the hardships of
my life ! What must I think, when I read that
the great world and renown are making me forget
all that doesn't form part thereof ! !—How and
where begin, to teach you otherwise ? !

Enough that the whole of my renown, and all
my successes in Germany, will not help to provide
me a corner wherein to assemble my wits and
prepare for fresh work. Right in the middle of
Germany, the invitation of the Metternichs to
pass a quiet and secluded time with them in Paris
was bound to strike me as a great good-fortune.
It lured me hither. Meanwhile the Princess's
mother died ; the father—mad—is brought to
Paris, obtains the rooms reserved for me, and I—
have to look round me in the world again to find
a decent chamber for myself and work, the only
thing remaining to me ! ! Failure of all my undertakings—rebuffs on all sides—nobody knowing
what to do with me anywhere !—No certainty, no

revenue ; trouble and care : no country, no family, nothing !—

Ah, what do you people know ?—

Child, *why* did you never come, in ten long years, to me in Switzerland ? *Cläre*, you know, found her way !—

'Twas ever thus !

No doubt I shall be coming to Berlin ere long, for all that ! Only, Berlin *may*—or rather, *might* be of too great importance to me, for me not to be on my guard against paying it too prompt a visit. That, alack, is policy !—

I think of transferring myself to Wiesbaden next month, to work in quiet there awhile. A speedy settling down is indispensable ; bad as my look-out may be with it, everything else is still worse for me.

Now take heart of grace, and be comforted : you are suffering with your nerves, child—one doesn't kick the bucket over that, however much one suffers. In fact, such sufferings will improve with time ; myself I now feel better, on the whole, than might have been expected. Have courage ! We shall see each other, too, this year. Nothing's settled, but many a straw is pointing to a Berlin visit. Keep up your pluck, and pull yourself together ; I'll make you laugh yet, take my word !—

Farewell, good Cile. Put up with this ; there's nothing of account to say about me ! Remembrances to Eduard ; is he doing well ? Tell him I'm doing badly ; which will balance things !

Adieu, take heart and hold me dear ! Thy brother   RICHARD.

97. To Eduard Avenarius

19 Quai Voltaire, Paris, 15. *January* 62.

Dear Eduard—Best thanks for your letter. Don't be cross if I only make the needful brief reply.

Be sure your invitation gave me heartfelt joy. It determines me to come and visit you both for a few days the beginning of February. I would come to you for months, if I weren't in a fever of work now. I stick to my idea of choosing a terrain for it where I can think of settling permanently and in keeping with my other plans and inclinations. Consequently I abide by Wiesbaden. You shall hear all my pros and cons as to a lengthier stay in Berlin by word of mouth.

On the occasion of this visit, however, I should also like to see my wife; I shall have much to discuss with her. Whether you can put us both up, even for a mere few days, I'm bound to doubt. Should there be nothing else for it, perhaps it would be better if you quartered *me* at some hotel close by, and took the wife unto yourselves.[1] After all, 'twould only be a matter of the nights; I should be with you from the first thing in the morning.—

I am also writing to my wife about it.

I shall be here till the end of this month.

---

[1] The visit did not come off; see No. 103, also letter 232 to Minna (Feb. 1, 62): "Cecilie has written me also, telling me that you have declined staying with them. You will have your own reasons for it,—but so far as I'm concerned now, this circumstance turns the scale with me *not* to go to Berlin for the present." —Tr.

As I hope to see both of you soon, I'll save all sorts of things for mouth that would be bootless here.

Adieu, dear Eduard ; best love to Cecilie and your children, and thanks once again for your kind letter. From his heart Thy   Richard W.

98. To Clara Wolfram

BIEBRICH, 2. *June* 1862.

My dear Cläre—Minna's tidings lead me to conclude that Mariechen's wedding is to take place in a few days. For my own part I'm so disused to all family life, in fact to all family feeling, that in truth it required a notable cause to re-direct me to that circle of human relations. Yet—rest assured—I should never have had the heart to let this epoch pass by without a warm greeting to my most faithful old sister. If we lived together, you'd receive more constant proofs of my attachment, beyond a doubt. The way I'm living now, bent upon nothing save quiet and freedom for work—my final refuge from the world—and yet a continual prey to incursions of all kinds, I'm bound at last to chafe at almost every contact with the outer world, and carefully avoid whatever might occasion frittering of my time or my attention. You can't believe how justified that care is, and how constantly I suffer from upset and failure ; so that I often tell myself, I'll give up every hope of coming to an understanding with my fellow-men, and in particular, avoid all new connections.

I returned to Biebrich a few days back from

Karlsruhe, where repeated experiences had finally compelled me to abandon every prospect founded on the Grand Duke's friendship, as in course of a most affecting conversation with him I could no longer help complaining of his Theatre-Director E. Devrient in a fashion that, since I cannot possibly wish to bring about this individual's downfall, made a total resignation of those prospects my bounden duty. Pondering my future on my journey back, really the sole true refuge I could see, was the chance of death not being over-long deferred. Arrived home, I found a letter of Minna's awaiting me, to boot, which set me in the most appalling alarm about her; for that letter really gave me the impression of coming from a mad-woman. She must be terribly excited again; God grant that her visit to Reichenhall may bring her improvement! Many a precedent allows me to hope so. For the rest, I'm bound to believe that a little slackening of our correspondence, limiting my side of it for the present to the merest needful, may contribute somewhat to her calming. Perhaps she'll regain some composure when she sets to work on the projected small establishment in Dresden.

Touching myself, I propose to complete at the least the main job of my new opera here, and then to join Minna in Dresden mid-autumn. With all my heart I hope and wish that Dresden may gradually re-shape itself into my habitat then. I have so literally no other plan or wish, that this hope is indeed the only thing to which I cleave still. The thought of native home and nearness to

one's family is very potent in it, and even if I
haven't spoken of it yet to any of my people, I
truthfully assure yourself that the prospect of
being near you all, and mixing with you, very
materially contributes to this special wish of mine
regarding Saxony and Dresden.

So I will solemnise my first act of re-entry into
the family circle to-day by begging you to convey
to Mariechen my most sincere felicitation on her
marriage. All that I have heard about her bridegroom points to that felicitation being amply
founded. Tell her that she and her young
husband also are of those with whom I hope to
feel again among my own belongings soon.

Very best remembrances to your good husband
too, and tell everybody all the nicest things you
can from me. Good luck to you, and comfort
yourself in all affliction with Thy heartily affectionate Brother   RICHARD.

99. To the Same

BIEBRICH A. RH., 11. *July* 1862.

How could you have been afraid, dear Cläre,
lest there might be the smallest thing in your
letter that I could take amiss? I have hitherto
refrained from mixing anyone in this affair, and
tried to find my way alone with that unhappy
woman who bootlessly is torturing herself and me
to death; but there is no end to be found to the
madness. So the only thing to do me good now,
in truth, is a frank discussion of this irretrievable
relation with others also and my people; and now

that I can hear your voices, it really seems as if a little light were dawning on me. It was solely Minna's painful malady, that imposed on me the duty of forbearance: her woful character, which visits everyone attached to me with grudge and hatred, had long been impotent for that. I now see, however, that I myself cannot possibly be the right person to have a beneficial effect on her heart-complaint; consequently a continuance or resumption of our living together is the most foolish and wrong-headed thing that could happen. Therefore it can only be a question of the *mode* in which it is annulled; and that depends on what Minna's good sense can eventually persuade her to. I have offered her a small establishment for herself in Dresden : she is to keep one room prepared for me : I shall make the experiment of seeing her there; if she behaves rationally (which I am compelled to doubt, alas), I may visit her frequently, and, while retaining a quiet haven elsewhere for my work, can still conceal the rupture from the world without any great slur on her. This is the last exertion [possible to] my good-will; yet I doubt that it will have any success. The idea of a divorce did not proceed from me,[1] obvious though it is, and excusable as it might be in me to harbour a wish to turn the remnant of my years to my works' advantage by the side of someone sympathetic to me. However, I crave no happiness, but simply liberation from a weight that makes me wretched. The right moment for that was missed long since; alike my good-nature and my sense of

---

[1] See pp. 750-2 of the " Minna " collection.—Tr.

justice betrayed me into allowing an incurable ill to augment to the point of unbearableness. Humanly speaking, I could adduce no other ground for a divorce now, than the reciprocal benefit of complete separation.

You see, dearest Cläre, how entirely I agree with you ; nay more, I admire you and your clear judgment in not having let yourself be confused by Minna's incredible falsifications of matters of fact between us. Enough : I hope to go to Dresden for a few days in the second half of August, and then to see yourself as well. Ask Cecilie to be there also, and beg her for Heaven's sake not to continue tormenting me à la Minna ; she seems to have no idea at all of the melancholy complications in my plight.

My study is just full of visitors, so please make shift with this, dear Cläre. Believe in my heartiest thanks for your dear letter, and that it has done me a power of good. Plenty of kind love ! Thy   RICHARD.

100. TO HIS NIECE FRANZISKA RITTER [1]

FRANKFORT, *Monday morning.*

DEAREST FRÄNZE—You are a clever creature, and have your heart in the right place. The 1000 thaler man is found, if you can bring him to the scratch. Listen ! Go to Dr X [Theo. Apel ?] ; he's rich, a friend of my young days, and fond of me. He made sacrifices to my giddy youth

---

[1] Albert Wagner's daughter. [See No. 59. The letter, undated, manifestly belongs to the first week in November 1862.—TR.]

before ; now let him make them to more noble interests.—Tell him I am prepared to give a grand concert at Leipzig in February if *he* will put an end to my atrocious plight now by an immediate advance of 1000 thlr. For this concert he should place himself at the head of a committee ; a gift of honour from my birthplace might perhaps be made its object not without some *sense.* I will promptly repay the 1000 thlr out of that February receipt ; or if it doesn't amount to that, I will make up the balance from my subsequent Berlin concert takings.

Tell him what the Ritters did for me so long, and how sorry you all are to be unable to do anything more now. In short, don't flinch : he *must !* Should the height of the sum prove an obstacle, lower it to 600 thaler if need be. If you bring off the 1000 thlr, Sascha [her husband, Alex. R.] shall have his 100 back at once. At the very worst, X must lend me 200 thlr, which should be promptly despatched to my wife—16. Walpurgisstrasse, Dresden ; in any event this remittance would have to go off from Leipzig at once.

Now look sharp !

I had a sleepless night, and this solution suddenly occurred to me as so simple,—but *you* alone can work it.

Please—telegraph me the result (discreetly worded) *immediately* to Biebrich. I hope for that despatch, let's say, to-morrow—Tuesday—noon.

Adieu. Best love to you good children !
Thy   RICHARD W.

101. To the Same

VIENNA, KAISERIN ELISABETH,
17. *Nov.* 62.

Heavens, dearest Fränze, how the world does rack me! Nix; nix! I don't get a step forwarder, have a frantic deal to do here, and can't give a thought to my money mess; so others must!

Good: try Steches. At least a basis:—a concert to be given at Leipzig early in February, —one might put Dr. Härtel on the committee; he has come round of late,—on the strength of which, prompt cash advance!—

Adieu, adieu; hold me dear, and forgive me the pother! Thy　　　　　RICHARD W.

102. To the Same

VIENNA, KAISERIN ELISABETH,
21. *Nov.* 62.

DEAREST FRÄNZE—I wrote you very wildly last time. Perhaps it vexed you. So I should like to fill up with all possible tameness what it behoves you to know.—

You will be aware of what I telegraphed back to Stör from Biebrich : the whole enquiry was idiotic, as you no doubt will perceive. I've a deal of trouble with the Grand Duke: he wants me to establish myself at Weimar as his official ; a vanity on his part to which I can lend no support. So *nothing* further has resulted from this honorarium question either. Moreover, it came through

Dingelstedt, and what results from that I've learnt before : misère.

Well, for the moment I'm so exclusively engrossed with my Vienna affair, in addition so terribly tired, and so crippled by this interminable money crisis, that I really require the intervention of a shrewd and heart-whole woman like yourself, to be able to assume that everything in any way possible is being done upon that side, while I surrender myself to my other cares. Whereas I am arranging combinations here which may drive me into the sacrifice of my stipulated fee so as to acquire Schnorr for Tristan, I want to be able to believe that help will be forthcoming from another quarter. I've left Minna still in debt, and without any subsidy ; myself I'm pressed in the extreme on various sides, and *must* have help as soon as possible. That idea with the Leipzig concert appears to me so very simple : a committee which, after my recent artistic success there, should arrange a grand concert to be conducted by me for my own benefit about the beginning of February, set on foot a subscription, place itself in communication with me regarding the programme, and invite me to come in the name, as it were, of my Leipzig friends. So, if the thing goes off well (and of that there can't be any doubt, providing it's skilfully started), the only question would be of first finding *some* or *several* persons to place the presumable profits— on a moderate computation—at my disposal by way of advance ; upon receipt of which sum I undertake to reach Leipzig the appointed day, and so on. I feel sure you understood my last few

lines in this sense, and per-haps I shall soon be
hearing something ?   Not before next week can I
make a regular commencement with rehearsals
here [for *Tristan*], but there is the strictest and most
serious good-will in upper regions, and I believe the
thing will come to pass.

For the rest, Vienna suits me ; not the " artists,"
but the people, in whose good books I stand quite
incredibly high.   A new fancy-shop has just been
opened with the sign of " Lohengrin " ; every
porter is delighted when he learns whose boots he's
blacking.   It is quite a remarkable populace, and
has given me a good few nice impressions already.

Now remembrances to Sascha and your children ;
be staunch and true.   You can give me a wonderful
lift now by succeeding ; and I require it !—

Adieu, good Fränze.   Hold me dear !   Thine
uncle   RICHARD.

102A. TO HIS BROTHER-IN-LAW HEINRICH
WOLFRAM [1]

[An undated fragment]

They have the best will towards me in Vienna,
but a total absence of the singers I require ; my
only hope remains here, all the same.

Give Cläre love from all my heart ; Lord, how
I should like to have such real good gossips with
her every day !   I keep hoping against hope that
things will go there [with Minna in Dresden ?] after all ;

---

[1] Numbering this " 104a," Herr Glasenapp places it after the letter
of Nov. 1863 to Cecilie Avenarius ; personally, however, I cannot help
thinking that the Russian allusion, combined with the " best will in Vienna,"
assigns the fragment to *February* of that year.—TR.

meanwhile I'm working might and main to lay a sound foundation for my future living free from care. Russia may prove a great help towards that ; only it's most unlucky for me that things there look so bad precisely now, and interest in art is the very last to be expected.

Now, kindest thanks. Best love to all, and the assurance that you yourself are ever prized and dear to me, from Thy   RICHARD WAGNER.

[Returned from Russia with replenished purse, in the Spring of 1863 Wagner takes up his abode at Penzing, near Vienna ; but fresh pecuniary difficulties drive him to another concert expedition in the autumn.—TR.]

103. TO CÄCILIE AVENARIUS

MAYENCE, 27. *Nov.* 63.

DEAR CECILIE—Your letter was sent after me on many a zigzag, and only caught me up to-day.—

You do me an injustice. I didn't think of paying you my first visit in 15 years for a mere night's shelter on my transit through Berlin ; I promise I will come to Berlin some day for a good long time, and put up then with you. In fact I expected to have occasion for a longish stay there on my journey back from Petersburg ; but all fell through again.

The reason I didn't come 2 years ago I withheld from you at the time [see p. 244 ; also *Minna*, p. 707].

It was impossible for me to come to Dresden this time [see *Minna*, p. 787] ; I am very sorry that you waited for me there. My fatigue after the Prague and Carlsruhe concerts was immense, and

makes me very shy of further undertakings of the
kind.

I'm still detained here by all sorts of difficult
negotiations with my publisher (Schott), so that
I can say nothing certain to-day even about
Löwenberg.

I am having a *shocking bad time!* That should
be thought of by all to whom points in my conduct
remain unaccountable. I had rather I were dead,
—for there'll really be no end to my troubles
before,—and you all seem to see them so little.

Kind love to Minna. I was in thorough earnest
about a somewhat longer visit to Dresden, and no
doubt it will come off before long,—but—under
easier circumstances than the present could have
been. If I were to keep explaining things in detail,
I should never find another moment's peace.

Farewell, and don't let yourself be misled into
injustices. I hope to pay you a tidy visit soon.
Thy brother   RICHARD.

104. TO HEINRICH WOLFRAM

PENZING, NEAR VIENNA, 16. *February* 1864.

DEAREST BROTHER-IN-LAW — Hearty thanks
for your amiable letter.

Unfortunately my whole enjoyment of its contents was dispelled by the account of Minna's state
of health. Lord knows how much I am in need
of kind solace myself now, but it seems I'm not to
come to rest! Hitherto I mostly had heard the
poor woman was doing tolerably ; in fact, after
quitting her a few months since, Ottilie Brockhaus

remarked to me on her robust appearance. That was a great comfort to me ; for all I proposed by our living apart was simply to avoid our mutual wearing of each other out. Thus, also, I have let her lack for nothing ; many people, indeed, reproach me with doing it too profusely, as they know how hard it has become in general to provide myself with money. At the least, then, I had the consolation that she was outwardly thriving ; to which, moreover, I might presume that even her erroneous estimate of my character and disposition, which she really will never decipher, would contribute in the end.

After all this, the brief account of her condition contained in your letter gave me quite a shock. I can't compose myself at all yet, and weep the whole day long. How I pity the unhappy woman, I cannot tell you !—Of course I wrote to her at once, and that comfortingly—I hope—and encouragingly.—If good Cläre could only revisit her, that I might know there was somebody near her again who could give me a lucid account of her ! Ah, if she only would grant me that sacrifice !

At present it's a positive question of life and death with me, whether I can keep to my work undisturbed and supply the theatres with the Meistersinger for next winter. I have been so cruelly and repeatedly interrupted in it, that I began to believe I must completely abandon the work. So I am doing all I can not to stir an inch, nor to let any great change occur in my position, before I've quite finished this work. Then—when that is done—there'll be no more reason for my

staying here, and—if it's possible and advisable—
I shall be prepared for even a removal to Dresden.
But everything—everything is getting so terribly
hard for me ; I've help from nowhere any more,
and nobody troubles about me. God knows if
even what I am bound to consider so imperative
now [completion of *Meistersinger* ?] will be possible to
me !—A catastrophe with Minna just now would
be my ruin for ever. O let her flourish in quiet
and leave all other troubles to me !

At your wish I enclose a few lines for Director
Grosse.—Only if you think it certain that you
could effect something against that Bensberg,
would I claim your services in that ; in which case
I would make you out the legal authority. But I
doubt its being of the smallest use ; I was treated
just the same before at Nuremberg. And then
these minor managers, good Lord, what can one
ever recover from them ? If only the big Court-
theatres would do their duty ! How abominable
the condition is there !

And yet—in truth—your news were on the
point of genuinely delighting me,—if that other
had not come with them !—

Most hearty thanks, accordingly, for everything.
Salute my good Cläre a thousand times, and tell
your children all that's nice from me. Farewell,
dearest friend. From his heart Thy faithful
brother-in-law, RICHARD WAGNER.

[Less than three months from the above, King
Ludwig the Second of Bavaria flew to the master's
rescue, installing him in his capital soon after.—TR.]

105. To Clara Wolfram [1]

Dear good Cläre—I can invite none of my family to "Tristan"; the present is so incredibly exciting a time to me, that, to be able to weather it, I'm compelled to steer clear of all the intercourse attendant on such visits. Before and after the rehearsals and performances I have to keep myself completely under lock and key; I cannot receive any visitor.

I should like to grant yourself, however, attendance at these wonderful performances . . . So listen. If you intend coming to Munich, I'll provide you with free board and lodging in a very quiet private hotel not far from here, where the Schnorrs are also staying. I shall see you, and we'll dine together twice or thrice,—according to circumstances; whilst Frau von Bülow will do everything else to look after you. The representations are set down for the 15th, 18th and 22nd May . . .

I tremble at the thought of the emotion which the sight of your poor sorely-tried self will occasion me again, and hesitated long about meeting you at such a time as *this*. You can't believe how I require to spare myself, with an undertaking so unheard of.—Still, I appeal to your heart! We can arrange things so that both of us may only taste the charm and sweets of this reunion!—

May you see by the above how dear you are to

[1] Reproduced from the *Tägl. Rundschau* of Oct. 15, 1902. [The dots are as in the German edition.—Tr.]

me, good Cläre!—With all his heart's kind love to you and yours, Thy brother   RICHARD.

MUNICH, 21 BRIENNERSTR.
   26. *April* 1865.

106. TO ALEXANDER AND FRANZISKA RITTER

DEAREST CHILDREN—The production is settled now for

Sunday, 10. June.

Come if you can, that I may see you both again and say goodbye.   With all his heart Your
       RICHARD W.

MUNICH,
4. *May*[1] 1865.

107. TO HEINRICH WOLFRAM

MY DEAR BROTHER-IN-LAW—Best thanks for your kind letter. On receiving it I felt alarmed as usual, especially when I get a letter from relatives, since I always dread some fresh misfortune. I'm so profoundly shattered by the ceaseless terrible experiences I've made of life, that the next piece of bad news will either do for me outright, or find me wholly callous.—Ever since Schnorr's death I have been avoiding all company, not to have to speak; for some time I fled to utter mountain solitude.—

You have reassured me a little about good Clara. I hope to pay a visit to the pair of you before we all die. Best love to the good faithful sister!—

---

[1] This *must* be a slip of the pen for "June," just as the "Sunday" is for "Saturday," the latter being the *Tristan* première's actual date.—TR.

Touching the representation of Lohengrin, please act entirely after your own judgment. I authorise you to grant the manager of your theatre permission, and to obtain me whatever sum seems fair to you. So far as I'm concerned, then, this matter's settled.—

Forgive me, dear old man, not writing more. I might have told you either very, very much, or the barest needful. I must stick to the latter.—

By working quietly awhile, I hope to recuperate. The affection of an inconceivably profound and lovely nature makes that possible ; it needed such a marvellously gifted mortal to be born for me, as this young King of Bavaria ! No one can grasp what he is to me : my guardian and my inspirer. I am basking in his love, and gaining strength to bring my task to end.—

Farewell and hold me dear, both of you. A thousand hearty greetings from Your

RICHARD W.

MUNICH, 10. *Sept.* 1865.

[Again less than three months later, a perfidious long-brewn court-intrigue drove Wagner from Bavaria.—TR.]

108. To LUISE BROCKHAUS

GENEVA, LES ARTICHAUTS.
3. *Jan.* 66.

Hearty thanks, dear Sister, in particular for your news.—I had had cheerful occasion of late to remember my family : in all the tumult of my curious Munich life, of an evening I dictated my biography, getting as far as my 21st year ; of

course you all appear in it, and it greatly touched
me to recall those youthful days, which stood
uncommonly clear in my memory. Down to that
time of life I could but choose a cheerful tone,
even when recording all my errors ; from that
time on (and this is still reserved for me !) my
life turns grave and bitter, and I'm accordingly
afraid the cheerful tone will quit me,—my marriage
looms ! Not a creature knows what I've suffered
through that !—

Naturally, this dictation isn't meant for publicity;
it is merely to serve as truthful record, after my
demise, for whoever may be called to write the
world my life.

Believe me, the death of good Fritz grieved
me much ; you know how he always affected me,
and how fond I was of him ! But so many upsets
and commotions overtook me at the time, that I
couldn't find an hour in which to send you my
condolence otherwise than with unseemly hurry.—

My departure from Munich had really been
deliberated by me daily : the King knew that it
meant a favour shewn me, not to keep me any
longer ; as it has been of use to him, he may even
have seen a momentary advantage in it to himself.
He must get older, and learn to read people a
little ; his ardour allowed me no peace, he was
offending everyone around him without being
able to adopt the right line of resistance. What
shall I say? Time will teach all. If he cannot
establish himself of his own strength, I can give
him no artificial stability. For the present I'm
urgently insisting on a few years of total with-

drawal for nothing but work ; every plan for
founding and producing [*Ring* theatre, etc.] must and
shall be postponed.   The King expects me back
in Munich at Easter ; only—I prefer living here,
or somewhere else, in complete retirement, as that's
my last chance of salvation.—

Let these few lines suffice you.   Little—but
prompt—I could manage that much !—

Farewell, good Luise ; rest assured of my
deepest condolence with your grievous loss, give
my love to your children, and stay good to Thy
brother   RICHARD.

[Three weeks after letter 108 Minna Wagner suddenly
died in Dresden.   The following April her husband
moved to Tribschen, a little promontory on the Lake of
Lucerne; where, with the exception of occasional outings
to Munich, etc., he remained for another six years.—TR.]

109. To Clara Wolfram

MY DEAR CLÄRE—It was wrong of me to be
so dilatory with my answer to your letter ; how
it came to pass, however, will be understood
by anyone in closer touch with my strangely
sequestered, yet continually so agitated life.   Therefore I'll waste no more time on excuses, but beg
you to believe it certainly was no defect of hearty
sympathy, that so long prevented me from hitting
off the hour for a letter to yourself.   There again
you would easily arrive at a correct judgment of
me, if you were a frequent witness of the evenings
when I dictate at my biography, and to my own
astonishment my past skims lifelike and distinct

before me. At the moment I have reached the period of my Dresden appointment : this retrospect often moves me strongly.

Another reason for my delay in writing was the half-formed project of revisiting my native land and kinsfolk soon. Hitherto I have been withheld from that also by work at my Meistersinger, which I was able to resume at length last summer, and at which I mean to stick till its completion. However, I am counting on the execution of my project this next summer, when I intend to stretch my limbs again a while. Then I shall come to you folk, and also tell yourself my heartfelt sympathy and sorrow for your grievous trials and troubles.

Minna's not having remembered you better with her bequests distresses me for many reasons ; but you are aware that her penchants never took the line of beings friendly with myself. God knows to whom she made away so many things which in other hands would probably have been more carefully cherished ; but it would have been repugnant to me in the last degree to discuss that with her in the slightest. With the grand piano [old Dresden one ?] I believe you haven't lost much, excepting for its value as a souvenir ; no doubt I shall be able to see to a suitable instrument for your house some future day. Your account of Minna's death quite moved me to horror afresh ; there was a calamity with that unhappy one which nothing could alter. In her fate lies something so disconsolate, that in my eyes it casts a shadow over all existence !

Whether you folk see clear anent my curious fortunes of the last few years, I must leave an open question : here and there I've hit on something fairly near the truth in newspapers. I had to make unconditional silence a law to myself, as I should have only committed my poor young friend by any public word. I had to let all depend upon the natural course of things, the gradual ripening of the young monarch's discernment and character, his ultimate dealings. It was a matter of nothing less than the ruin of the last and single hope among our German princes : all guileless, he was being betrayed and enmeshed by his own most intimate officials ; to open his eyes in the long run, was no light task for me, and nothing but his unbounded affection gave me at last the power to move him to those decisive steps which finally have doubtless saved him from the utmost dangers. I am of the best hope for his welfare now, and for my own part merely wish he may leave me in peace here for a number of years, where I am living as out of the world and at last have regained leisure and relish for work.—

However brief, the above is really all I can tell you by letter ; were I to go into particulars, I should never make an end. Let us hope for a speedy reunion ; it is among the most agreeable prospects I hold before me. Take good care of yourself, and—shew a bold front to the last trials of life ! Greet your belongings, and remain ever good to Thy faithful brother   RICHARD.

LUCERNE, 15. *Jan.* 1867.

110. To Luise Brockhaus [1]

Hearty thanks for your greeting, dear Sister ; I have a profound need, myself, to see my native land and kinsfolk once again. I shall come on a visit next summer, for certain. I wrote and told Cläre so, whom I had been owing a letter for ever so long, only a day or two back.

I fully understand your troubles of the recent past ; only, you are mistaken if you think my life a tranquil one, even in my present retreat. This time my cares have only touched myself so far as they concerned my profound love and sympathy for the young King of Bavaria ; in which regard no month elapsed last summer that didn't bring me some mortal alarm. His singular affection for me alone has made it possible to me at last to rouse in him the strength to free himself and country from extremest shame. I may hope that all has now arrived at the best of turnings for him, and tell myself that at the cost of pangs whereof no soul knows anything, nor shall know, I have won him the assurance of a noble fate.

It will prove hard to claim the sole reward I wish for it, as I want nothing beyond leave to remain here, where I have found peace and new zest for my work ; whereas the whole stiff victory has no meaning in his estimation unless I return full soon to him entirely. Still, I am hoping to incline him to my own desire, since he is equal to any sacrifice for me.

---

[1] An enclosure, directed "To/Madame Luise Brockhaus/whose address/ I have mislaid."

Amid these strangely agitating outer circumstances my Meistersinger, the composition of which I couldn't resume before moving here, is approaching completion at last, and I am hoping to bring my most popular work to production—at Nuremberg, if I can get my way—this very year.

There you have the pick of what I could tell you in haste ; make the most of it !—Thanks again for the agreeable surprise your letter gave me ; be assured of my heartiest reciprocation of your sisterly devotion ; greet your household ; and hope with me for speedy Wiedersehen.   With all his heart Thy faithful brother

RICHARD.

LUCERNE,
17. *Jan.* 1867.

The lost address, please !

111. To CLARA WOLFRAM

MY DEAR CLÄRE—Your faithful old friend Mejo has just informed me of the approaching celebration of your fortieth wedding-day.   That was fine of him ; it was a fresh corroboration of my dearness to yourself, when your own friends believe a hearty word from me would specially rejoice you on that day.   How heartily I am attached to you, in turn, no doubt you'll bear me witness.   If my life is growing more and more isolated, on the one hand my increasing soreness toward a world that always meets me with misunderstandings and insanities may be held to blame for it, but on the other I feel that isolation all the keener as I'm void of family. I know the idea of Family only from my old association with my brothers and sisters ; but how much has Life been forced to loose that ! Gladly would I have freshened it up : without exactly wanting to summon a family-conclave, a visit to you all in series keeps running in my head. I was nearly executing it the other day, and Mejo's news already strengthened my intention to look in on you at Chemnitz soon.

So many serious affairs, however, which I must let resolve in full calm and composure now, have withheld me from that project's execution through the fear lest such a journey might perforce expose me to great commotion. This amount of talking to a quantity of people is the very thing that always sets me in a fever of fatigue ; and that no doubt arises from my never having been able to settle down to a regular intercourse at any main centre, and therefore being pumped and stared at as a stranger wherever I may go : which intensely annoys and upsets me, particularly as no one takes the pains to ascertain exactly what I am or do, and everybody therefore fumbles round me as the merest curiosity. Such a position as mine may look all very well from a distance ; but whence could it come that I produce something different from others, if I were not also different in myself, but simply cared for racket, gossip, buzz and praise, like all of those with whom I'm confounded even by Herr W., for instance, as I greatly fear. Ah, that *would* be lovely, to get through the writing of a work like this (beneath what trials !), exhaust one's patience with a pack of hounds to bring it nobly and intelligently to execution— against the creatures' every custom,—and then just squat and be delighted if folk come and praise one! No, dear Cläre, nobody must ask that of me. What *I* desire on such occasions, I shewed yourself : by main force I made my dear old sister come, to give her pleasure and myself a cordial through her loyal true appreciation of my work. And few were the words that was done with, a look, just a squeeze of the hand ! So— we'll pass by the excellent W. ; if he's fond of me, so much the better for him.

And precisely as you came to see my Meister-singer, would I gladly have come for your feast-day in turn ; but believe me, it has proved impossible. I am sending you instead the Mastersingers themselves, who—as that wasn't done according to a previous order—will act quite well as bride-guard. Hans Sachs, above all, is just the man to fill my place to-day ; the Apprentices, too, in God's name let them figure at the festival ; whilst the street shindy might fit in pat enough, perhaps, as intermezzo in memory of Nuremberg.[1] When you hear the night-watchman, think of me !

Dear Cläre, it really isn't altogether meaningless, that just my Meistersinger should be coming for your fortieth wedding - day. Draw thence the spirit of a calmly-smiling resignation : 'twas that

---

[1] See the account in " *Mein Leben* " of the young man's adventures at Nuremberg in the company of his brother-in-law Wolfram, summer 1835.—Tr.

inspired me with this work ; and what can better beseem us in our looking back on a life of toil and care that has accomplished so few of our wishes? Our having suffered all things, only to bid goodbye in the end to every fond hope, strictly shews that one true boon *alone* was gainable : peace of mind in renouncing ! And truly, from that there's a further great and sole untarnishable joy to be distilled : calm, disinterested pleasure in the good and beautiful. See, something like that I was able to offer you when I bade you come to Munich, since I *had* something to offer for such a taste. Now I send you the work to live through again : dip oft therein, and when the Golden Wedding comes along, just open it once more and maybe it will ring out of itself !—

Greet the honourable old Heinrich and all your children. Bride and bridegroom, your health !! Thy faithful brother   RICHARD.

LUCERNE, 20. *Oct.* 1868.

112. TO SISTER OTTILIE BROCKHAUS

TRIBSCHEN (LUCERNE), 6. *Dec.* 1868.

MY DEAR OTTILIE—Don't be vexed at the seemingly trivial fashion in which I recalled myself to your memory by all manner of profane com- missions. Recognising that the thing could be approached from the humorous side alone, I even got those errands laid on you through Hermann ; whereby it naturally acquired so grotesque a character, that the joke must be obvious : into which in fact, to my merriest edification, your admirable Hermann entered with as much alacrity as good-humour in his reply.—As for the matter itself, all my earthly wishes have been perfectly fulfilled, as everything arrived in prime condition and best quality ; the bookseller was first to shew up, then the cigar-dealer, and finally the delicacies came in fullest natural luxuriance.

Whilst tendering you and good Clemens [her son, in holy orders] my heartiest thanks, I find it hard to promise to spare you such orders in future without first having imparted another want. My heart, to wit, is set on " compressed vegetables " of any and every kind, especially the fine. I'm so wretchedly off here for that sort of thing ; my housekeeper has tried now and then to get some from Basle, but there always was such a palaver about it, and such countless and costly mistakes with the orders, that I address this last request to you, were it only to keep you in practice with that care for good victuals into which you fell with a positive passion during my last visit !—

Things are going quite tolerably with me at present ; I have had glorious weather for some time past, and enjoy the pleasures, so seldom known to others, of a winter spent in such a wonderful landscape. Work, too, is forging ahead. The less I experience of the world, the better I feel in general, and by dint of firm measures I've steeled myself well to ward off every nuisance ; should I have caused you disturbance, in turn, I am heartily sorry. I have nothing before me in this world, and nurse no so-called life-plans ; on the contrary, in the strict consistency of my feelings

as regards this world's relations, I am ready at
each instant to accept my fate. Indeed in many
things I share the Buddhist monks' curious pride,
who beg for alms, not since they need them, but
to confer on bestowers the merit of giving.

— The other day there fell into my hands an
extract from Laube's now fairly famous criticism
of my " Meistersinger " and what it stands for ; it
was really most painful to read, and the thought
that this absolute recreant could now be treated in
my sister's house with a certain social impartiality
in respect of her brother acquired something quite
distressing to me. I don't like setting up a kind
of claim on this point, yet could wish that the
next time his peculiar want of tact betrays him into
speaking on that subject in your house, you would
impose the strictest silence on him with regard to
me, ay, forbid him to mention my name. Should
that embargo need a means, please use the question
whether he would care for me to publish his this
year's letters to myself and Frau v. Bülow, also
his applications addressed to the latter through
Charlotte v. Hagen for the post of Munich
Theatre-Intendant, with their accompanying pro-
testations of his ardour for my work and views ?
Perhaps, indeed, he might accept this ; since he
knows perfectly well that, even with his consent,
I am incapable of such low tricks, — a piece of
knowledge emboldening many a one to have his
fling at me,—but enough of that also !—

It will heartily delight me to receive good news
from you ; may I hope that " Tayia," too, is
making progress in the truest sense ? If you only

can pull yourselves quite together, I reckon on a
thoroughly complex visit from you in my lovely
hermitage next summer.   I beseech you to keep
that uppermost in all your thoughts.—

And now best remembrances to all, including
even Ritschl and Nietzsche, both of whom pleased
me very much.   Hold me dear, all of you ; and
for yourself, dear Sister, think ever kindly of Thy
brother   RICHARD.

113. To CÄCILIE AVENARIUS

DEAR CECILIE—It certainly was a wish to
revive the home-like sense of being with my
kinsfolk, that formed the chief incentive of my
recent trip to Leipzig.   I left it to depend on how
I felt, whether I should visit Dresden as well,
perhaps also Berlin.   After a brief sojourn at
Leipzig, however, I discovered the great fatigue
it causes one, when he has been out of all touch
with his people for a number of years, and, to
establish a few points to converse on as relatives,
must first give a history of all that has happened
to one to those he has grown quite a stranger to,
and who practically have paid no closer heed
whatever to any of our ups and downs ; and yet
I had seen the Hermann Brockhaus's repeatedly
in these last 10 years, also had come a few times
into contact both with Cläre and Luise.   For the
nonce I was tired, and resolved on return.   Moreover, Berlin is a supremely fatal place to me, where
I could only set my foot again in great emergency ;
in the past 6 years I've travelled through it twice,

but merely as a posting-stage, dead-beat, altogether incapable of combining a stay. Least of all could I have thought of readjusting family relations so long interrupted on such a rush through ; particularly as the question still remained un-answered, why my relatives had never come *to me* when I was shut both off and out. Her having paid me a proper visit at that time in Switzerland knit a decided bond between myself and Cläre ; further, I found her in Dresden when it was a matter of making endurable an extremely painful meeting with my lamented wife. To yourself, dear Cecilie, the day and hour were also given that come to every mortal once in serious relations with another, and when it has to be determined what will be the word he speaks. Not only did you miss that opportunity, much to the detriment of your relations with me, but you made every-thing then weighing on me even more oppressive through your blind judgment of my bearings toward Minna.——

In the summer of last year I was sorry to learn that your husband had intended calling on me with his son ; I could have wished that he had announced his intention beforehand, not merely regarded me as a casual object of interest upon a Swiss excursion : when I should have answered him, and arranged a meeting at my house.——

Now I entreat you not to take all this too much to heart. Herewith I send you—don't be angry !—what portraits of myself I have on hand. Ottilie ordered my bust for herself while in Munich with me, when she visited the sculptor's

T

studio ; Luise wanted to give her daughter Cläre
one for Christmas, and ordered it from the sculptor
herself. It would be difficult for me to see to
such a thing from here now, as I am totally cut
off from Munich.

That my memories of yourself are solely kind
ones, I fancy I proved to your son Richard on his
visit to Munich (1865). Remember me to him
and Eduard, and the almost completely unknown
other members of your family, and believe in the
brotherly attachment of Thy   RICHARD.

LUCERNE, 22. *Dec.* 1868.

114. TO LUISE BROCKHAUS

DEAREST LUISE — The requisite answer in
haste : — Next time that fatal stampede occurs
(particularly with a Sunday audience) please do
me the favour of retiring to the back of your box,
closing your eyes, and attending to nothing but
H. Sachs's final speech. Then, if you find his
words express the true and deeper meaning of the
whole, laid bare at last ; if, at the point in the
music where the Nuremberg Mastersingers' theme
directly weds itself to that of Walther's prize-
song, you hear that broader drift melodically
depicted to your feeling,—say, what would you
think of me, if, to mollify the crudeness of one
section of the public (which really throngs to me
unbidden), I straightway sacrificed a beauty which
forms a gift for those invited by me ? These,
to whom alone my work can be addressed, should

therefore fitly do their best to get the beautiful preserved to them unmaimed. If, already in his cloak, the King of Saxony turned back to applaud again, undoubtedly it may have been intended for Herr K[apell-] M[eister] Rietz, perhaps also for Mitterwurzer, who likewise claims this honour; but *I* believe, what moved him to such interest for sure received its strongest impulse from my Sachs's final speech : for, to such folk was that speech addressed.

So let the non-elect crowd out and welcome; that happens everywhere. At the best subscription-concerts the audience becomes restive toward the close of a Beethoven symphony ; when one goes to the theatre, one should know beforehand that one will have to mingle with a pack of groundlings in the lump. To uphold the good and genuine, however, and protect it against their evil habits, is the very task for nobler and better-cultured minds. Wherefore, instead of appealing to me [for mutilation], you rather ought to try and move some clever and courageous person to give this public a public lecture on its crudeness, and make it grasp what it is destroying and losing.—

Be sure that all I hear from any of you delights me heartily ; and no less does it please me, of course, to gather that my work at least was given in such a manner that a fine effect was a certainty.

I shall be much obliged by further details, with which I'm none too lavishly provided otherwise. If the Management had better education and sense of honour, doubtless I should have received a report from their side also ; but that's a thing, you see, which people seem to know no more.

Farewell, dearest Luise. Kind love to you and yours! Thy   RICHARD.

LUCERNE, 28. *Jan.* 1869.

115. TO EDUARD AVENARIUS [1]

DEAR EDUARD—Now that you have paid me another visit, and everything went off so nicely (except your never coming back), please allow me to remember you also sans ceremony when seeking advice.

I have already told you of my wish to issue an edition of my Collected Writings. I feel more and more bound to take thought for supplying the present and subsequent ages with an authentic record of my aims and work, as I cannot prevent other people from busying their pens with me in the most ignorant and slovenly fashion, and the confusion about me simply augments every day.— I have mapped out the arrangement of the said edition on the accompanying sheet of paper. You will observe that the staple is varied enough, yet connected. The material for the 1st volume lies completely ready, as also nearly all the rest. So it's a question of finding the right publisher for it. I narrated to you my previous wearisome experiences with J. J. Weber ; I should be very sorry to have to go on in that Charity sort of style : to be chucked into a horrid big business as a mere by-

[1] Enclosing a manuscript prospectus of the "Gesammelte Schriften und Dichtungen."

blow, annoys me. My ideal would be a young beginner who wants to stake a little on attracting rapid notice to his firm : but he must be able to "make a splash." Please give a moment's thought to what and whom you could suggest to me. The plan of issue, *i.e.* its hastening or retarding, would have entirely to go by circumstances. The volumes wouldn't need to be published in their ultimate order ; for instance, vol. IV. (Opera and Drama) might wait till quite the end. The 3 Opera-poems [*Communication*, *etc.*], Art-work of the Future, also Art and Revolution, are completely sold out, and I receive many complaints of it, especially from foreigners ; there'd be a good market in France, England and Russia. One could begin straight off with volume I. ; it offers an entire course of entertaining light literature (God, when I think how those utterly weak and empty letters of Mendelssohn have been bought !). But—things would have to be made a bit easy for me, and the transaction shew some likelihood of profit.—Hence my fervent request to you to befriend me with advice and deed.—

I hope Vevey improved your somewhat ailing health ? Cecilie, on the contrary, surprised me greatly by her capital robust appearance. It was very gratifying to have seen you both again at last : the "spell" is broken. Since you left, though, I have had unheard-of bothers [Munich *Rheingold*] ; Lord knows when I shall end by being left at peace. Nothing can occur in my life without cramp and convulsions,—it seems my fate ! I am also enclosing a "Declaration" of mine, from the Allg. Ztg, which mayn't have come under your eyes. You see what impish tricks I've had to guard against ; but I'm glad that my determination never again to take part in the performance of my works (as everything is really so abominable !) has had such effect on the other side. Only in this way can I guarantee myself the calm I need so ; in furtherance whereof, however, it's also requisite to give all genuine sympathisers with me a lucid survey of my aims and work.

So, best remembrances, dear Eduard ! Pass them on to Cile and the children, and let all of you stay good to Thy brother-in-law

WAGNER.

TRIBSCHEN,
12. *Oct.* 1869.

116. To CÄCILIE AVENARIUS

DEAR CECILIE—I still owe you my earnest thanks for an incomparably precious Christmas present. Not till these last few days did I get into the frame of mind in which I proposed reading those letters right through. You will interpret that aright, as you know how desirous I am, on the other hand, of collecting the mementos of our family to defend them from dispersal. This craze, awoken and intensified in me since several years, has remained unknown to none of our relatives, who have the rather wondered that such souvenirs should be so eagerly enquired after. I therefore thank you deeply for your characteristic sacrifice in copying out these touching documents, the originals whereof will be of great value to your children, in your opinion, though they have no personal recollection of those whose hand-writing affects ourselves so much because it takes us straight into the presence of persons we once were in close contact with.

The contents of those letters have not only touched, however, but truly thrilled me. Such an example of the most complete self-sacrifice for a nobly-taken aim but rarely stands so plain before our eyes in private life, as here. I confess I feel wellnigh inconsolable at this self-sacrifice of our father Geyer, and his letters to Albert in particular filled me with positive gall. Quite especially am I moved, too, by the high and delicate refinement in these letters, particularly in those to our mother; I cannot comprehend how this tone of genuine culture could have sunk so greatly in our family's later converse. At the same time, however, I have been able to derive from these very letters to our mother a penetrating glimpse into the relation of those two in arduous times. I believe I see perfectly clear now, even tho' I feel it extremely difficult to express my view of that relation. To me it seems as if our father Geyer believed he was atoning for a trespass by his sacrifice for the whole family.—

The " Massacre of the Innocents " [Geyer's comedy] I obtained at like time in its printed form. So, the manuscript copy your sisterly forethought no doubt procured with greatest trouble having no kind of autographic value, yet being of a certain interest for reason of its rarity, I beg you to allow me to return it to you.—

Strictly, I still owe Eduard a reply to his most friendly and circumstantial letter regarding the edition of my Collected Writings; but all I've to tell him is deuced short : namely, that I see it isn't time for the fulfilment of my wish. That's the real summa summarum I have deduced from the proposals he made me. Be so kind, then, as to give your good husband my best regards, and simply inform him of this coming to my senses.

But I have yet another, and a big request : that you will excuse me to your son Richard, of whom I hold a high opinion, as you know.—He sent me his philosophic treatise, and accompanied it with a letter which I decidedly cannot answer before I have arrived at thorough study of that treatise. But *study* it I must ; I am no schooled philosopher : for a thing like that the time must come to me, as come it did erewhile ; at present it is far away. So apology for apology, and merely the general assurance of my sterling delight in his letter.—

And now I pray you, give my cordial greetings to all your household, and rest assured of the faithful brotherly love with which greets thee Thy   RICHARD W.

TRIBSCHEN,
14. *Jan.* 1870.

117. TO CLARA WOLFRAM [1]

[*Autumn* 1870.]

MY DEAR GOOD CLÄRE—Don't be cross with me for having only let you know of my new marriage through a general announcement, to

[1] An undated fragment.

begin with, and don't believe it signified disparagement or cooling down of any kind. No, I really haven't even yet had time to overtake my tenderer outward obligations : in and for itself so long retarded, the act of legal union with my present wife of late had so depended on the furnishing of needful patrial certificates etc., that I couldn't fix the wedding-day beforehand ; and at last, when all had got in order, thought best to choose the earliest possible date, over-night as it were, that this formality might finally be gone through with no more delay. In such circumstances you will understand that, just as I let the wedding itself pass off quietly, without festivity or ceremony, so I simply cleared off everything connected with it in a trice; which is not to say, of course, that I didn't also mean to send kind word to those who loyally and sympathetically have stuck to me of the great blessing which now adorns my life and fills it with an object never dreamt before.

This I do herewith, dear Sister, and pray you to continue your sisterly love for myself and my wife. Of what for years had passed between us, as preliminary to our at-last-to-be-cemented bond, there were no explanations to be given : a devotion and self-sacrifice without example might be regarded and judged by the world as it is wont to do ; *we* had only to look to it that at least the friendly-minded should learn at some time what had here been rescued and preserved. Luckily, the hour has struck when everybody may convince himself thereof!

(*Conclusion missing.*)

118. To sister Ottilie Brockhaus

KIND LOVE, DEAR OTTILIE !—I'm always glad to
hear from you, particularly when I get something
good to hear.   That was a truly beautiful letter
you wrote to Cosima ; she burst into tears over
it again to-day.   Yes, hers is a marvellous nature !
I often think I'm merely dreaming she is mine.
We shall come down on you next Spring.
I want to shew my wife whate'er I value from my
earlier days, alike people and places.   Then it will
also be time for me to look round me in " the
world " again for what I still may bring to pass
there.   God knows what fruit it will bear.   In the
meantime I'm sparing and assembling my forces.
At Christmas I shall send you people something.[1]—
Many kind regards to our dear Hermann, your
sons and daughters.   To Clemens my especial
thanks.   He really ought to have baptised my
son, whose name is Helferich Siegfried Richard
Wagner.   He's a beauty and strong, and is to be
a healer of wounds : what besides, is his affair.
What prodigious good luck for me ! !—
       Kisses from Thy brother   RICHARD.

TRIBSCHEN, 25. *October* 1870.

119.[2] To the Same

DEAR OTTILIE—We should be very glad of
a thorough good *talk* with you, so I'll cut my
writing short to-day.   Is it possible for you to put

---

[1] Evidently the *Beethoven* essay.—Tr.
[2] In the German edition no. " 119 " is represented by the letter I am
ranging as no. 121, see footnote to which ; my numbers 119 and 120
therefore correspond with the German 120 and 121.—Tr.

myself and wife up on a few days' visit ? We are
proposing a voyage "in's Reich," which would
bring us to Leipzig toward the 20th April and
anchor us there a few days—as said—if we could
be sure of not incommoding your household ; as
in the contrary event—without yourselves—an
actual stay there would have no meaning for us.
Perhaps your good Anna will step into the breach
again ? The room she so magnanimously devolved
on me before would do perfectly for the pair of us.
Then we should like to pay Dresden a few days'
visit too, if Luise is there, and finally honour Berlin,
where I have something not unimportant in mind.

Be so good as to give me a friendly hint if it is
possible ; be greeted and greet most warmly from
ourselves ! Thy faithful brother   RICHARD.

LUCERNE,
26. *March* 1871.

120.[1] TO THE SAME

DEAR OTTILIE—Clemens is returning in a day
or two, and I hope will report to you how glad we
were to have him with us here.

At the moment I have a request for you.
Could you recommend us a reliable person for the
children ? We have been obliged to discharge the
one hitherto in our service because she didn't give
us satisfaction, and *I* am particularly anxious—
seeing how Cosima is over-exerting herself without
such assistance—that a good replacer should arrive
as soon as possible. The young person doesn't
need to be a so-called "governess" ; the elder

---

[1] No. "121" in the German edition ; see last and next footnotes.—Tr.

daughters are being taught by my wife single-handed : at the outside she would have to ground the younger girls in the rudiments of reading and writing, besides starting them in feminine tasks. So there is no question whatever of "piano," "French," and such - like ; only it must be a methodical person, as her chief duties will be to bathe and wash the children, dress and undress them, keep their things in order, do a little tailoring and stitching, assist at their meals, and all that sort of thing.   Above all, however, she must speak good German (not Saxon, then), be a *Protestant*, and have tidy, decent manners.   *Here*, and round about, we find it uncommonly hard to pick up such an individual, since the stratum directly in front of us is South German and Catholic : which, to anyone who knows, is saying everything. Neither will it be easy for yourself, dear Ottilie, to find the right article if you have to *seek ;* only there might be a chance of your knowing just the type of person, for whom you even wanted a good situation ; that does occur at times, and therefore I appeal to you.   If you really had the proper person, all I would ask of you is to provide her at once with her travelling-money and send her here without delay, when all her terms *approved by you* would be fulfilled without demur.

Don't be astonished at *my* laying this matter before you : I'm certain that Cosima would never arrive at it to-day or to-morrow, as her time's so excessively occupied with attending to the children ; and that's the very reason I've felt urged to take her place with you for this once.

One thing more :—

I want to apply to FEUSTEL of Bayreuth for information as to eligible building-sites, and other services in which a man of his position may be of great utility to me. True, I might approach him simply on the strength of my "celebrity"; but I prefer being "socially" introduced or commended to the gentleman also, especially as that's made so easy by your former close acquaintance with him. So please be good enough to write the man a few kind words in that sense, to which (as soon as you had given me notice) I could refer when I wrote him myself. I should also be glad if you would take this opportunity to supply the man's correct full name, and title, if any.—

For the rest, you'll soon hear quite enough of us by mouth, my dear ; which I therefore take into account when assuring you and yours of the heartiest love and attachment of myself and mine. Cosima has formed a truly proud affection for her "nephews," and prizes them seriously high; which is no more than they deserve, for they're excellent and lovable good fellows.—

Farewell and stay good to Thy faithful brother
RICHARD WAGNER.

LUCERNE,
8. *Oct.* 1871.

121. TO HIS NIECE OTTILIE BROCKHAUS

MY DEAR OTTILIE — I have just received through Hermann the mournful tidings of the death of your beloved mother, my dear sister [Luise]. It came upon me altogether unexpectedly, as one of those blows that numb us of a sudden, plunging us into a profound reverie from which we return at last to our habitual consciousness of life with the sense of a great, an almost icy void. Our first stir is then directed to those who naturally must feel that void the keenest ; and thus our commiseration with the grief of these nearest alone awakes us to full warmth of life again.

How painfully this stupendous loss must have affected yourself, dear Ottilie ! Believe me, I feel it with you most sincerely, and most heartily desire to do you any good I can.—This I certainly can only do by praying you to believe in the deep verity of my own mourning for the dear departed, whose noble heart had beat in such sincere compassion for myself as well. She was very good, your dear mother ! How rare a comfort must it be to me, that I was allowed to be so intimately near to her again last spring ; even if that very solace sharpens the acuteness of my grief, it has also tenderly dissolved the numbness all such grievous loss evokes in us at first, and made it sooner possible to turn to you in full affliction and declare my deep condolence.

Give my truest love to your good sisters, and tell them what I've said for them as well as you. The sadder all you dear ones must be, think all the kinder now and ever of your faithful Uncle

RICHARD.

LUCERNE,
5. *Jan.* 1872 [1] (evening).

---

[1] The German gives " 1871," but that is plainly one of the misdatings so common at the turn of a year, since Luise Brockhaus is enquired after in the letter of March 1871 ; see No. 119.—Tr.

The most heartfelt remembrances and assurances of her condolence accompany my greetings from the part of my dear wife.

122. To Alexander Ritter [husband of Franziska Wagner]

BAYREUTH, 9. *March* 1873.

CHERISHED NEPHEW—I most earnestly beseech you to consult a local expert, and hunt me out a suitable table-wine (white) from among the Wurzburg vineyards. I am told the "Klostergarten" possesses and produces a really *light* wine; please forward me 12 bottles of it as sample, the sender to be paid per the post on receipt. I've come to the conclusion, you see, that under the title of Rhine wine I have long been drinking nothing but concocted and adulterated stuff; whereas the Würzburger, owing to its unpopularity, has at least the reputation of being put up undoctored and pure.

God bless you! In bother and haste Thy sublime Uncle   R. WAGNER.

123. To Prof. Hermann Brockhaus

MY DEAR HERMANN—A letter from yourself, —an agreeable surprise indeed! It rejoiced us the more, as we had been waiting in vain for a sign of life from Ottilie or Fritz to reassure us that they both had returned from their visit with friendly recollections of us.

Thanks, dearest Brother-in-law, that Maximilian Order appears at all events to have had more considerable effect on the interest you take in me, than was the case with myself. The Chapter of this Order had chosen me once before —exactly nine years back—and submitted my name to the King of Bavaria. At that time—not having the smallest knowledge of this order or its statutes—I was merely informed by the Cabinet-Secretary that the King wished to confer the order on me (of his own initiative, as I was left to infer) : should I care about it ? Thereon I had the King asked to refrain from that fresh token of favour— at a moment when his relations with me were creating fuss enough : moreover I had got so old, said I, that, after my pupils had been decorated with orders of all kinds, I might very well content myself therewith for the remainder of my life. Delighted at such an opportunity of embroiling me with the Chapter and making my position in Munich more untenable, the Cabinet turned this declaration to all the evil use it could, and not till later did I learn how greatly Liebig, Kaulbach and the rest, had felt insulted by me. Well—the gentlemen having repeated their choice after nine years, had really something touching for me, and since it was announced to me in proper form, this time I calmly let the matter take its course ; whereby I've been robbed of the pride, though, of being laid in my grave some fine day without that sort of patent of honour.

We are very glad that your Rectorship [Univ.] suited you so well and left such pleasant memories behind. I can well imagine that a life into which so little pleasure enters as my own may disconcert you on looking it over.[1] Sundry things might have been made easier for me, to be sure : it needs a tough constitution and a long life, to extort from stupidity and malignant callousness what might just as well have come to pass with less exertion, had the fallows of our age but been manured with rather more good-will.—For all that, I wish from my heart that things may have gone as well with all of you as I may fairly say about my household. If I hadn't my big undertaking in front of me [*Festspiel*], I truly should have everything now that can gladden one's spirit at the goal of a difficult life. Next Spring, moreover, we expect to move into our house [Wahnfried], the fitting-up of which has cost no little patience and vexation. Then we perhaps shall see yourself here some day, shan't we ?

Best love to yours and ours from me and Cosima ; hold us dear yourself, and rest ever assured of my reciprocal affection. With all his heart, Thy brother-in-law

RICHARD WAGNER.

BAYREUTH,
30. *Dec.* 1873.

124. TO CLARA WOLFRAM [2]

(BAYREUTH, 27. *October* 1874.)

How strange, dear Cläre ! Only yesterday I was thinking of *yourself* most vividly, and made up my mind to invite you to visit us here next

---

[1] "Im Ueberblicke" seems to point to a copy of the privately-printed *Mein Leben* having been sent to sister Ottilie and her husband.—Tr.

[2] From the *Tägl. Rundschau* of Oct. 15, 1902.

U

summer and stay as long as you liked in our at last completed house. You were to bring your Röschen with you ; it was all settled, and I was recalling so many chapters in my life which you had helped go through, and thinking how you really are my greatest intimate of all my brothers and sisters. My childhood, too, of which my wife so often wants to hear, you alone could have distinct remembrance of. So—I was rejoicing in the thought of writing you soon,—and behold !— there comes this sable message.—Good Wolfram, —how glad I am I saw him once again last year, after so long an interval !—He was a good, an upright, and, for sure, a gifted man : for certain he has reached the bourn of peace !

Blest be his memory !

And now I ask myself if you oughtn't, perhaps, to come to us this very autumn—so lovely here now. Everything is in readiness to offer you quite tolerable accommodation. I think you'd better—rise, take Röschen with you, and come right soon to see how things are looking at and round Bayreuth. Then we'll have many a long talk,—and that's often a wonderful help.

Be most heartily embraced, and give most faithful greetings to your sorrow-stricken family from Thy brother   RICHARD W.

APPENDIX

EXPLANATORY NOTES

(By C. F. GLASENAPP)

ON THE LETTERS' RECIPIENTS

PERSONALIA

(By Herr GLASENAPP)

THE reader will naturally find fuller particulars of the individuals to whom these "Family Letters" were addressed, and of their respective relations to the Master, in *Das Leben Richard Wagners* by the present editor (Breitkopf & Härtel, Leipzig). Here we can only offer a few very general indications anent the various members of the family, and their descendants so far as involved.

(1) To the mother, JOHANNA GEYER, four letters of the present collection are directed: nos. 4, 6, 15, 52. For all particulars of her personality, character, mental attributes and their cultivation, we must refer to the source above-mentioned, especially to vol. i, pp. 36 and 89-90, fourth edition [German].

(2) ALBERT WAGNER, the eldest brother, born the 2nd of March 1799, was educated at the Meissen Prince's School, studied medicine for a while at Leipzig, then singing under Mieksch at Dresden, and appeared at various minor theatres such as Breslau, Wurzburg, Halle. In furtherance of his step-daughter Johanna's career, he afterwards removed to Dresden, and subsequently to Berlin, where he ultimately became stage-manager under Botho von Hülsen. He died the 31st October 1874.— To him are addressed letters 30, 35, 48; another letter, sent to him Feb. 20, 1834, is known to have been in the possession of the Avenarius's some decads back, and can scarcely be considered lost for good.

Daughters : Johanna [reputed], Franzisca, Marie. JOHANNA W., afterwards married to Landrath Jachmann of Berlin, is a familiar figure in the history of the operatic stage. No letters to her, either in the original or in transcript, have been discovered in the Wahnfried archives; but doubtless some have been preserved elsewhere, and may be incorporated in a future edition.

FRANZISCA W., a remarkable character and richly-gifted artist, engaged as actress at the Grand-ducal theatre of Schwerin, bade an early farewell to the stage after her marriage to Alexander Ritter [son of R. Wagner's old friend, Frau Julie R.]. To her are addressed letters 59, 69-71, 75, 77, 100-102 ; to her and her husband no. 106 ; to him the billet 122.

MARIE W., married Herr Jakoby of Hamburg. We know nothing of letters addressed by the Master to her.

(3) ROSALIE Wagner, born the 4th of March 1803. For details of her career as actress the reader is referred to vol. i of *Das Leben*, her final engagement being at the Leipzig theatre, when she formed the half-orphaned family's main support after Ludwig Geyer's death. Married to Dr. Oswald MARBACH, she died in the first year of wedlock, Oct. 12, 1837, five days after giving birth to a daughter Rosalie. The letters addressed to her, nos. 2, 3 and 5, attest the youthful Richard's deep attachment to this sister.—Letters to Prof. Marbach of later years (1869) still exist, but have proved inaccessible to us as yet.

(4) The name of brother JULIUS Wagner (born Aug. 7, 1804) is of repeated occurrence in our collection. He received free education at a Masonic institute in Dresden, his deceased father having belonged to the brotherhood, which likewise assisted the rest of the family. He learnt the goldsmith's art from a brother of stepfather Geyer, also made a journey to Paris, but mostly lived in the house of his brother-in-law, Fr. Brockhaus, where he gained the reputation of "an agreeable companion, but useless in practical life,"—confirmed by the

fact of his brothers and sisters allowing him an annuity, to which the Master contributed even at epochs of personal pinch (cf. p. 226). Letters were written by him to Julius at various times (cf. p. 204), but hitherto have proved unprocurable.

(5) LUISE Wagner, born December 14, 1805, actress at Breslau and elsewhere, left the Leipzig Town-theatre in 1828 to marry Friedrich BROCKHAUS of the well-known local firm of publishers, survived her husband († end of 1865) about [six] years, and died the beginning of January [1872]. Five of our letters, nos. 72, 95, 108, 110 and 114, are addressed to her, whilst her death forms the subject of letter [121].[1] All other letters to herself and husband seem to have vanished past recall, though we have numerous indications of their former existence in plenty, from youthful days, from Paris, and in particular from Dresden.

Only the two youngest of her daughters, Clara and Ottilie, seem to have received letters from their uncle. To CLARA BROCKHAUS (md v. Kessinger) are addressed letters 65, 78, 84, 87, and manifestly that no. 80 we found at an autograph-dealer's. As the last-named, like so many other letters, had plainly passed into the owner-ship of some collecting friend, future recovery even of the second half of letter 87 (see footnote to p. 213) does not appear beyond the bounds of probability.

To Luise's youngest daughter, OTTILIE BROCKHAUS, is addressed letter 121.

(6) CLARA Wagner, born November 29, 1807, artistically most gifted of all the sisters, in her outward lot least favoured. Likewise a pupil of Mieksch, she made her appearance as singer with distinction at the age of 17, but early lost her voice's freshness and had to content herself with minor stages such as those of Augsburg, Nuremberg and Magdeburg. At Augsburg

---

[1] For the figures I have here enclosed in square brackets Herr Glasenapp gives "five," "1871," and "119"; my reason for the emendation will be found in letter 119 itself and in my footnote to no. 121.—Tr.

she gave her hand to Heinrich Wolfram, then also engaged there as singer, subsequently leaving the stage with him when he went into business at Chemnitz. The letters to her from the Master, breathing a confidence above any bestowed on the rest of his family, constitute the finest of monuments to her lovable nature ; but her unselfishness betrayed her into giving many of them away (according to her children's statements), so that a goodly number have passed into unknown private hands, whence we can only trust that a few may some day re-emerge.[1] In our present collection nos. 58, 88, 90, 98, 99, 105, 109, 111, 117 and 124, are addressed to herself, nos. 102a, 104 and 107 to her husband, with whose death our very latest letter is concerned. Countless earlier letters to sister and brother-in-law, from 1835 onward, have disappeared for the present without a trace.

Her daughters Rosalie (Röschen) and Marie are named in the letters to Clara ; of letters addressed to themselves we know nothing whatever.

(7) Ottilie Wagner, born March 14, 1811, never made public appearance. She lived for some time in the house of her sister Luise Brockhaus, whence she was married the 11th of April 1836, at the church of S. Nicholas in Leipzig,[2] to her brother-in-law Professor Hermann Brockhaus, a learned Sanscritist of genuine culture, who seems to have stood the nearest to the Master of all his various brothers-in-law, and whose sudden death (Jan. 5, 1877) moved him deeply. Letters 1, 112 and 118-20 in our collection are addressed to sister Ottilie, nos. 60 and 123 to her husband ; many an intervening other, for

---

[1] For example, we know the history of *two* such letters, presented by her to an intimate friend, Frau H. From the latter they were well-nigh extorted by force, through an intermediate acquaintance, to pass into the possession of a feminine English collector in return for an insignificant sum.

[2] *Not in Dresden*, as would appear from a slip or misprint in *Das Leben* i, 256, overlooked even in the latest edition (4th), there being no "Nicolaikirche" in Dresden at all. Presumably the young couple removed to Dresden, however, directly after marriage. [Herr Glasenapp's own footnote.]

instance, that referred to on p. 222 (passed on to the *firm ?*), has disappeared for the time being.

Among her sons, FRIEDRICH and CLEMENS both stood on the best of footings with their famous uncle, and Clemens in particular is sure to have been the recipient of a letter or two ; but we have found these as yet unobtainable.

(8) CÄCILIE GEYER, half-sister to the Master, born February 26, 1815, married the 5th of March 1840 Eduard AVENARIUS, at that time chief of the little Paris branch " Librairie allemande de Brockhaus & Avenarius." Close-linked in childhood—*cf.* p. 190—brother and half-sister were again brought very near each other by the many vicissitudes of their Paris stay ; whilst, in comparison with the rest of the family, in this instance a sense of piety has treasured up so rich a store of proofs of brotherly attachment and tenderness, that we may abstain from all enumeration of the letters to sister Cäcilie and her husband Eduard. In fact, even those we possess to the mother, to Albert, and one of those to Rosalie (no. 5), spring from the Avenarius collection preserved by " Cile's " forethought, which therefore constitutes the very backbone of our publication. The originals are at present in the possession of Dr. Ferdinand Avenarius, who most kindly placed them at the editor's disposal, after permitting faithful copies to be made for the Wahnfried archives long before.

(9) [Herr Glasenapp's final note deals with the eight letters to Wagner's first wife MINNA included in the German edition, in anticipation of the immeasurably fuller correspondence published since ; to which he adds, that " even these letters are not preserved in absolute entirety, some of them—like so many others—having trickled into unknown private hands as autographs."—Tr.]

INDEX

In this Index, "*n.*," following a numeral, signifies "footnote"; whilst curved brackets, when enclosing numerals, indicate that the subject is only mentioned indirectly on that page of the text : thus

Dresden, 167 *n.*, (198), would stand for
Dresden, 167 footnote, 198 (an allusion).

In the case of the more largely represented headings I have thought it unnecessary to include here all the simpler "greetings."—W. A. E.

THE END